ESSAYS OF E. B. WHITE

# ESSAYS
# OF
# E. B. White

HARPER COLOPHON BOOKS
HARPER & ROW, PUBLISHERS
NEW YORK, HAGERSTOWN, SAN FRANCISCO, LONDON

A hardcover edition of this book was originally published by Harper and Row Publishers, Inc.

First HARPER COLOPHON edition published 1979

ISBN: 0-06-090662-6

79 80 81 82 83 10 9 8 7 6 5 4 3 2 1

# CONTENTS

Foreword      *vii*

## I. *THE FARM*

GOOD-BYE TO FORTY-EIGHTH STREET      3

HOME-COMING      7

A REPORT IN SPRING      14

DEATH OF A PIG      17

THE EYE OF EDNA      25

COON TREE      34

A REPORT IN JANUARY      46

THE WINTER OF THE GREAT SNOWS      53

RIPOSTE      60

THE GEESE      62

## II. *THE PLANET*

LETTER FROM THE EAST      71

BEDFELLOWS      80

SOOTFALL AND FALLOUT      90

UNITY      100

## III. *THE CITY*

THE WORLD OF TOMORROW     III

HERE IS NEW YORK     118

## IV. *FLORIDA*

ON A FLORIDA KEY     137

THE RING OF TIME     142

WHAT DO OUR HEARTS TREASURE?     150

## V. *MEMORIES*

AFTERNOON OF AN AMERICAN BOY     157

FAREWELL, MY LOVELY!     162

THE YEARS OF WONDER     169

ONCE MORE TO THE LAKE     197

## VI. *DIVERSIONS AND OBSESSIONS*

THE SEA AND THE WIND THAT BLOWS     205

THE RAILROAD     208

## VII. *BOOKS, MEN, AND WRITING*

THE ST. NICHOLAS LEAGUE     225

A SLIGHT SOUND AT EVENING     234

SOME REMARKS ON HUMOR     243

DON MARQUIS     250

WILL STRUNK     256

MR. FORBUSH'S FRIENDS     262

# FOREWORD

❦

The essayist is a self-liberated man, sustained by the childish belief that everything he thinks about, everything that happens to him, is of general interest. He is a fellow who thoroughly enjoys his work, just as people who take bird walks enjoy theirs. Each new excursion of the essayist, each new "attempt," differs from the last and takes him into new country. This delights him. Only a person who is congenitally self-centered has the effrontery and the stamina to write essays.

There are as many kinds of essays as there are human attitudes or poses, as many essay flavors as there are Howard Johnson ice creams. The essayist arises in the morning and, if he has work to do, selects his garb from an unusually extensive wardrobe: he can pull on any sort of shirt, be any sort of person, according to his mood or his subject matter—philosopher, scold, jester, raconteur, confidant, pundit, devil's advocate, enthusiast. I like the essay, have always liked it, and even as a child was at work, attempting to inflict my young thoughts and experiences on others by putting them on paper. I early broke into print in the pages of *St. Nicholas*. I tend still to fall back on the essay form (or lack of form) when an idea strikes me, but I am not fooled about the place of the essay in twentieth-century American letters—it stands a short distance down the line. The essayist, unlike the novelist, the poet, and the playwright, must be content in his self-imposed role of second-class citizen. A writer who has his sights trained on the Nobel Prize or other earthly triumphs had best write a novel, a poem, or a play, and leave the essayist to ramble about, content with living a free life and enjoying the satisfactions of a somewhat undisciplined existence. (Dr. Johnson called the essay "an irregular, undigested piece"; this happy practitioner has no wish to quarrel with the good doctor's characterization.)

There is one thing the essayist cannot do, though—he cannot indulge himself in deceit or in concealment, for he will be found out in no time. Desmond MacCarthy, in his introductory remarks to the 1928 E. P. Dutton & Company edition of Montaigne, observes that Montaigne "had the gift of natural candour. . . ." It is the basic ingredient. And even the essayist's escape from discipline is only a partial escape: the essay, although a relaxed form, imposes its own disciplines, raises its own problems, and these disciplines and problems soon become apparent and (we all hope) act as a deterrent to anyone wielding a pen merely because he entertains random thoughts or is in a happy or wandering mood.

I think some people find the essay the last resort of the egoist, a much too self-conscious and self-serving form for their taste; they feel that it is presumptuous of a writer to assume that his little excursions or his small observations will interest the reader. There is some justice in their complaint. I have always been aware that I am by nature self-absorbed and egoistical; to write of myself to the extent I have done indicates a too great attention to my own life, not enough to the lives of others. I have worn many shirts, and not all of them have been a good fit. But when I am discouraged or downcast I need only fling open the door of my closet, and there, hidden behind everything else, hangs the mantle of Michel de Montaigne, smelling slightly of camphor.

The essays in this collection cover a long expanse of time, a wide variety of subjects. I have chosen the ones that have amused me in the rereading, along with a few that seemed to have the odor of durability clinging to them. Some, like "Here Is New York," have been seriously affected by the passage of time and now stand as period pieces. I wrote about New York in the summer of 1948, during a hot spell. The city I described has disappeared, and another city has emerged in its place— one that I'm not familiar with. But I remember the former one, with longing and with love. David McCord, in his book *About Boston* tells of a journalist from abroad visiting this country and seeing New York for the first time. He reported that it was "inspiring but temporary in appearance." I know what he means. The last time I visited New York, it seemed to have suffered a personality change, as though it had a brain tumor as yet undetected.

Two of the Florida pieces have likewise experienced a sea change. My remarks about the condition of the black race in the South have happily been nullified, and the pieces are merely prophetic, not definitive.

To assemble these essays I have rifled my other books and have added a number of pieces that are appearing for the first time between covers. Except for extracting three chapters, I have let "One Man's Meat" alone, since it is a sustained report of about five years of country living—a report I prefer not to tamper with. The arrangement of the book is by subject matter or by mood or by place, not by chronology. Some of the pieces in the book carry a dateline, some do not. Chronology enters into the scheme, but neither the book nor its sections are perfectly chronological. Sometimes the reader will find me in the city when he thinks I am in the country, and the other way round. This may cause a mild confusion; it is unavoidable and easily explained. I spent a large part of the first half of my life as a city dweller, a large part of the second half as a countryman. In between, there were periods when nobody, including myself, quite knew (or cared) where I was: I thrashed back and forth between Maine and New York for reasons that seemed compelling at the time. Money entered into it, affection for *The New Yorker* magazine entered in. And affection for the city.

I have finally come to rest.

E. B. WHITE

*April 1977*

# ACKNOWLEDGMENTS

Of the thirty-one essays in this collection, twenty-two appeared originally in *The New Yorker*. "Farewell, My Lovely!" a collaboration with Richard L. Strout, appeared first in *The New Yorker* under that title, later as a small book called *Farewell to Model T*, published by G. P. Putnam's Sons. "Death of a Pig" appeared in the *Atlantic Monthly*. "Riposte" was published on the *New York Times* Op-Ed Page, under the title "Farmer White's Brown Eggs." "Here Is New York" appeared first as an article in *Holiday*, then as a small book, published by Harper & Brothers. Two essays, "On a Florida Key" and "Once More to the Lake," were originally published in *Harper's Magazine*, in the One Man's Meat series. "The Sea and the Wind that Blows" first appeared in the *Ford Times*, and "A Slight Sound at Evening" was originally published in the *Yale Review* under the title "Walden—1954." The remarks on humor in Chapter VII formed part of an introduction to *A Subtreasury of American Humor*, published by Coward McCann. The piece on Don Marquis in the same chapter was taken from an introduction to the *lives and times of archy and mehitabel*, published by Doubleday.

I

❧❦❧

# THE FARM

# GOOD-BYE TO FORTY-EIGHTH STREET

*Turtle Bay, November 12, 1957*

For some weeks now I have been engaged in dispersing the contents of this apartment, trying to persuade hundreds of inanimate objects to scatter and leave me alone. It is not a simple matter. I am impressed by the reluctance of one's worldly goods to go out again into the world. During September I kept hoping that some morning, as by magic, all books, pictures, records, chairs, beds, curtains, lamps, china, glass, utensils, keepsakes would drain away from around my feet, like the outgoing tide, leaving me standing silent on a bare beach. But this did not happen. My wife and I diligently sorted and discarded things from day to day, and packed other objects for the movers, but a six-room apartment holds as much paraphernalia as an aircraft carrier. You can whittle away at it, but to empty the place completely takes real ingenuity and great staying power. On one of the mornings of disposal, a man from a second-hand bookstore visited us, bought several hundred books, and told us of the death of his brother, the word "cancer" exploding in the living room like a time bomb detonated by his grief. Even after he had departed with his heavy load, there seemed to be almost as many books as before, and twice as much sorrow.

Every morning, when I left for work, I would take something in my hand and walk off with it, for deposit in the big municipal wire trash basket at the corner of Third, on the theory that the physical act of disposal was the real key to the problem. My wife, a strategist, knew better and began quietly mobilizing the forces that would eventually put our goods to rout. A man could walk away for a thousand mornings carrying something with him to the corner and there would still

[ 3 ]

be a home full of stuff. It is not possible to keep abreast of the normal tides of acquisition. A home is like a reservoir equipped with a check valve: the valve permits influx but prevents outflow. Acquisition goes on night and day—smoothly, subtly, imperceptibly. I have no sharp taste for acquiring things, but it is not necessary to desire things in order to acquire them. Goods and chattels seek a man out; they find him even though his guard is up. Books and oddities arrive in the mail. Gifts arrive on anniversaries and fête days. Veterans send ball-point pens. Banks send memo books. If you happen to be a writer, readers send whatever may be cluttering up their own lives; I had a man once send me a chip of wood that showed the marks of a beaver's teeth. Someone dies, and a little trickle of indestructible keepsakes appears, to swell the flood. This steady influx is not counterbalanced by any comparable outgo. Under ordinary circumstances, the only stuff that leaves a home is paper trash and garbage; everything else stays on and digs in.

Lately we haven't spent our nights in the apartment; we are bivouacked in a hotel and just come here mornings to continue the work. Each of us has a costume. My wife steps into a cotton dress while I shift into midnight-blue tropical pants and bowling shoes. Then we buckle down again to the unending task.

All sorts of special problems arise during the days of disposal. Anyone who is willing to put his mind to it can get rid of a chair, say, but what about a trophy? Trophies are like leeches. The ones made of paper, such as a diploma from a school or a college, can be burned if you have the guts to light the match, but the ones made of bronze not only are indestructible but are almost impossible to throw away, because they usually carry your name, and a man doesn't like to throw away his good name, or even his bad one. Some busybody might find it. People differ in their approach to trophies, of course. In watching Edward R. Murrow's "Person to Person" program on television, I have seen several homes that contained a "trophy room," in which the celebrated pack rat of the house had assembled all his awards, so that they could give out the concentrated aroma of achievement whenever he wished to loiter in such an atmosphere. This is all very well if you enjoy the stale smell of success, but if a man doesn't care for that air he is in a real fix when disposal time comes up. One day a couple of weeks ago, I sat for a while staring moodily at a plaque that had entered my life largely as a result of some company's zest for promotion. It was bronze on walnut, heavy enough to make an anchor for a rowboat, but I didn't need a rowboat anchor, and this thing had my name on it. By deft work with a screwdriver, I finally succeeded in prying the nameplate off; I pocketed this, and carried the mutilated remains to the corner, where the wire basket waited. The work exhausted me more than did the labor for which the award was presented.

Another day, I found myself on a sofa between the chip of wood gnawed by the beaver and an honorary hood I had once worn in an academic procession. What I really needed at the moment was the beaver himself, to eat the hood. I shall never wear the hood again, but I have too weak a character to throw it away, and I do not doubt that it will tag along with me to the end of my days, not keeping me either warm or happy but occupying a bit of my attic space.

Right in the middle of the dispersal, while the mournful rooms were still loaded with loot, I had a wonderful idea: we would shut the apartment, leave everything to soak for a while, and go to the Fryeburg Fair, in Maine, where we could sit under a tent at a cattle auction and watch somebody else trying to dispose of something. A fair, of course, is a dangerous spot if a man is hoping to avoid acquisition, and the truth is I came close to acquiring a very pretty whiteface heifer, safe in calf—which would have proved easily as burdensome as a chip of wood gnawed by a beaver. But Fryeburg is where some of my wife's ancestors lived, and is in the valley of the Saco, looking west to the mountains, and the weather promised to be perfect, and the premium list of the Agricultural Society said, "Should Any Day Be Stormy, the Exercises for That Day Will Be Postponed to the First Fair Day," and I would rather have a ringside seat at a cattle sale than a box at the opera, so we picked up and left town, deliberately overshooting Fryeburg by 175 miles in order to sleep one night at home.

The day we spent at the Fryeburg Fair was the day the first little moon was launched by the new race of moon-makers. Had I known in advance that a satellite was about to be added to my world, in this age of additives, I might have stayed in New York and sulked instead of going to the Fair, but in my innocence I was able to enjoy a day watching the orbiting of trotting horses—an ancient terrestrial phenomenon that has given pleasure to unnumbered thousands. We attended the calf scramble, the pig scramble, and the baby-beef auction; we ate lunch in the back seat of our flashy old 1949 automobile, parked in the infield; and then I found myself a ringside seat with my feet in the shavings at the Hereford sale, under the rattling tongue and inexorable hammer of auctioneer Dick Murray, enjoying the wild look in the whites of a cow's eyes.

The day had begun under the gray blanket of a fall overcast, but the sky soon cleared. Nobody had heard of the Russian moon. The wheels wheeled, the chairs spun, the cotton candy tinted the faces of children, the bright leaves tinted the woods and hills. A cluster of amplifiers spread the theme of love over everything and everybody; the mild breeze spread the dust over everything and everybody. Next morning, in the Lafayette Hotel in Portland, I went down to breakfast and found May Craig looking solemn at one of the tables and Mr. Murray, the auctioneer, looking cheerful at another. The newspaper headlines told of the moon. At that hour of the morning, I could not take in the exact significance, if any, of a national heavenly body. But I was glad I had spent the last day of the natural firmament at the One Hundred and Seventh Annual Exhibition of the West Oxford Agricultural Society. I see nothing in space as promising as the view from a Ferris wheel.

But that was weeks ago. As I sit here this afternoon in this disheveled room, surrounded by the boxes and bales that hold my undisposable treasure, I feel the onset of melancholy. I look out onto Forty-eighth Street; one out of every ten passers-by is familiar to me. After a dozen years of gazing idly at the passing show, I have assembled, quite unbeknownst to them, a cast of characters that I depend on. They are the nameless actors who have a daily walk-on part in my play—the greatest of dramas. I shall miss them all, them and their dogs. Even more, I think, I shall miss the garden out back—the wolf whistle of the starling, the summer-night murmur of the fountain; the cat, the vine, the sky, the willow. And the visiting birds of spring and fall—the small, shy birds that drop in for one drink and stay two weeks. Over a period of thirty years, I have occupied eight caves in New York, eight digs— four in the Village, one on Murray Hill, three in Turtle Bay. In New York, a citizen is likely to keep on the move, shopping for the perfect arrangement of rooms and vistas, changing his habitation according to fortune, whim, and need. And in every place he abandons he leaves something vital, it seems to me, and starts his new life somewhat less encrusted, like a lobster that has shed its skin and is for a time soft and vulnerable.

# HOME-COMING

*Allen Cove, December 10, 1955*

On the day before Thanksgiving, toward the end of the afternoon, having motored all day, I arrived home and lit a fire in the living room. The birch logs took hold briskly. About three minutes later, not to be outdone, the chimney itself caught fire. I became aware of this development rather slowly. Rocking contentedly in my chair, enjoying the stupor that follows a day on the road, I thought I heard the dull, fluttering roar of a chimney swift, a sound we who live in this house are thoroughly accustomed to. Then I realized that there would be no bird in residence in my chimney at this season of the year, and a glance up the flue made it perfectly plain that, after twenty-two years of my tenure, the place was at last afire.

The fact that my chimney was on fire did not greatly surprise or depress me, as I have been dogged by small and large misadventures for the past ten years, the blows falling around my head day and night, and I have learned to be ready for anything at any hour. I phoned the Fire Department as a matter of routine, dialing a number I had once forehandedly printed in large figures on the edge of the shelf in the telephone closet, so that I would be able to read it without my glasses. (We keep our phone in a closet here, as you might confine a puppy that isn't fully house-trained. The dial system is unpopular anyway in this small rural Maine community, and as far as I am concerned, the entire New England Telephone & Telegraph Co. deserves to be shut up in a closet for having saddled us with dials and deprived us of our beloved operators, who used to know where everybody was and just what to do about everything, including chimney fires.)

My call was answered promptly, but I had no sooner hung up than I observed that the fire appeared to be out, having exhausted itself, so I called back to cancel the run, and was told that the department would like to come anyway. In the country, one excuse is as good as another for a bit of fun, and just because a fire has grown cold is no reason for a fireman's spirits to sag. In a very short time, the loud, cheerful apparatus, its red signal light blinking rapturously, careened into the driveway, and the living room filled rapidly with my fire-fighting friends. My fire chief is also my barber, so I was naturally glad to see him. And he had with him a robust accomplice who had recently been up on my roof installing a new wooden gutter, dry and ready to receive the first sparks from a chimney fire, so I was glad to see *him*. And there was still a third fire-eater, and everyone was glad to see everyone else, as near as I could make out, and we all poked about learnedly in the chimney for a while, and then the department left. I have had dozens and dozens of home-comings at the end of an all-day ride on U.S. 1, but strangely enough this was one of the pleasantest.

Shortly before he died, Bernard DeVoto gave the Maine coast a brisk going over in his *Harper's* column, using some four-letter words that raised the hackles of the inhabitants. Mr. DeVoto used the word "slum" and the word "neon." He said that the highway into Maine was a sorry mess all the way to Bucksport, and that the whole strip was overpopulated and full of drive-ins, diners, souvenir stands, purulent amusement parks, and cheap-Jack restaurants. I was thinking about this indictment at lunch the other day, trying to reconstruct my own cheap-Jack impressions of the familiar route after my recent trip over it. As I sat at table, gnawing away at a piece of pie, snow began falling. At first it was an almost imperceptible spitting from the gray sky, but it soon thickened and came driving in from the northeast. I watched it catch along the edge of the drive, powder the stone wall, dust the spruce cover on the flower borders, coat the plowed land, and whiten the surface of the dark frozen pond, and I knew that all along the coast from Kittery on, the worst mistakes of men were being quietly erased, the lines of their industrial temples softened, and U.S. 1 crowned with a cold, inexpensive glory that DeVoto unhappily did not live to see.

Even without the kindly erasures of the snow, the road into Maine does not seem a slum to me. Like highways everywhere, it is a mixed dish: Gulf and Shell, bay and gull, neon and sunset, cold comfort and warm, the fussy façade of a motor court right next door to the pure geometry of an early-nineteenth-century clapboard house with barn attached. You can certainly learn to spell "moccasin" while driving into Maine, and there is often little else to do, except steer and avoid death.

Woods and fields encroach everywhere, creeping to within a few feet of the neon and the court, and the experienced traveler into this land is always conscious that just behind the garish roadside stand, in its thicket of birch and spruce, stands the delicate and well-proportioned deer; just beyond the overnight cabin, in the pasture of granite and juniper, trots the perfectly designed fox. This is still our triumphant architecture, and the Maine man does not have to penetrate in depth to be excited by his coastal run; its flavor steals into his consciousness with the first ragged glimpse of properly textured woodland, the first whiff of punctually drained cove.

Probably a man's destination (which is ever in the motorist's thoughts) colors the highway, enlarges or diminishes its defects. Gliding over the tar, I was on my way home. DeVoto, traveling the same route, was on his way to what he described rather warily as "professional commitments," by which he probably meant that he was on his way somewhere to make a speech or get a degree. Steering a car toward home is a very different experience from steering a car toward a rostrum, and if our findings differ, it is not that we differed greatly in powers of observation but that we were headed in different emotional directions. I sometimes suspect that when I am headed east, my critical faculties are retarded almost to the vanishing point, like a frog's heartbeat in winter.

What happens to me when I cross the Piscataqua and plunge rapidly into Maine at a cost of seventy-five cents in tolls? I cannot describe it. I do not ordinarily spy a partridge in a pear tree, or three French hens, but I do have the sensation of having received a gift from a true love. And when, five hours later, I dip down across the Narramissic and look back at the tiny town of Orland, the white spire of its church against the pale-red sky stirs me in a way that Chartres could never do. It was the Narramissic that once received as fine a lyrical tribute as was ever paid to a river—a line in a poem by a schoolboy, who wrote of it, "It flows through Orland every day." I never cross that mild stream without thinking of his testimonial to the constancy, the dependability of small, familiar rivers.

Familiarity is the thing—the sense of belonging. It grants exemption from all evil, all shabbiness. A farmer pauses in the doorway of his barn and he is wearing the right boots. A sheep stands under an apple tree and it wears the right look, and the tree is hung with puckered frozen fruit of the right color. The spruce boughs that bank the foundations of the homes keep out the only true winter wind, and the light that leaves the sky at four o'clock automatically turns on the yellow lamps within, revealing to the soft-minded motorist interiors of perfect security, kitchens full of a just and lasting peace. (Or so it seems to the homing traveler.)

Even journalism in Maine has an antic quality that gives me the feeling of being home. The editorial in our weekly paper, after taking DeVoto to task for his disparaging remarks, ended on a note of delirious maladroitness. The editorialist strongly urged DeVoto to return—come back and take a second look, see the *real* Maine. Then he added, "Note: DeVoto has died since this article was written."

Benny DeVoto, a good fighter in all good causes, would enjoy that one thoroughly if he could indeed return for one more look around.

The deer season is all over for 1955. One day last week, half the hunters in town converged on the swamp south of here, between the road and the shore, for a final drive. As I rode into the village that afternoon, there was a rifleman at every crossing, and the cries of the beaters could be heard from the woods, the voice of one of them much louder and clearer than the others—a buglelike sound that suggested the eagerness of a hound. During November, a deer can't move anywhere in this community without having its whereabouts flashed via the grapevine. As the season draws to a close, a sort of desperateness infects the male population. That afternoon it was almost as though the swamp contained an escaped convict. I heard two shots just before dark, but I learned later that neither of them took effect, and was secretly glad. Still, this business of favoring the deer over the hunter is a perplexing one; some of my best friends are deerslayers, and I never wish a man bad luck. As a spectator at the annual contest between deer and man, I am in the same fix as at the Harvard-Yale game—I'm not quite sure which club I'm rooting for.

In the village, I found three big trucks loading fir-balsam wreaths for Boston. They were lined up in formation, headed out, ready for the starter's gun. The loads were already built high in the air. Fir balsam is like no other cargo; even a workaday truck is exalted and wears a consecrated look when carrying these aromatic dumplings to the hungry dwellers in cities. This is the link that must not be broken. The head man in charge of wreaths was standing in front of his platoon, directing operations. He was one of those who had officiated at my chimney fire. His cheeks were red with cold. I asked him if he would be going to Boston himself with one of the trucks, and he said no, he couldn't go, because he had pneumonia.

"You really got pneumonia?" I asked as the wicked wind tugged at our shirts.

"Yes, indeed," he replied cheerfully. "Can't seem to shake it."

I report this conversation so the people of Boston will not take their Christmas greens for granted. Wreaths do not come out of our wood lots and roll up to Boston under their own steam; they must be pried out and boosted on their way by a man with pneumonia. I noted that several of the crew were fellows whom I had last seen a few weeks ago shingling the roof of my ell in Indian summer. Hereabouts a man must know every trade. First he tacks cedar shingles to a neighbor's roof, then he's off to Boston to shingle the front doors of Beacon Hill with the living green.

Maine sends about a million Christmas trees out of the state every year, according to my latest advices. It is an easy figure to remember, and an easy one to believe as you drive about the county and see the neatly tied bundles along the road, waiting to be picked up, their little yellow butts so bright and round against the darkling green. The young fir balsam is a standard cash crop, just like the middle-aged clam. The price paid for trees "at the side of the road" ranges from a dollar a bundle (four or five trees) to $3.75. A man can be launched, or catapulted, into the Christmas-tree business quite by surprise. I wandered across the road the other day and up into the maple woods beyond my hayfield, and discovered that a miracle had taken place while my back was turned: the grove was alive with young firs, standing as close together as theatergoers between the acts.

The Christmas-tree harvest is hard on the woods, though. People tend to cut wastefully, hacking away wherever the going is good. And the enemy is always at our gates in the form of bugs and blights. I have just read a report on the forest-insect situation, sent me by the county agent. We have all sorts of picturesque plagues. The balsam woolly aphid. Birch dieback. Dutch elm disease. Spruce budworm. (A spruce "bud" in Maine parlance is a spruce cone—the thing a red squirrel eats the seeds of, sitting on a rock, and the thing Boston and New York celebrants like to put on their mantelpieces. The budworm comes into the state in the form of a moth, on the northeast wind, in summertime. I don't know whether a squirrel or a wood-lot owner has more at stake in this particular crisis.)

There are only a few small items of news to report at this season. Canada jays have been observed in the vicinity, and they managed to get into the paper, under the headline "UNUSUAL BIRD SEEN." I felt pretty good about this, because I had spotted two of these whiskey-jacks (not to be confused with cheap-Jacks) way back in October. The liquor store in the county seat was held up by a masked gunman recently and robbed of $2,672.45, which turned out to be the day's receipts and, of course, gave a much clearer picture of the amount of drinking done around here than any previous event. It would appear that the whiskey-jacks are here advisedly; they just like the sound of the place. Under the big shade trees in front of the house, the lawn is littered with dozens of half-eaten apples. I studied these, wondering what had been going on. Then I discovered that it was the work of crows. The crows pick little yellow apples from the old tree by the shed and carry them to some high perch before rifling them for seeds. In this respect they are no different from the people of San Francisco, who like to drink at the Top of the Mark, where they can really see what they are doing.

Here in New England, each season carries a hundred foreshadowings of the season that is to follow—which is one of the things I love about it. Winter is rough and long, but spring lies all round about. Yesterday, a small white keel feather escaped from my goose and lodged in the bank boughs near the kitchen porch, where I spied it as I came home in the cold twilight. The minute I saw the feather, I was projected into May, knowing that a barn swallow would be along to claim the prize and use it to decorate the front edge of its nest. Immediately, the December air seemed full of wings of swallows and the warmth of barns. Swallows, I have noticed, never use any feather but a white one in their nest-building, and they always leave a lot of it showing, which makes me believe that they are interested not in the feather's insulating power but in its reflecting power, so that when they skim into the dark barn from the bright outdoors they will have a beacon to steer by.

P.S. (April 1962).　　A trip home over the highway still warms me in the same indescribable way, but the highway itself changes from year to year. The seductive turnpike, which used to peter out conveniently at Portland, introducing the traveler to the pleasures of Route 1, now catapults him clear through to Augusta and will soon shoot him to Bangor if he isn't careful. The Narramissic still flows through Orland every day, but the last time I drove home I did not "dip down across" the river; instead I found myself hustling along on a new stretch of improved highway that cut out around Orland to the north and rushed me across the stream on a new bridge. The steep hill and sharp turns had been ironed out by the ironers, effecting a saving of probably three minutes in running time. So I was home three minutes earlier but have no idea how I spent those three extra minutes or whether they profited me as much as the old backward glance at Orland —its church spire, its reliable river, its nestling houses, its general store, and its bouquet of the flowering of New England.

The whiskey-jack showed up again around here a couple of years ago. I encountered one down in the cedar swamp in the pasture, where

I had gone to look for a fox's den. The bird, instead of showing alarm at my intrusion, followed me about, jumping silently from branch to branch in the thick woods, seemingly eager to learn what I was up to. I found it spooky yet agreeable to be tailed by a bird, and a disreputable one at that. The Canada jay looks as though he had slept in his clothes.

# A REPORT IN SPRING

*New York, May 10, 1957*

I bought a puppy last week in the outskirts of Boston and drove him to Maine in a rented Ford that looked like a sculpin. There had been talk in our family of getting a "sensible" dog this time, and my wife and I had gone over the list of sensible dogs, and had even ventured once or twice into the company of sensible dogs. A friend had a litter of Labradors, and there were other opportunities. But after a period of uncertainty and waste motion my wife suddenly exclaimed one evening, "Oh, let's just get a dachshund!" She had had a glass of wine, and I could see that the truth was coming out. Her tone was one of exasperation laced with affection. So I engaged a black male without further ado.

For the long ordeal of owning another dachshund we prepared ourselves by putting up for a night at the Boston Ritz in a room overlooking the Public Garden, where from our window we could gaze, perhaps for the last time, on a world of order and peace. I say "for the last time" because it occurred to me early in the proceedings that this was our first adoption case in which there was a strong likelihood that the dog would survive the man. It had always been the other way round. The garden had never seemed so beautiful. We were both up early the next morning for a final look at the fresh, untroubled scene; then we checked out hastily, sped to the kennel, and claimed our prize, who is the grandson of an animal named Direct Stretch of the Walls. He turned out to be a good traveler, and except for an interruption caused by my wife's falling out of the car in Gardiner, the journey went very well. At present, I am a sojourner in the city again, but here in

the green warmth of a city backyard I see only the countenance of
spring in the country. No matter what changes take place in the world,
or in me, nothing ever seems to disturb the face of spring.

The smelts are running in the brooks. We had a mess for Monday
lunch, brought to us by our son, who was fishing at two in the morning.
At this season, a smelt brook is the nightclub of the town, and when the
tide is a late one, smelting is for the young, who like small hours and
late society.

No rain has fallen in several weeks. The gardens are dry, the road
to the shore is dusty. The ditches, which in May are usually swollen
to bursting, are no more than a summer trickle. Trout fishermen are
not allowed on the streams; pond fishing from a boat is still permissible.
The landscape is lovely to behold, but the hot, dry wind carries the smell
of trouble. The other day we saw the smoke of a fire over in the direction
of the mountain.

Mice have eaten the crowns of the Canterbury bells, my white-
faced steer has warts on his neck (I'm told it's a virus, like everything
else these days), and the dwarf pear has bark trouble. My puppy has
no bark trouble. He arises at three, for tennis. The puppy's health, in
fact, is exceptionally good. When my wife and I took him from the
kennel, a week ago today, his mother kissed all three of us good-bye,
and the lady who ran the establishment presented me with complete
feeding instructions, which included a mineral supplement called Per-
vinal and some vitamin drops called Vi-syneral. But I knew that as soon
as the puppy reached home and got his sea legs he would switch to the
supplement *du jour*—a flake of well-rotted cow manure from my boot,
a dead crocus bulb from the lawn, a shingle from the kindling box,
a bloody feather from the execution block behind the barn. Time has
borne me out; the puppy was not long in discovering the delicious sup-
plements of the farm, and he now knows where every vitamin hides,
under its stone, under its loose board. I even introduced him to the tonic
smell of coon.

On Tuesday, in broad daylight, the coon arrived, heavy with
young, to take possession of the hole in the tree, but she found another
coon in possession, and there was a grim fight high in the branches. The
new tenant won, or so it appeared to me, and our old coon came down
the tree in defeat and hustled off into the woods to examine her wounds
and make other plans for her confinement. I was sorry for her, as I
am for any who are evicted from their haunts by the younger and
stronger—always a sad occasion for man or beast.

The stalks of rhubarb show red, the asparagus has broken through.
Peas and potatoes are in, but it is not much use putting seeds in the

ground the way things are. The bittern spent a day at the pond, creeping slowly around the shores like a little round-shouldered peddler. A setting of goose eggs has arrived by parcel post from Vermont, my goose having been taken by the fox last fall. I carried the package into the barn and sat down to unpack the eggs. They came out of the box in perfect condition, each one wrapped in a page torn from the *New England Homestead*. Clustered around me on the floor, they looked as though I had been hard at it. There is no one to sit on them but me, and I had to return to New York, so I ordered a trio of Muscovies from a man in New Hampshire, in the hope of persuading a Muscovy duck to give me a Toulouse gosling. (The theme of my life is complexity-through-joy.) In reply to my order, the duck-farm man wrote saying there would be a slight delay in the shipment of Muscovies, as he was "in the midst of a forest-fire scare." I did not know from this whether he was too scared to drive to the post office with a duck or too worried to fit a duck into a crate.

By day the goldfinches dip in yellow flight, by night the frogs sing the song that never goes out of favor. We opened the lower sash of the window in the barn loft, and the swallows are already building, but mud for their nests is not so easy to come by as in most springtimes. One afternoon, I found my wife kneeling at the edge of her perennial border on the north side, trying to disengage Achillea-the-Pearl from Coral Bell. "If I could afford it," she said bitterly, "I would take every damn bit of Achillea out of this border." She is a woman in comfortable circumstances, arrived at through her own hard labor, and this sudden burst of poverty, and her inability to indulge herself in a horticultural purge, startled me. I was so moved by her plight and her unhappiness that I went to the barn and returned with an edger, and we spent a fine, peaceable hour in the pretty twilight, rapping Achillea over the knuckles and saving Coral Bell.

One never knows what images one is going to hold in memory, returning to the city after a brief orgy in the country. I find this morning that what I most vividly and longingly recall is the sight of my grandson and his little sunburnt sister returning to their kitchen door from an excursion, with trophies of the meadow clutched in their hands —she with a couple of violets, and smiling, he serious and holding dandelions, strangling them in a responsible grip. Children hold spring so tightly in their brown fists—just as grownups, who are less sure of it, hold it in their hearts.

# DEATH OF A PIG

❦

*Autumn 1947*

I spent several days and nights in mid-September with an ailing pig and I feel driven to account for this stretch of time, more particularly since the pig died at last, and I lived, and things might easily have gone the other way round and none left to do the accounting. Even now, so close to the event, I cannot recall the hours sharply and am not ready to say whether death came on the third night or the fourth night. This uncertainty afflicts me with a sense of personal deterioration; if I were in decent health I would know how many nights I had sat up with a pig.

The scheme of buying a spring pig in blossomtime, feeding it through summer and fall, and butchering it when the solid cold weather arrives, is a familiar scheme to me and follows an antique pattern. It is a tragedy enacted on most farms with perfect fidelity to the original script. The murder, being premeditated, is in the first degree but is quick and skillful, and the smoked bacon and ham provide a ceremonial ending whose fitness is seldom questioned.

Once in a while something slips—one of the actors goes up in his lines and the whole performance stumbles and halts. My pig simply failed to show up for a meal. The alarm spread rapidly. The classic outline of the tragedy was lost. I found myself cast suddenly in the role of pig's friend and physician—a farcical character with an enema bag for a prop. I had a presentiment, the very first afternoon, that the play would never regain its balance and that my sympathies were now wholly with the pig. This was slapstick—the sort of dramatic treatment that instantly appealed to my old dachshund, Fred, who joined the

[ 17 ]

vigil, held the bag, and, when all was over, presided at the interment. When we slid the body into the grave, we both were shaken to the core. The loss we felt was not the loss of ham but the loss of pig. He had evidently become precious to me, not that he represented a distant nourishment in a hungry time, but that he had suffered in a suffering world. But I'm running ahead of my story and shall have to go back.

My pigpen is at the bottom of an old orchard below the house. The pigs I have raised have lived in a faded building that once was an icehouse. There is a pleasant yard to move about in, shaded by an apple tree that overhangs the low rail fence. A pig couldn't ask for anything better—or none has, at any rate. The sawdust in the icehouse makes a comfortable bottom in which to root, and a warm bed. This sawdust, however, came under suspicion when the pig took sick. One of my neighbors said he thought the pig would have done better on new ground—the same principle that applies in planting potatoes. He said there might be something unhealthy about that sawdust, that he never thought well of sawdust.

It was about four o'clock in the afternoon when I first noticed that there was something wrong with the pig. He failed to appear at the trough for his supper, and when a pig (or a child) refuses supper a chill wave of fear runs through any household, or ice-household. After examining my pig, who was stretched out in the sawdust inside the building, I went to the phone and cranked it four times. Mr. Dameron answered. "What's good for a sick pig?" I asked. (There is never any identification needed on a country phone; the person on the other end knows who is talking by the sound of the voice and by the character of the question.)

"I don't know, I never had a sick pig," said Mr. Dameron, "but I can find out quick enough. You hang up and I'll call Henry."

Mr. Dameron was back on the line again in five minutes. "Henry says roll him over on his back and give him two ounces of castor oil or sweet oil, and if that doesn't do the trick give him an injection of soapy water. He says he's almost sure the pig's plugged up, and even if he's wrong, it can't do any harm."

I thanked Mr. Dameron. I didn't go right down to the pig, though. I sank into a chair and sat still for a few minutes to think about my troubles, and then I got up and went to the barn, catching up on some odds and ends that needed tending to. Unconsciously I held off, for an hour, the deed by which I would officially recognize the collapse of the performance of raising a pig; I wanted no interruption in the regularity of feeding, the steadiness of growth, the even succession of days. I wanted no interruption, wanted no oil, no deviation. I just wanted to keep on raising a pig, full meal after full meal, spring into summer into fall. I didn't even know whether there were two ounces of castor oil on the place.

Shortly after five o'clock I remembered that we had been invited out to dinner that night and realized that if I were to dose a pig there was no time to lose. The dinner date seemed a familiar conflict: I move in a desultory society and often a week or two will roll by without my going to anybody's house to dinner or anyone's coming to mine, but when an occasion does arise, and I am summoned, something usually turns up (an hour or two in advance) to make all human intercourse seem vastly inappropriate. I have come to believe that there is in hostesses a special power of divination, and that they deliberately arrange dinners to coincide with pig failure or some other sort of failure. At any rate, it was after five o'clock and I knew I could put off no longer the evil hour.

When my son and I arrived at the pigyard, armed with a small bottle of castor oil and a length of clothesline, the pig had emerged from his house and was standing in the middle of his yard, listlessly. He gave us a slim greeting. I could see that he felt uncomfortable and uncertain. I had brought the clothesline thinking I'd have to tie him (the pig weighed more than a hundred pounds) but we never used it. My son reached down, grabbed both front legs, upset him quickly, and when he opened his mouth to scream I turned the oil into his throat —a pink, corrugated area I had never seen before. I had just time to read the label while the neck of the bottle was in his mouth. It said Puretest. The screams, slightly muffled by oil, were pitched in the hysterically high range of pig-sound, as though torture were being carried out, but they didn't last long: it was all over rather suddenly, and, his legs released, the pig righted himself.

In the upset position the corners of his mouth had been turned down, giving him a frowning expression. Back on his feet again, he regained the set smile that a pig wears even in sickness. He stood his ground, sucking slightly at the residue of oil; a few drops leaked out of his lips while his wicked eyes, shaded by their coy little lashes, turned on me in disgust and hatred. I scratched him gently with oily fingers and he remained quiet, as though trying to recall the satisfaction of being scratched when in health, and seeming to rehearse in his mind the indignity to which he had just been subjected. I noticed, as I stood there, four or five small dark spots on his back near the tail end, reddish brown in color, each about the size of a housefly. I could not make out what they were. They did not look troublesome but at the same time they did not look like mere surface bruises or chafe marks. Rather they seemed blemishes of internal origin. His stiff white bristles almost completely hid them and I had to part the bristles with my fingers to get a good look.

Several hours later, a few minutes before midnight, having dined well and at someone else's expense, I returned to the pighouse with a flashlight. The patient was asleep. Kneeling, I felt his ears (as you might put your hand on the forehead of a child) and they seemed cool, and then with the light made a careful examination of the yard and the house for sign that the oil had worked. I found none and went to bed.

We had been having an unseasonable spell of weather—hot, close days, with the fog shutting in every night, scaling for a few hours in midday, then creeping back again at dark, drifting in first over the trees on the point, then suddenly blowing across the fields, blotting out the world and taking possession of houses, men, and animals. Everyone kept hoping for a break, but the break failed to come. Next day was another hot one. I visited the pig before breakfast and tried to tempt him with a little milk in his trough. He just stared at it, while I made a sucking sound through my teeth to remind him of past pleasures of the feast. With very small, timid pigs, weanlings, this ruse is often quite successful and will encourage them to eat; but with a large, sick pig the ruse is senseless and the sound I made must have made him feel, if anything, more miserable. He not only did not crave food, he felt a positive revulsion to it. I found a place under the apple tree where he had vomited in the night.

At this point, although a depression had settled over me, I didn't suppose that I was going to lose my pig. From the lustiness of a healthy pig a man derives a feeling of personal lustiness; the stuff that goes into the trough and is received with such enthusiasm is an earnest of some later feast of his own, and when this suddenly comes to an end and the food lies stale and untouched, souring in the sun, the pig's imbalance becomes the man's, vicariously, and life seems insecure, displaced, transitory.

As my own spirits declined, along with the pig's, the spirits of my vile old dachshund rose. The frequency of our trips down the footpath through the orchard to the pigyard delighted him, although he suffers greatly from arthritis, moves with difficulty, and would be bedridden if he could find anyone willing to serve him meals on a tray.

He never missed a chance to visit the pig with me, and he made many professional calls on his own. You could see him down there at all hours, his white face parting the grass along the fence as he wobbled and stumbled about, his stethoscope dangling—a happy quack, writing his villainous prescriptions and grinning his corrosive grin. When the enema bag appeared, and the bucket of warm suds, his happiness was complete, and he managed to squeeze his enormous body between the two lowest rails of the yard and then assumed full charge of the irrigation. Once, when I lowered the bag to check the flow, he reached in and hurriedly drank a few mouthfuls of the suds to test their potency. I have noticed that Fred will feverishly consume any substance that is associated with trouble—the bitter flavor is to his liking. When the bag was above reach, he concentrated on the pig and was everywhere at once, a tower of strength and inconvenience. The pig, curiously enough, stood rather quietly through this colonic carnival, and the enema, though ineffective, was not as difficult as I had anticipated.

I discovered, though, that once having given a pig an enema there is no turning back, no chance of resuming one of life's more stereotyped roles. The pig's lot and mine were inextricably bound now, as though the rubber tube were the silver cord. From then until the time of his death I held the pig steadily in the bowl of my mind; the task of trying to deliver him from his misery became a strong obsession. His suffering soon became the embodiment of all earthly wretchedness. Along toward the end of the afternoon, defeated in physicking, I phoned the veterinary twenty miles away and placed the case formally in his hands. He was full of questions, and when I casually mentioned the dark spots on the pig's back, his voice changed its tone.

"I don't want to scare you," he said, "but when there are spots, erysipelas has to be considered."

Together we considered erysipelas, with frequent interruptions from the telephone operator, who wasn't sure the connection had been established.

"If a pig has erysipelas can he give it to a person?" I asked.

"Yes, he can," replied the vet.

"Have they answered?" asked the operator.

"Yes, they have," I said. Then I addressed the vet again. "You better come over here and examine this pig right away."

"I can't come myself," said the vet, "but McFarland can come this evening if that's all right. Mac knows more about pigs than I do anyway. You needn't worry too much about the spots. To indicate erysipelas they would have to be deep hemorrhagic infarcts."

"Deep hemmorrhagic what?" I asked.

"Infarcts," said the vet.

"Have they answered?" asked the operator.

"Well," I said, "I don't know what you'd call these spots, except they're about the size of a housefly. If the pig has erysipelas I guess I have it, too, by this time, because we've been very close lately."

"McFarland will be over," said the vet.

I hung up. My throat felt dry and I went to the cupboard and got a bottle of whiskey. Deep hemorrhagic infarcts—the phrase began fastening its hooks in my head. I had assumed that there could be nothing much wrong with a pig during the months it was being groomed for murder; my confidence in the essential health and endurance of pigs had been strong and deep, particularly in the health of pigs that belonged to me and that were part of my proud scheme. The awakening had been violent and I minded it all the more because I knew that what could be true of my pig could be true also of the rest of my tidy world. I tried to put this distasteful idea from me, but it kept recurring. I took a short drink of the whiskey and then, although I wanted to go down to the yard and look for fresh signs, I was scared to. I was certain I had erysipelas.

It was long after dark and the supper dishes had been put away when a car drove in and McFarland got out. He had a girl with him. I could just make her out in the darkness—she seemed young and pretty. "This is Miss Owen," he said. "We've been having a picnic supper on the shore, that's why I'm late."

McFarland stood in the driveway and stripped off his jacket, then his shirt. His stocky arms and capable hands showed up in my flashlight's gleam as I helped him find his coverall and get zipped up. The rear seat of his car contained an astonishing amount of paraphernalia, which he soon overhauled, selecting a chain, a syringe, a bottle of oil, a rubber tube, and some other things I couldn't identify. Miss Owen said she'd go along with us and see the pig. I led the way down the warm slope of the orchard, my light picking out the path for them, and we all three climbed the fence, entered the pighouse, and squatted by the pig while McFarland took a rectal reading. My flashlight picked up the glitter of an engagement ring on the girl's hand.

"No elevation," said McFarland, twisting the thermometer in the light. "You needn't worry about erysipelas." He ran his hand slowly over the pig's stomach and at one point the pig cried out in pain.

"Poor piggledy-wiggledy!" said Miss Owen.

The treatment I had been giving the pig for two days was then repeated, somewhat more expertly, by the doctor, Miss Owen and I handing him things as he needed them—holding the chain that he had looped around the pig's upper jaw, holding the syringe, holding the bottle stopper, the end of the tube, all of us working in darkness and in comfort, working with the instinctive teamwork induced by emergency conditions, the pig unprotesting, the house shadowy, protecting, intimate. I went to bed tired but with a feeling of relief that I had turned over part of the responsibility of the case to a licensed doctor. I was beginning to think, though, that the pig was not going to live.

He died twenty-four hours later, or it might have been forty-eight —there is a blur in time here, and I may have lost or picked up a day in the telling and the pig one in the dying. At intervals during the last day I took cool fresh water down to him and at such times as he found the strength to get to his feet he would stand with head in the pail and snuffle his snout around. He drank a few sips but no more; yet it seemed to comfort him to dip his nose in water and bobble it about, sucking in and blowing out through his teeth. Much of the time, now, he lay indoors half buried in sawdust. Once, near the last, while I was attending him I saw him try to make a bed for himself but he lacked the strength, and when he set his snout into the dust he was unable to plow even the little furrow he needed to lie down in.

He came out of the house to die. When I went down, before going to bed, he lay stretched in the yard a few feet from the door. I knelt, saw that he was dead, and left him there: his face had a mild look, expressive neither of deep peace nor of deep suffering, although I think he had suffered a good deal. I went back up to the house and to bed, and cried internally—deep hemorrhagic intears. I didn't wake till nearly eight the next morning, and when I looked out the open window the grave was already being dug, down beyond the dump under a wild apple. I could hear the spade strike against the small rocks that blocked the way. Never send to know for whom the grave is dug, I said to myself, it's dug for thee. Fred, I well knew, was supervising the work of digging, so I ate breakfast slowly.

It was a Saturday morning. The thicket in which I found the gravediggers at work was dark and warm, the sky overcast. Here, among alders and young hackmatacks, at the foot of the apple tree, Lennie had dug a beautiful hole, five feet long, three feet wide, three feet deep. He was standing in it, removing the last spadefuls of earth while Fred patrolled the brink in simple but impressive circles, disturbing the loose earth of the mound so that it trickled back in. There had been no rain in weeks and the soil, even three feet down, was dry and powdery. As I stood and stared, an enormous earthworm which had been partially exposed by the spade at the bottom dug itself deeper and made a slow withdrawal, seeking even remoter moistures at even lonelier depths. And just as Lennie stepped out and rested his spade against the tree and lit a cigarette, a small green apple separated itself from a branch overhead and fell into the hole. Everything about this last scene seemed overwritten—the dismal sky, the shabby woods, the imminence of rain, the worm (legendary bedfellow of the dead), the apple (conventional garnish of a pig).

But even so, there was a directness and dispatch about animal burial, I thought, that made it a more decent affair than human burial: there was no stopover in the undertaker's foul parlor, no wreath nor spray; and when we hitched a line to the pig's hind legs and dragged him swiftly from his yard, throwing our weight into the harness and leaving a wake of crushed grass and smoothed rubble over the dump, ours was a businesslike procession, with Fred, the dishonorable pallbearer, staggering along in the rear, his perverse bereavement showing in every seam in his face; and the post-mortem performed handily and swiftly right at the edge of the grave, so that the inwards that had caused the pig's death preceded him into the ground and he lay at last resting squarely on the cause of his own undoing.

I threw in the first shovelful, and then we worked rapidly and without talk, until the job was complete. I picked up the rope, made it fast to Fred's collar (he is a notorious ghoul), and we all three filed back up the path to the house, Fred bringing up the rear and holding back every inch of the way, feigning unusual stiffness. I noticed that although he weighed far less than the pig, he was harder to drag, being possessed of the vital spark.

The news of the death of my pig traveled fast and far, and I received many expressions of sympathy from friends and neighbors, for no one took the event lightly and the premature expiration of a pig is, I soon discovered, a departure which the community marks solemnly on its calendar, a sorrow in which it feels fully involved. I have written this account in penitence and in grief, as a man who failed to raise his pig, and to explain my deviation from the classic course of so many raised pigs. The grave in the woods is unmarked, but Fred can direct the mourner to it unerringly and with immense good will, and I know he and I shall often revisit it, singly and together, in seasons of reflection and despair, on flagless memorial days of our own choosing.

# THE EYE OF EDNA

❧

*Allen Cove, September 15, 1954*

Two hurricanes have visited me recently, and except for a few rather hasty observations of my own (which somehow seem presumptuous), all I know about these storms is what I've heard on the radio. I live on the Maine coast, to the east of Penobscot Bay. Formerly, this coast was not in the path of hurricanes, or if it was we didn't seem to know it, but times change and we must change with them. My house is equipped with three small, old-fashioned radios, two of them battery sets, one a tiny plug-in bedside model on which my wife sometimes manages to get the Giants after I have turned in. We do not have television, and because of this curious omission we are looked upon as eccentrics, possibly radicals.

Hurricanes, as all of us know to our sorrow, are given names nowadays—girls' names. And, as though to bring things full circle, newborn girl babies are being named for hurricanes. At the height of the last storm, one of the most dispiriting crumbs of news that came to me as the trees thrashed about and the house trembled with the force of the wind was that a baby girl had been born somewhere in the vicinity of Boston and had been named Edna. She is probably a nice little thing, but I took an instant dislike to her, and I would assume that thousands of other radio listeners did, too. Hurricanes are the latest discovery of radio stations and they are being taken up in a big way. To me, Nature is continuously absorbing—that is, she is a twenty-four-hour proposition, fifty-two weeks of the year—but to radio people, Nature is an oddity tinged with malevolence and worthy of note only in her more violent moments. The radio either lets Nature alone or gives her the full

[ 25 ]

treatment, as it did at the approach of the hurricane called Edna. The idea, of course, is that the radio shall perform a public service by warning people of a storm that might prove fatal; and this the radio certainly does. But another effect of the radio is to work people up to an incredible state of alarm many hours in advance of the blow, while they are still fanned by the mildest zephyrs. One of the victims of Hurricane Edna was a civil-defense worker whose heart failed him long before the wind threatened him in the least.

I heard about Edna during the morning of Friday, September 10, some thirty-six hours before Edna arrived, and my reaction was normal. I simply buttoned up the joint and sat down to wait. The wait proved interminable. The buttoning-up was not difficult—merely a couple of hours of amusing work, none of it heavy. I first went to the shore, hauled my twelve-foot boat up above high-water mark, and tied it to a stump. I closed and barricaded the boathouse doors. Then I came back up through the meadow, tolled the sheep into the barn, hooked the big doors on the north side, and drove nails in next to the hooks, so they couldn't pull out when the doors got slatting around. I let the geese in and fed them some apples—windfalls left over from Hurricane Carol. There was no good reason to shut the geese in, as they had roamed all over the place during Carol, enjoying the rough weather to the hilt and paying frequent visits to the pond at the height of the storm, but I shut them in from tidiness, and because the radio was insisting that everyone stay indoors. I got a couple of two-by-fours and some pegs, and braced the cedar fence on the west side of the terrace. Anticipating power failure, I drew extra water for drinking and cooking, and also set a pail of water next to each toilet, for a spare flush. My wife, who enters quickly into the spirit of disaster, dug up a kerosene lamp, and there was a lot of commotion about cleaning the globe and the chimney— until it was discovered that there was no wick. The potted fuchsia was moved indoors, and also the porch rocker, lest these objects be carried aloft by the wind and dashed against windows. The croquet set was brought in. (I was extremely skeptical about the chance of croquet balls coming in through the window, but it presented a vivid picture to the imagination and was worth thinking about.) The roof of the pullet house had blown off during Carol, and the pullets had developed a prejudice against hurricanes, so I shut them up early. I went to bed that night confident that all was in readiness.

Next morning, everything was in place, including the barometric pressure. The power was on, the telephone was working, the wind was moderate. Skies were gray and there was a slight rain. I found my wife curled up in bed at ten of seven with her plug-in going, tuned to disaster.

In the barn, I received an ovation from the geese, and my failure to release them caused an immense amount of gossip. After breakfast, the whole household, with the exception of our dachshund, settled down to the radio, not in a solid family group but each to his own set and his own system of tuning. No matter where one wandered, upstairs or down, back or front, a radio voice was to be heard, bringing ominous news. As near as I could make out, the storm was still about a thousand miles away and moving north-northeast at about the speed of a medium-priced automobile. Deaths had been reported in New Jersey. A state of emergency had been declared in New London, Connecticut, and in Portland, Maine. Something had happened to the second shift at the Commercial Filters Corporation plant in Melrose, Massachusetts, but I never learned what. A man named Irving R. Levine wished me "good news." The temperature in Providence, Rhode Island, was sixty-eight degrees.

It became evident to me after a few fast rounds with the radio that the broadcasters had opened up on Edna awfully far in advance, before she had come out of her corner, and were spending themselves at a reckless rate. During the morning hours, they were having a tough time keeping Edna going at the velocity demanded of emergency broadcasting. I heard one fellow from, I think, Riverhead, Long Island, interviewing his out of doors man, who had been sent abroad in a car to look over conditions on the eastern end of the island.

"How would you say the roads were?" asked the tense voice.

"They were wet," replied the reporter, who seemed to be in a sulk.

"Would you say the spray from the puddles was dashing up around the mudguards?" inquired the desperate radioman.

"Yeah," replied the reporter.

It was one of those confused moments, emotionally, when the listener could not be quite sure what position radio was taking—*for* hurricanes or *against* them.

A few minutes later, I heard another baffling snatch of dialogue on the air, from another sector—I think it was Martha's Vineyard.

"Is it raining hard there?" asked an eager voice.

"Yes, it is."

"Fine!" exclaimed the first voice, well pleased at having got a correct response.

At twenty-one and a half seconds past eleven o'clock, a New England prophet named Weatherbee, the WBZ weatherman, reported that the storm was moving north-northeast at fifty miles an hour and said that New England as a whole would not get the sustained force of the wind. This prediction was followed by a burst of inspirational music, and I wandered away and into the kitchen, where I found Mrs. Freethy mixing up a spongecake. "Heard from Edna?" she asked with wry amusement as she guided the electric mixer on its powerful way through the batter. Mrs. Freethy takes her hurricanes where she finds them.

When I returned to the radio, a man was repeating the advice I had heard many times. Fill the car with gas before the pumps lose their power. Get an old-fashioned clock that is independent of electricity. Set the refrigerator adjustment to a lower temperature. I weighed all these bits of advice carefully. The car had already been fueled. The clocks in my house have never been contaminated by so much as a single jolt of electric current. And I decided against monkeying with the refrigerator, on the ground that the control knob was probably buried behind about eighteen small, hard-to-handle items of food left over from previous meals and saved against a rainy day like this one.

I switched to Rockland, 1450 on my dial. The town manager of Camden was speaking. He said preparations had been made for mass feeding, and that you could get fed at either the Grange Hall or the Congregational Parish House, and you were invited to bring your own food. A bulletin said the core of the storm would pass to the east of Rhode Island. From Bangor, the news was that the Gene Autry show would continue as planned. The Boston Fire Commissioner advised me to keep calm and follow instructions, and I thought again about my obstinacy in the matter of the refrigerator. In Nantucket, winds were seventy-seven miles per hour.

At noon, I took a short vacation from the radio and looked out at the familiar scene, which, because it bore so little relation to the radio scene, assumed a sort of unreality. It was thirty hours or more since I'd slipped into a hurricane mood, and I could feel the telling effects of such sustained emotional living. I went outdoors. A light breeze was blowing from the southeast. Rain fell in a drizzle. The pasture pond was unruffled but had the prickly surface caused by raindrops, and it seemed bereft without geese. The sky was a gloomy gray. Two rose-bushes bowed courteously to each other on the terrace. I got a berry basket and walked out to the pullet yard, where I collected a few damp eggs. The pullets stood about in beachcombing attitudes, their feathers in disorder. As I walked back to the house, I measured with my eye the point on the roof where the biggest balm-of-Gilead tree would strike when it toppled over. I made a mental note to evacuate my people from front rooms if the wind should shift into the west, but was doubtful as to my chances of evacuating my wife from any room whatsoever, as she doesn't readily abandon well-loved posts, especially if they are furnished with traditional objects that she admires and approves of, and she is inclined to adopt a stiff-backed attitude about any change of location based on my calculations. Furthermore, she can present an overwhelming array of evidence in support of her position.

Back indoors, the storm, from which I had enjoyed momentary relief by taking a stroll in it, was on me again in full force—wild murmurings of advance information, almost impossible to make head or tail of. Edna's eye was at sea, and so was I. The eye was in New Jersey. No, it was in Long Island. No, it was not going to hit western Long Island or central Massachusetts. It was going to follow a path between Buzzards Bay and Nantucket. (This called for an atlas, which I produced.) All of New England will get the weaker part of the storm, but the Maine coast, "down Bar Harbor way," can be hit hard by Edna late this afternoon. I bridled at being described as "down Bar Harbor way."

Not only were the movements of the storm hard to follow but the voices were beginning to show the punchy condition of the poor, overworked fellows who had been blowing into their microphones at seventy miles per hour for so many hours. "Everything," cried one fellow, "is pretty well battered down in Westerly." I presumed he meant "battened down," but there was no real way of knowing. Another man, in an exhausted state, told how, in the previous hurricane, the streets of Providence had been "unindated." I started thinking in terms of unindated streets, of cities pretty well battered down. The wind now began to strengthen. The barometer on my dining-room wall was falling. From Rockland I got the "Top of the Farm News": 850,000 bales of cotton for August; a new variety of alfalfa that will stand up to stem nematode and bacterial wilt; a new tomato powder—mix it with water and you get tomato juice, only it's not on the market yet. Low tide will be at 4:23 this afternoon. The barometer now reads 29.88 and falling. A chicken shoot is canceled for tomorrow—the first chicken shoot I had ever heard of. All Rockland stores will close at three o'clock, one of them a store carrying suits with the new novelty weave and novel button and pocket trim. If this thing gets worse, I thought, I'll have to go outdoors again, even though they tell you not to. I can't take it in here. At 1:55 P.M., I learned that visiting hours at the Portsmouth Hospital, two hundred miles to the southwest of me, had been canceled, and, having no friend there, I did not know whether to be glad about this or sorry.

The time is now two o'clock. Barometer 29.50, falling. Wind ESE, rising. It seems like a sensible moment to do the afternoon chores—get them over with while the going is good. So I leave the radio for a spell and visit the barn, my peaceable kingdom, where not a nematode stirs.

When I resumed my vigil, I discovered to my great surprise that Rockland, which is quite nearby, had dropped Edna for the time being and taken up American League baseball. A Red Sox–Indians game was on, with the outfield (I never learned which outfield) playing it straight-away. My wife, who despises the American League, was listening on her set, and dialing erratically. I heard a myna bird being introduced, but the bird failed to respond to the introduction. Then someone gave the rules of a limerick contest. I was to supply the missing line for the following limerick:

> I knew a young lady named Joan
> Who wanted a car of her own.
> She was a sharp kid
> So here's what she did
> .   .   .   .   .   .   .   .   .

The line came to me quickly enough: She ordered a Chevy by phone. I was to send this to Box 401 on a postcard, but I didn't know what city and I wasn't at all sure that it was a General Motors program—could have been a competitor. The whole thing made no sense anyway, as cars were at that moment being ordered off the roads—even Joan's car.

At 2:30, it was announced that school buildings in the town of Newton were open for people who wanted to go to them "for greater personal security or comfort." Ted Williams, who had been in a slump, singled. WBZ said the Boston police had lost touch with Nantucket, electric power had failed in South Natick, Portland was going to be hit at five o'clock, Wells Beach had been evacuated, a Republican rally for tonight in Augusta had been canceled, the eye of Edna was five miles north of Nantucket, a girl baby had been born, Katharine Cornell had been evacuated by police from her home on Martha's Vineyard, and all letter carriers had been called back to their stations in Boston on the old sleet-snow-wind theory of mail delivery. I made a trip to the barometer for a routine reading: 29.41, falling.

"The rain," said the Mayor of Boston in a hearty voice, "is coming down in sheets."

"That gigantic whirlpool of air known as Hurricane Edna," said Weatherbee, from his South Shore observation point, "is over the town hall of Chatham." Weatherbee also dropped the news that the eastern end of the Maine coast would probably get winds of hurricane velocity about six hours from now.

"Weatherbee," said a proud voice from the WBZ Communications

Center, "is still batting a thousand." (At this juncture I would have settled for Ted Williams, who wasn't doing nearly so well.)

The rest of the afternoon, and the evening, was a strange nightmare of rising tempest and diminishing returns. The storm grew steadily in force, but in our neck of the woods a characteristic of hurricanes is that they arrive from the southwest, which is where most radio lives, and radio loses interest in Nature just as soon as Nature passes in front of the window and goes off toward the northeast. Weatherbee was right. The storm did strike here about six hours later, with winds up to ninety miles an hour, but when the barometer reached its lowest point and the wind shifted into the NW and began to tear everything to pieces, what we got on the radio was a man doing a whistling act and somebody playing the glockenspiel. All the livelong day we had had our mild weather to the sound of doom, and then at evening, when the power failed and the telephone failed and the tide flooded and the gale exploded, we heard the glockenspiel. Governor Cross, a Republican, who also lives to the westward, had already announced that the worst of the storm was over and that, except for a few benighted areas along the coast, everything was hunky-dory. I notice he got voted out of office a couple of days later, probably by an enormous outpouring of Republican turncoats from the coastal towns to the east of him, whose trees were being uprooted at the time he was speaking.

My own evening was an odd one. As Edna moved toward me across the Gulf of Maine, I watched the trees and the rain with increasing interest, albeit with no radio support except from the glockenspiel. At half past six, I evacuated my wife from a front room, without police action, and mixed us both a drink in a back room. At 6:55, she leaned forward in her chair and began neatening the books in a low bookshelf, pulling the volumes forward one by one and lining them up with the leading edge of the shelf, soldiers being dressed by their sergeant. By half past seven the wind had slacked off to give Edna's eye a good peep at us, the glass was steadying, and ten minutes later, watching the vane on the barn, I saw the wind starting to back into the north, fitfully. The rain eased up and we let the dachshund out, taking advantage of the lull. (Unlike the geese, she had no use for rough weather, and she had obeyed the radio faithfully all day—stayed put under the stove.)

At 7:45, the Governor of New Hampshire thanked everyone for his cooperation, and Logan International Airport announced the resumption of flights. At eight o'clock, my barometer reached bottom—28.65. The Governor of Massachusetts came on to thank *his* people, and somebody announced that the Supreme Market in Dorchester would be open for business in the morning (Sunday). Another voice promised that at eleven o'clock there would be a wrap-up on Hurricane Edna.

At this point, I decided to take a stroll. The night was agreeable—moon showing through gray clouds, light rain, hurricane still to come. My stroll turned out to be a strange one. I started for the shore, thinking I'd look over things down there, but when I got to the plank bridge over the brook I found the bridge under water. This caused me to wonder whether my spring, which supplies the house and which is located in the low-lying woods across the road, was being unindated. So, instead of proceeding to the shore, I crossed the road and entered the woods. I had rubber boots on and was carrying a flashlight. The path to the spring is pretty well grown over and I had difficulty finding it. In fact, I'm not sure that I ever did find it. I waded about in the swampy woods for ten or fifteen minutes, most of the time in water halfway up to my knees. It was pleasant in there, but I was annoyed that I was unable to find the spring. Failing in this, I returned to the house, kicked off my boots, and sank back into radioland. The Bangor station predicted ninety-mile winds within half an hour, and I discovered a scrap of paper on which my wife had scribbled "Bangor 9437, 7173, and 2313"— emergency numbers taken down just as though we were really in telephone communication with the outside world. (The phone had been gone for a long time.)

At 8:44, the power failed, the house went dark, and it was a whole lot easier to see Edna. In almost no time the storm grew to its greatest height: the wind (NW by this time) chased black clouds across the ailing moon. The woods to the south of us bent low, as though the trees prayed for salvation. Several went over. The house tuned up, roaring with the thunder of a westerly wind. For a little while, we were both battened down and battered down.

There are always two stages of any disturbance in the country—the stage when the lights and the phone are still going, the stage when these are lost. We were in the second stage. In front of the house, a large branch of the biggest balm-of-Gilead tree snapped and crashed down across the driveway, closing it off. On the north side, an apple tree split clean up the middle. And for half an hour or so Edna held us in her full embrace.

It did not seem long. Compared to the endless hours of the radio vigil, it seemed like nothing at all. By ten o'clock, the wind was moderating. We lighted the dog up to her bed by holding a flashlight along the stairs, so she could see where to leap. When we looked out of a north bedroom, there in the beautiful sky was a rainbow lit by the moon.

It was Taylor Grant, earlier in the evening, who pretty well summed things up for radio. "The weather bureau estimates that almost forty-six million persons along the east coast have felt some degree of concern over the movement of the storm," said Mr. Grant. "Never before has a hurricane had that large an audience." As one member of this vast audience, I myself felt a twinge of belated concern the next morning when I went over to the spring to fetch a pail of water. There in the woods, its great trunk square across the path, its roots in the air, lay a big hackmatack.

I never did get to hear the wrap-up.

# COON TREE

❦

*Allen Cove, June 14, 1956*

The temperature this morning, here in the East, is 68 degrees. The relative humidity is 64 percent. Barometer 30.02, rising. Carol Reed is nowhere in sight. A light easterly breeze ruffles the water of the cove, where a seine boat lies at anchor, her dories strung out behind like ducklings. Apple blossoms are showing, two weeks behind schedule, and the bees are at work—all six of them. (A bee is almost as rare a sight these days as a team of horses.) The goldfinch is on the dandelion, the goose is on the pond, the black fly is on the trout brook, the Northeast Airliner is on course for Rockland. As I write these notes, the raccoon is nursing one of her hangovers on the branch outside the hole where her kittens are.

My doctor has ordered me to put my head in traction for ten minutes twice a day. (Nobody can figure out what to do with my head, so now they are going to give it a good pull, like an exasperated mechanic who hauls off and gives his problem a smart jolt with the hammer.) I have rigged a delightful traction center in the barn, using a canvas halter, a length of clothesline, two galvanized pulleys, a twelve-pound boat anchor, a milking stool, and a barn swallow. I set everything up so I could work the swallow into the deal, because I knew he would enjoy it, and he does. While his bride sits on the eggs and I sit on the milking stool, he sits on a harness peg a few feet away, giggling at me throughout the ten-minute period and giving his mate a play-by-play account of man's fantastic battle with himself, which in my case must look like suicide by hanging.

I think this is the fourth spring the coon has occupied the big

[ 34 ]

tree in front of the house, but I have lost count, so smoothly do the years run together. She is like a member of our family. She has her kittens in a hole in the tree about thirty-five feet above the ground, which places her bedchamber a few feet from my bedchamber but at a slightly greater elevation. It strikes me as odd (and quite satisfactory) that I should go to sleep every night so close to a litter of raccoons. The mother's comings and goings are as much a part of my life at this season of the year as my morning shave and my evening drink. Being a coon, she is, of course, a creature of the night; I am essentially a creature of the day, so we Cox and Box it very nicely. I have become so attuned to her habits—her departure as the light fades at quarter past eight, her return to the hungry kittens at about 3 A.M., just before daylight, after the night's adventures—that I have taken to waking at three to watch her home-coming and admire her faint silhouette against the sky as she carefully sniffs the bark all around the hole to learn if anything has been along during her absence and if any child of hers has disobeyed the instructions about *not* venturing out of the hole.

My introduction to raccoons came when, as a child, I read in a book by the late Dr. William J. Long a chapter called "A Little Brother to the Bear." I read all the books of William J. Long with a passionate interest, and learned the Milicete Indian names for the animals. (Dr. Long always called a bear Mooween, he always called a chickadee Ch'geegee-lokh-sis. This device stimulated me greatly, but if I remember right, it annoyed Theodore Roosevelt, who was also interested in nature.) I must have read the raccoon story twenty times. In those days, my imagination was immensely stirred by the thought of wildlife, of which I knew absolutely nothing but for which I felt a kind of awe. Today, after a good many years of tame life, I find myself in the incredibly rich situation of living in a steam-heated, electrically lit dwelling on a tarred highway with a raccoon dozing in her penthouse while my power lawn mower circles and growls noisily below. At last I am in a position to roll out the green carpet for a little sister to the bear. (I have even encountered Dr. Long's daughter Lois in my travels, but it was not among raccoons that we met, and she seemed to have no mark of the Milicete Indian about her whatsoever, and never in my presence has she referred to a great horned owl as Kookooskoos, which saddens me.)

There are two sides to a raccoon—the arboreal and the terrestrial. When a female coon is in the tree, caring for young, she is one thing. When she descends and steps off onto solid earth to prowl and hunt, she is quite another. In the tree she seems dainty and charming; the circles under her eyes make her look slightly dissipated and deserving of sympathy. The moment she hits the ground, all this changes; she seems predatory, sinister, and as close to evil as anything in Nature (which contains no evil) can be. If I were an Indian, naming animals, I would call the raccoon He Who Has the Perpetual Hangover. This morning, conditions inside the hole are probably unbearable. The kittens are quite big now, the sun is hot, and the hole is none too roomy anyway —it's nothing but a flicker hole that time has enlarged. So she has emerged, to lie in full view on the horizontal limb just under her doorway. Three of her four legs are draped lifelessly over the limb, the fourth being held in reserve to hang on with. Her coat is rough, after the night of hunting. In this state she presents a picture of utter exhaustion and misery, unaccompanied by remorse. On the rare occasions when I have done a little hunting myself at night, we sleep it off together, she on her pallet, I on mine, and I take comfort in her nearness and in our common suffering.

I guess I have watched my coon descend the tree a hundred times; even so, I never miss a performance if I can help it. It has a ritualistic quality, and I know every motion, as a ballet enthusiast knows every motion of his favorite dance. The secret of its enchantment is the way it employs the failing light, so that when the descent begins, the performer is clearly visible and is a part of day, and when, ten or fifteen minutes later, the descent is complete and the coon removes the last paw from the tree and takes the first step away, groundborne, she is almost indecipherable and is a part of the shadows and the night. The going down of the sun and the going down of the coon are interrelated phenomena; a man is lucky indeed who lives where sunset and coonset are visible from the same window.

The descent is prefaced by a thorough scrub-up. The coon sits on her high perch, undisturbed by motorcars passing on the road below, and gives herself a complete going over. This is catlike in its movements. She works at the tail until it is well bushed out and all six rings show to advantage. She washes leg and foot and claw, sometimes grabbing a hind paw with a front paw and pulling it closer. She washes her face the way a cat does, and she rinses and sterilizes her nipples. The whole operation takes from five to fifteen minutes, according to how hungry she is and according to the strength of the light, the state of the world below the tree, and the mood and age of the kittens within the hole. If the kittens are young and quiet, and the world is young and still, she finishes her bath without delay and begins her downward journey. If the kittens are restless, she may return and give them another feeding. If they are well grown and anxious to escape (as they are at this point in June), she hangs around in an agony of indecision. When a small head appears in the opening, she seizes it in her jaws and rams it back inside. Finally, like a mother with no baby-sitter and a firm date at the theater, she takes her leave, regretfully, hesitantly. Sometimes, after she has made it halfway down the tree, if she hears a stirring in the nursery she hustles back up to have another look around.

A coon comes down a tree headfirst for most of the way. When she gets within about six feet of the ground, she reverses herself, allowing her hind end to swing slowly downward. She then finishes the descent tailfirst; when, at last, she comes to earth, it is a hind foot that touches down. It touches down as cautiously as though this were the first contact ever made by a mammal with the flat world. The coon doesn't just let go of the tree and drop to the ground, as a monkey or a boy might. She steps off onto my lawn as though in slow motion— first one hind paw, then the other hind paw, then a second's delay when she stands erect, her two front paws still in place, as though the tree were her partner in the dance. Finally, she goes down on all fours and strides slowly off, her slender front paws reaching ahead of her to the limit, like the hands of an experienced swimmer.

I have often wondered why the coon reverses herself, starting headfirst, ending tailfirst. I believe it is because although it comes naturally to her to descend headfirst, she doesn't want to arrive on the ground in that posture, lest an enemy appear suddenly and catch her at a disadvantage. As it is, she can dodge back up without unwinding herself if a dog or a man should appear.

Because she is a lover of sweet corn, the economic status of my raccoon is precarious. I could shoot her dead with a .22 any time I cared to. She will take my corn in season, and for every ear she eats she will ruin five others, testing them for flavor and ripeness. But in the country a man has to weigh everything against everything else, balance his pleasures and indulgences one against another. I find that I can't shoot this coon, and I continue to plant corn—some for her, what's left for me and mine—surrounding the patch with all sorts of coon baffles. It is an arrangement that works out well enough. I am sure of one thing: I like the taste of corn, but I like the nearness of coon even better, and I cannot recall ever getting the satisfaction from eating an ear of corn that I get from watching a raccoon come down a tree just at the edge of dark.

Today I've been rereading a cheerful forecast for the coming century, prepared by some farsighted professors at the California Institute of Technology and published not long ago in the *Times*. Man, it would appear, is standing at the gateway to a new era of civilization. Technology will be king. Everything man needs (the report says) is at hand. All we require is air, sea water, ordinary rock, and sunlight. The population of the earth will increase and multiply, but that'll be no problem—the granite of the earth's crust contains enough uranium and thorium to supply an abundance of power for everybody. If we just pound rock, we're sitting pretty.

It is a splendid vision: technology the king, Jayne Mansfield the queen. (It is also the same old conflict.) Right in the middle of the forecast, the professors paused long enough to let drop a footnote. Their prediction, they said, applies *only* if world catastrophe is avoided. At any rate, the civilization at whose gateway I am said to be standing will pose one rather acute problem for me: *What position am I going to take in the matter of rock?* I have taken my stand on raccoon; now I have to take my stand on rock. These acres on which I live are well supplied and underlaid with rock. The pasture is full of granite, the vegetable garden has some splendid rocks in it, the foundation of the house is granite, the doorstone is granite, there is a granite outcropping in the lawn where the whippoorwill comes to sit and repeat himself in the hour before daybreak, several of the fields are ledgy in places, and if you wander into the woods, you come on old stone walls made of tons and tons of rock. A ton of granite, according to my advices, contains about four grams of uranium and twelve grams of thorium. Is my next move to extract this stuff, or can I leave my stones be? I assume that if I am to dwell contentedly and adjust to the new era, I must pick the uranium and thorium from my rocks and convert them into power, but I'm not sure I am ready to fall in with any such hare-brained scheme. The only time I ever fooled with rocks in a big way on this place, I simply made a lot of noise, created a memorable era of confusion, and ended up about where I started. (I got fooling with rocks because I had bought a cow, and in the country one thing leads to another.) The only place for a nuclear reactor here would be the brooder house, and I need the brooder house for my chicks. If the modern way to get electric power to run my brooder stove is to tap the energy in my pasture rocks, I may very well consider returning to the old natural method of raising chicks, using a couple of broody hens—in which case I am standing at the gateway to the long past rather than the long future. There is one big boulder down in the pasture woods where I sometimes go to sit when I am lonely or sick or melancholy or disenchanted or frightened, and in combination with sweet fern, juniper, and bayberry this old rock has a remarkably restorative effect on me. I'm not sure but that this is the true energy, the real source of man's strength. I'm not sure rocks would work out so well for me if I were to drag them up out of the pasture and pry the fissionable materials out of them.

I am not convinced that atomic energy, which is currently said to be man's best hope for a better life, is his best hope at all, or even a good bet. I am not sure energy is his basic problem, although the weight of opinion is against me. I would feel more optimistic about a bright future for man if he spent less time proving that he can outwit Nature and more time tasting her sweetness and respecting her seniority. Almost every bulletin I receive from my county agent is full of wild schemes for boxing Nature's ears and throwing dust in her eyes, and the last issue of the *Rural New-Yorker* contained a tiny item saying that poultrymen had "volunteered" to quit feeding diphenyl-para-phenylene-diamine to chickens, because it can cause illness in "persons"—one of the tardiest pieces of volunteer activity I ever heard of. Yesterday, it was reported in the news that atomic radiation is cumulative and that no matter how small the dose, it harms the person receiving it and all his descendants. Thus, a lifetime of dental X-rays and other familiar bombardments and fallouts may finally spell not better teeth and better medicine but no teeth and no medicine, and a chicken dinner may become just another word for bellyache. The raccoon, for all her limitations, seems to me better adjusted to life on earth than men are; she has never taken a tranquilizing pill, has never been X rayed to see whether she is going to have twins, has never added DPPD to the broiler mash, and is not out at night looking for thorium in rocks. She is out looking for frogs in the pond.

Dr. Fritz Zwicky, the astrophysicist, has examined the confused situation on this planet, and his suggestion is that we create one hundred *new* planets. Zwicky wants to scoop up portions of Neptune, Saturn, and Jupiter and graft them onto smaller planets, then change the orbits of these enlarged bodies to make their course around the sun roughly comparable to that of our earth. This is a bold, plucky move, but I would prefer to wait until the inhabitants of *this* planet have learned to live in political units that are not secret societies and until the pens on the writing desks in banks are not chained to the counter. Here we are, busily preparing ourselves for a war already described as "unthinkable," bombarding our bodies with gamma rays that everybody admits are a genetical hazard, spying on each other, rewarding people on quiz programs with a hundred thousand dollars for knowing how to spell "cat," and Zwicky wants to make a hundred *new* worlds. Maybe he gained confidence to go ahead when he heard that in Florida they had succeeded in putting an elephant on water skis. Any race of creatures that can put an elephant on water skis is presumably ready to construct new worlds.

Dr. Vannevar Bush, who is in a far better position to discuss science and progress than I am, once said, "Man may, indeed, have evolved from the primordial ooze, and this may be accepted as good if we assume that it is good to have complex life on earth, but this again is an arbitrary assumption." Many of the commonest assumptions, it seems to me, are arbitrary ones: that the new is better than the old, the untried superior to the tried, the complex more advantageous than the simple, the fast quicker than the slow, the big greater than the small, and the world as remodeled by Man the Architect functionally sounder and more agreeable than the world as it was before he changed everything to suit his vogues and his conniptions.

I have made a few private tests of my own, and my findings differ somewhat from those of the Cal Tech men. We have two stoves in our kitchen here in Maine—a big black iron stove that burns wood and a small white electric stove that draws its strength from the Bangor Hydro-Electric Company. We use both. One represents the past, the other represents the future. If we had to give up one in favor of the other and cook on just one stove, there isn't the slightest question in anybody's mind in my household which is the one we'd keep. It would be the big black Home Crawford 8-20, made by Walker & Pratt, with its woodbox that has to be filled with wood, its water tank that has to be replenished with water, its ashpan that has to be emptied of ashes, its flue pipe that has to be renewed when it gets rusty, its grates that need freeing when they get clogged, and all its other foibles and deficiencies. We would choose this stove because of the quality of its heat, the scope of its talents, the warmth of its nature (the place where you dry the sneakers, the place where the small dog crawls underneath to take the chill off, the companionable sounds it gives forth on cool nights in fall and on zero mornings in winter). The electric stove is useful in its own way, and makes a good complementary unit, but it is as cold and aseptic as a doctor's examining table, and I can't imagine our kitchen if it were the core of our activity.

The American kitchen has come a long way, and it has a long way to return before it gets to be a good room again. Last fall, the American Society of Industrial Designers met in Washington and kicked the kitchen around a bit. One of the speakers, I remember, said that we will soon get to the point of eating "simply and fast." He said we would push a button and peas would appear on a paper plate. No preparation at all.

It really comes down to what a man wants from a plate of peas, and to what peas have it in their power to give. I'm not much of an eater, but I get a certain amount of nourishment out of a seed catalogue on a winter's evening, and I like to help stretch the hen wire along the rows of young peas on a fine morning in June, and I feel better if I sit around and help with the shelling of peas in July. This is all a part of the pageantry of peas, if you happen to like peas. Our peas didn't get planted until May 9 this spring—about three weeks later than the normal planting time. I shall hardly know what day in July to push the button and watch them roll out onto the paper plate.

Another speaker at the designers' conference said, "The kitchen as we know it today is a dead dodo." (One solution this man offered for the house of the future is to have a place called a "dirty room." This would be equipped with appliances for all cleaning problems, and into it would be dumped everything dirty. But in most American homes the way to have a dirty room is to have a small boy; that's the way *we* worked it for a number of happy years.) I think the kitchen, like the raccoon, is a dead dodo only if you choose to shoot it dead. Years ago, at the time I bought this house, I examined my kitchen with a wondering and skeptical eye and elected to let it live. The decision stands as one of the few sensible moves I've made on this place. Our kitchen today is a rich, intoxicating blend of past, present, and future; basically it belongs to the past, when it was conceived and constructed. It is a strange and implausible room, dodolike to the modern eye but dear to ours, and far from dead. In fact, it teems with life of all sorts— cookery, husbandry, horticulture, canning, planning. It is an arsenal, a greenhouse, a surgical-dressing station, a doghouse, a bathhouse, a lounge, a library, a bakery, a cold-storage plant, a factory, and a bar, all rolled up into one gorgeous ball, or ballup. In it you can find the shotgun and shell for shooting up the whole place if it ever should become obsolete, in it you can find the molasses cookie if you decide just to sit down and leave everything the way it is. From morning till night, sounds drift from the kitchen, most of them familiar and comforting, some of them surprising and worth investigating. On days when warmth is the most important need of the human heart, the kitchen is the place you can find it; it dries the wet socks, it cools the hot little brain. During heat waves, the wood fire is allowed to go out, and with all doors open the kitchen sucks a cool draft through from one side of the house to the other, and General Electric is king for a day.

Our kitchen contains such modern gadgets as an electric refrigerator, a Macy cabinet, and a Little Dazey ice smasher, and it contains such holdovers from the past as the iron stove, the roller towel, the iron sink, the wooden drainboard, and the set tubs. (You can wash a dog in my kitchen without any trouble except from the dog.) It is remarkably free of the appliances that you see in exhibits whose name ends in "ama." It *does* have an egg beater, an electric mixer, and a garbage can that opens miraculously at a slight pressure from the toe. It also has the electric stove, with the dials that you turn. I can't read these dials without my glasses, and it is usually more practical for me to build a fire in the wood stove than to hunt up my glasses. For that matter, the wood stove almost always has steam up, our climate being what it is, and is all ready to go without any fire-building. You just add a stick of wood, open the draft, and shove the kettle a few inches to the left, toward the heat.

I don't think I am kidding myself about this stove. If I had to go to the woods myself, cut the wood, haul it out, saw it, and split it, I wouldn't be able to afford a wood stove, because I lack the strength and the skill for such adventures. In a way, the stove is my greatest luxury. But I'm sure I've spent no more on it than many a man has spent on more frivolous or complex devices. A wood stove is like a small boat; it costs something to keep, but it satisfies a man's dream life. Mine even satisfies all the cooks in this family—and there are half a dozen of them—which is a more telling argument and a more substantial reward.

I read a statement by Jim Bailey not long ago, after he had run his mile in 3:58.6. "I have no sensation of speed when I run," he said, "and I never know how fast I'm going." Such is the case with most of us in this queer century of progress. Events carry us rapidly in directions tangential to our true desires, and we have almost no sensation of being in motion at all—except at odd moments when we explode an H-bomb or send up a hundred new planets or discard an old stove for a new one that will burn thorium instead of spruce.

My stove, which I'm sure would be impractical in many American homes, is nevertheless a symbol of my belief. The technologists, with their vision of happiness at the core of rock, see only half the rock—half of man's dream and his need. Perhaps success in the future will depend partly on our ability to generate cheap power, but I think it will depend to a greater extent on our ability to resist a technological formula that is sterile: peas without pageantry, corn without coon, knowledge without wisdom, kitchens without a warm stove. There is more to these rocks than uranium; there is the lichen on the rock, the smell of the fern whose feet are upon the rock, the view from the rock.

Last night, to amuse the grandson who is presently handling the problem of our "dirty room," we read the first chapter of *The Peterkin Papers*, and I was amazed to discover what a perfect fable it is for these times. You recall that Mrs. Peterkin poured herself a delicious cup of coffee and then, just as she was ready to drink it, realized that she had put salt in it instead of sugar. Here was a major crisis. A family conference was held, and the chemist was called in on the case. The chemist put in a little chlorate of potassium, but the coffee tasted no better. Then he added some tartaric acid and some hypersulphate of lime. It was no better. The chemist then tried ammonia and, in turn, some oxalic, cyanic, acetic, phosphoric, chloric, hyperchloric, sulphuric, boracic, silicic, nitric, formic, nitrous nitric, and carbonic acid. Mrs. Peterkin tasted each, but it still wasn't coffee. After another unsuccessful round of experimentation, this time with herbs, Elizabeth Eliza took the problem to the lady from Philadelphia, who said, "Why doesn't your mother make a fresh cup of coffee?"

The lady's reply is arresting. Certainly the world's brew is bitter today, and we turn more and more to the chemist and the herbwoman to restore its goodness. But every time I examine those Cal Tech elements—sun, sea, air, and rock—I am consumed with simple curiosity, not about whether there is thorium in the rock but whether there is another cup of coffee in the pot.

P.S. (March 1962).      Six years have elapsed. It is a pleasure to report that the coon tree is still in business and so is our black iron stove. When I wrote that a coon comes down a tree headfirst and then reverses herself when near the ground, touching down with one hind foot, I had observed only one coon in the act of leaving a tree. The coon I wrote about is no longer with us; she was ousted by another female (probably a younger one and perhaps her own daughter) after a fierce battle high in the tree at the entrance to the hole, both females being pregnant and ready to lie in. The new young coon, the one we have now, descends the tree headfirst but does not reverse when near the ground. She continues headfirst and steps off onto the lawn with one front foot. Moral: a man should not draw conclusions about raccoons from observing one individual. The day may come when we'll have a coon that completes the descent of the tree with a half gainer.

Every year the coon hole gets larger, from wear and tear and from the tendency of balm-of-Gilead trees to grow hollow in their old age. The chamber, or nursery, now boasts two openings, the big one that serves as entrance in the south face of the tree and a smaller one higher up in the northeast face. The smaller hole is of occasional interest to woodpeckers—hairies and pileateds—who stop by and inspect it. They peer in, and soon become agitated. If the chamber contains a raccoon with kittens, the visiting bird is jolted by the unexpected sight of live animals inside a tree. If no coons are there, I think the bird is surprised and disappointed by the light that enters from the larger aperture, making the chamber unnaturally bright and unsuitable for woodpecker occupancy.

Last spring, when the young coons were about three weeks old, we had a torrential three-day rainstorm. It was so bad, even the coon hole shipped water. The mother made the hard decision to evacuate the young ones, which she did by carrying them, one by one, in her mouth down the tree and depositing them a few hundred yards down the road in a drier location under the floor of a neighbor's house. Three days later in broad daylight she brought them all back and reinstated them—a monumental job of planning and execution over an obstacle course bristling with dogs, men, and vehicles. There were four kittens, which meant for her a total of fourteen trips over the road, all told.

As for my kitchen, it is really two kitchens—the front one and the back one. The front kitchen, where the black stove is, has survived the pressures of time; it is the same as ever, warm, comfortable, convenient, and unimproved. The back kitchen, however, fell on evil days and modern appliances, as I knew it would eventually. It now looks like the setting for a television commercial. We removed the old black iron sink and substituted a shiny stainless one. We rebuilt the counters, covering them with Formica, or Micarta, or something that ends in "a," I forget what. We threw out the old wooden drainboard, which had grown almost as soft as a sponge, and replaced it with a yellow rubber mat that has no pitch. We tore out the set tubs; in their place is an automatic washing machine that goes on the blink every five weeks and an automatic dryer that blows lint into the woodshed through an exhaust pipe every time it is used. Next to the new sink, under the counter, we installed an automatic dishwasher. This machine works quite nicely, but it celebrates each new phase of the wash with a great clanking noise; it grunts and groans incessantly at its labors, and it leaves a hot smell of detergent in the wake of its toil, so that when you pass it on your way out to the woodshed the air in the room tickles the inside of your nose. It takes the design off the china and leaves ring marks on the glassware. Strong detergents have replaced weak soaps in the back kitchen, vibration has replaced quietude, sanitation broods over all, the place smells of modernity and Ajax, and there is no place to wash the dog. (I give our current dachshund one bath a year now, in an old wash boiler, outdoors, finishing him off with a garden-hose rinse. He then rolls in the dirt to dry himself and we are where we started.)

I liked the back kitchen better the way it was before we improved it, but I knew it was doomed. I will have to admit that the old wooden drainboard had quite an impressive accumulation of gurry in its seams. Germs must have loved it. I know *I* did. Incidentally, I was pleased to learn, not long ago, that children in unsanitary homes acquire a better resistance to certain diseases (polio and hepatitis among them) than children in homes where sanitation is king. Whether or not our old drainboard was a guardian of our health I will never know; but neither my wife nor I have enjoyed as good health since the back kitchen got renovated. I would hate to think that it's just a coincidence.

# A REPORT IN JANUARY

❧

*Allen Cove, January 30, 1958*

Margaret Mitchell once made a remark I have treasured. Someone asked her what she was "doing," and she replied, "Doing? It's a full-time job to be the author of *Gone With the Wind*." I remembered this cheerful statement this morning as I lay in bed, before daylight, marshaling in my head the problems and projects and arrangements of the day and wondering when I would again get a chance to "do" something— like sit at a typewriter. I felt a kinship with Miss Mitchell and comforted myself with the pleasing thought that just to live in New England in winter is a full-time job; you don't have to "do" anything. The idle pursuit of making-a-living is pushed to one side, where it belongs, in favor of living itself, a task of such immediacy, variety, beauty, and excitement that one is powerless to resist its wild embrace.

Right this minute I am making a brief show of resistance; I have resolved to keep the wolf from the door. But what I'm really trying to keep from my door is the fox—a very different proposition. A loaded gun is at my side, and my typewriter is placed strategically at a window that commands a view of the strip of woods from which the fox usually emerges. He has been thrice in our dooryard within the week. Thrice have I muffed him. He came first during a snow squall, and carried off a little buff Cochin Bantam hen who was outdoors trying her snowshoes. I witnessed the murder from an upstairs window, feeling as helpless as I'd felt on a day years ago when I stood at a window in St. Luke's Hospital overlooking Morningside Park and watched a thief beat up a woman. Yesterday I got a shot at the fox, but I hurried the shot (in anger) and he ran off into the woods grinning.

One of the most time-consuming things is to have an enemy. The fox is mine. He wants to destroy my form of society—a society of free geese, of Bantams unconfined. So I react in the natural way, building up my defenses, improving my weapons and my aim, spending more and more time on the problem of supremacy. This morning the wolf and the fox compete for my attention; I am a hunter divided against himself. Either animal could slip easily through my guard while I am thinking about the other. When I realize what a vast amount of time the world would have for useful and sensible tasks if each country could take its mind off "the enemy," I am appalled. I shot a fox last fall —a long, lucky shot with a .22 as he drank at the pond. It was cold murder. All he wanted at that moment was a drink of water, but the list of his crimes against me was a long one, and so I shot him dead, and he fell backward and sank slowly into the mud.

The war between me and the fox is as senseless as all wars. There is no way to rationalize it. The fox is not even the biggest and meanest killer here—I hold that distinction myself. I think nothing of sending half a dozen broilers to the guillotine. Come June, heads will be rolling behind my barn. Foxes are now carrying a disease called hardpad, but even that is insufficient reason for shooting a fox. My puppy, I presume, could pick up hardpad from sniffing around in the dooryard, and then I would have a dachshund that was not only hard-headed but hard-footed, too, which would try my patience. But if you were to solve the problem of disease by shooting the sick, you'd have to shoot Aunt Mollie when she got the flu. I have plenty of convictions but no real courage, and I find it hard to live in the country without slipping into the role of murderer. From where I sit I can see a piece of suet hanging on a crab-apple tree. A hairy woodpecker is digging away at it contentedly. The suet is from a steer we killed last fall—I gave the order for the hatchet job. Imagine killing a steer to feed a woodpecker! (We also got 367 pounds of beef for our freezer, but I can't see that that changes the matter any. The fox and I are up to the same mischief; we differ only in technique.)

Hunters in this state killed 40,142 deer during the 1957 season. It was the third-highest kill on record. Maine is a bit touchy about its deerslaying and prefers to break the record each year. In 1951 the hunters tagged 41,730 deer, and that figure still stands as the one to beat. I don't know why people feel unhappy when the curve of a graph fails to keep going up, but they do. Even when we find something we'd like to reduce, such as highway fatalities, it doesn't always sound as though we had our heart in it. On the eve of every holiday, the National Safety Council broadcasts its prediction that such-and-such a number of motorists are "expected" to die over the weekend, almost as though it were a man's duty to go out and get killed in order to make the estimate come out right. I didn't shoot a deer, but someone brought me a hindquarter and it was good. A moose came to town right in the middle of the battle, and somebody shot him and cut his head off, leaving the meat to spoil. Everybody was stirred up about the incident of the moose: there is a heavy fine for killing a moose nowadays, but there is an even heavier resentment against anyone's wasting good meat.

Shortly after the close of the deer season, there was a lead editorial in the paper complaining that there had been a drop in out-of-state hunting licenses and urging that Maine get busy and appropriate more money for development, to attract hunters to the state. The theory is that if you shoot forty thousand deer one year you aren't getting ahead unless you shoot fifty thousand the next, but I suspect there comes a point where you have shot just exactly the right number of deer. Our whole economy hangs precariously on the assumption that the higher you go the better off you are, and that unless more stuff is produced in 1958 than was produced in 1957, more deer killed, more automatic dishwashers installed, more out-of-staters coming into the state, more heads aching so they can get the fast fast fast relief from a pill, more automobiles sold, you are headed for trouble, living in danger and maybe in squalor. If that theory is sound, Maine won't be in a solid position until we kill at least forty million deer and with a good prospect of making it fifty million the following year. But that would be the end of the wilderness, and without its wilderness Maine would feel awfully naked.

The editorial pointed to Florida as an example of a state that had sense enough to spend large sums on promotion. "Florida ads all but smother Maine's," said the editorial. I guess this is true. Another thing that is true is that Florida recently "developed" the beach where I used to swim, and as a result I no longer care about going there. Some fellow with strong promotional instincts put a bulldozer to work on the beach and leveled the sand dunes in order to improve the parking facilities and make a place for a hot-dog stand. Formerly it was very pleasant to prop yourself against a sand dune and look out at the beautiful sea, but now you have to lie perfectly flat and look out at the beautiful candy wrappers swirling in the eddies of the wind. The last time I gazed at the scene, I realized that I had lost interest in that particular strip of beach. (And if the surf hath lost its savor, wherewith shall we be surfeited?) So I am lingering in Maine this winter, to fight wolves and foxes. The sun here is less strong than Florida's, but so is the spirit of development, and I can stare at the sea without peering through the wire mesh of a trash basket. Of course, it is conceivable that Florida will get along nicely without me. But if the various state development programs are to work properly a man would have to be in all forty-eight states at the same time.

The urge to solve a problem with a bulldozer or some other piece of heavy machinery is strong. I succumbed to it last fall when I hired a man to scoop out my pasture pond with a device called a back hoe. What I was trying to do was restore the pond to the condition it was in when I first laid eyes on it, many years ago. So far, all I have accomplished is to stir the pond up. The banks look like a place where enormous children have been making enormous mud pies. The pond has a clay bottom, and when this got agitated by the back hoe the water became cloudy. On certain days, when the light is right, it looks as though someone had poured milk into the pond. Every morning, I look out to see if the pond has cleared during the night, but it stays milky. When it froze, it made cloudy ice—which is just as good for skating as clear ice, but that is no solace, because for the first time in thirty-five years I can't find my shoe hockeys. Everything points to the conclusion that when thieves entered our apartment in New York last summer they were so sore at me for not having stocked the place with mink coats they took my skates to get even.

The winter has been mild so far, and excessively wet. Snow lies on the ground today, but for the most part we have had rain and wind. Everybody says he can't remember any winter like it in all his life, but that's what you always hear, no matter what the weather is like. The rains have been almost continuous; water stands everywhere. The barnyard is the consistency of oatmeal gruel, and my two Hereford heifers slide around like a couple of otters. The geese do not have to walk clear down to the pond; they just go as far as the bottom of the lane, where a pool has formed deep enough for their carnivals, which at this season include dalliance.

Work is not plentiful here in town this winter. The Christmas-greens business, however, hit an all-time high last month. A good many people—men, women, and children—earn their Christmas-shopping money by cutting brush (spruce and fir) to be trucked to Boston for use in wreaths and other decorations. My best information is that the take was around $9,000.

Scalloping was poor in December—too much wind. Lately it has improved a bit; there have been days when the sea was quiet enough for the boats to go out. Winter fishing, even under good conditions, is hazardous, and our town has just lost a man to the sea. He fell overboard last night from the slippery deck of a dragger tied up in Rockland and was drowned. Like many a fisherman, he couldn't swim a stroke.

I heard yesterday that the school-lunch program, which has been a fixture for a number of years, had been abruptly discontinued; no two people agree on which the reason is, but it seems to be partly a lessening of government support, partly a rise in the price of food. In a nearby town, the lunch program received a tremendous shot in the arm last fall when a couple of deer were run over by motorists. The alert school board soon had venison on the menu two or three times a week, at the going rate—twenty-five cents a meal.

Until yesterday's snowfall the woods had been bare. We got out our year's supply of firewood on wheels—two old wire wheels off a Model A Ford. Years ago, people depended on sleds for bringing wood out from the wood lots, but very few do it that way any more. They use scoots, which are a sort of drag, or they use a two-wheel trailer drawn by a tractor. My tractor is quite old now, and has faded to a pretty color—zinnia pink, like a red shirt that has been much washed. When I bought it, it was fire-engine red, but now it can slink away into the woods and go out of sight as quickly as a little animal. An hour or so later it reappears, dragging a load of wood to add to the pile. Arthur Cole arrived one blustery afternoon after work, trailing his sawing machine behind his coupé, and sawed almost all of our six and a half cords before dark. Arthur is seventy-six and dearly loves to saw wood. He still has all ten fingers. He is working on his twenty-three-thousandth cord, having been at it—mostly at odd moments, before or after work—for forty-nine years. He has a record of every stick of wood that has been through his machine, and can show it to you, in cords and in dollars—the plain accounting of a man who has never been able to leave work alone. When he started sawing, forty-nine years ago, he used to get fifty cents a cord. Now he gets two dollars. "You handle a lot of big money now," he said as I handed him thirteen dollars, "but you're no better off." He has had many accidents, and on a couple of occasions has had to be sewn together, so that he could be out early the next morning to saw more wood. Once, the saw threw a stick at him and caught his upper plate, driving it into his jaw. Dry wood is more treacherous than green wood, and sometimes Arthur wears a catcher's mask when he finds the saw throwing knucklers at him. He does not always take money for his work—just swings in with his machine at the house of someone who is disabled, and starts sawing.

At this season of the year, darkness is a more insistent thing than cold. The days are short as any dream. A new house has been built about twenty miles from here by a man who has plenty of money to spend, and he has equipped it with an automatic light-boosting system, so that as soon as the sun begins losing its strength in the afternoon, electric lights come on all through the place, maintaining an even intensity of illumination at all times. I wouldn't care for that one bit. I like to come in from chores and find the early dark in the rooms, when the only gleam is a single lamp over an amaryllis bulb on which my wife is practicing some sort of deception. I like groping my way into the barn cellar at six, where my two whiteface heifers are feeding at the rack, their great white heads visible, their dark bodies invisible—just two heads suspended in air, as neatly as John the Baptist's. I should think a house in which the light never varies would be as dull as a woman in whom the emotions were always the same. I am reasonably sure, however, that the trick lighting system will go on the blink every once in a while, and that the owner will creep around with a flashlight, the way all the rest of us do, to find the seat of darkness.

It's been fifteen years since we last wintered in this house. Settling in again to live steadily right around the year, as we used to do, has been full of excitement and the sense of our changed condition. (Anybody who is fifteen years older is in a changed condition, no matter what his condition.) There is no schoolboy in the house now to keep the air stirred up. The room he once occupied now contains a television set; we sit there in stupefaction, listening to "April Love" and learning how to set our hair. Other gadgets have crept in, most of them in the back kitchen.

The days ahead unroll in the mind, a scroll of blessed events in garden and in barn. Wherever you look, you see something that advertises the future: in the heifer's sagging sides you see the calf, in the cock's shrill crow you hear the pipping egg, in the cache of warm topsoil down cellar next the furnace you see the seedling, and even on the darkest day the seed catalogue gives off a gleam from some tomato of the first magnitude. The brightness of the dream is exceeded only by its complexity. Farming, even my kind, is infinitely complex, and it grows more so with every year. A few days after I had mailed my order for fifty day-old Silver Cross chicks, I received a long letter from the hatcheryman. (My order amounted to $9.50—nineteen cents a chick —and must have been one of the smallest orders received by that hatchery, so there was no obligation to write anything but a postcard of acknowledgment.) The letter said my chicks would be shipped on Monday, March 31, and would probably arrive the following morning. Then it went on:

As you perhaps know, our Silver Cross is made by top-crossing a Rhode Island Red female with a Schoonmaker White Rock male which is pure for Silver and Restricted Black. The reciprocal of this cross breed is the Golden (or Buff) Sex Link, which looks not unlike the Rhode Island Red. Of the two, the Buff lays the larger egg. Cockerel chicks in both crosses are identical in color (Columbian). For what it is worth we have developed a Silver Rhode Island Red from four generations of backcrosses to the Rhode Island Red. Bird looks like a Silver Cross, but breeds true for its plumage pattern. We also have a Canadian Columbian Rock (a yellow-skinned Sussex segregate), which produces a remarkably pure Columbian pattern in crosses with the Rhode Island Red female. The alleles of Silver and Gold fascinate the geneticist, for any number of multiple crosses can be made, using the linkage of color and sex. We are, for example, testing three three-way crosses, made from top-crossing a "synthetic" Rhode Island Red (unrelated to our own strain) with different Silver cockerels. We then top-cross the Silver Cross females (derived from this original two-way cross) with Parmenter Red cockerels. All females come Gold (or Buff) like the sire. We expect considerable hybrid vigor, probably expressed as good livability. . . .

This struck me as a real chatty letter. It is clear from its contents that to run a hatchery these days a man must know something more than how to carry a pail of water to a thirsty hen. Even though I got lost in the tangle of those backcrosses, I liked getting the letter. Livability is what I am after: I greatly admire a live bird. But my program is to simplify, and I am not much interested in the space-hen, which will probably be the next cross. The other day I read a piece in the *New England Homestead* saying that of Cornell's 268 agricultural graduates last year only twenty-five went into farming. Young people, the article said, hesitate to go into farming because of the low income. I think some of them may be more worried about the high complexity than the low income.

In one respect my henpen in the barn is ahead of the most modern egg-producing plant: from it come eggs that are 98 percent clean-shelled, with no trace of dirt. Today many commercial egg raisers have quit worrying about dirty eggs; they simply install a washing machine and run every egg through. I stood in the laundry room of a large egg factory not long ago and watched the eggs come off the assembly line by the hundred. Each wire basket of eggs (clean and dirty mixed) was immediately placed in the washing machine that was standing there throbbing its heart out. Here, in a detergent bath at a temperature of 120 degrees, the eggs remained for three minutes. When they were removed from their hot tub, the shells had the fine patina of a cheap plastic toy. If that's an egg, I'm a rabbit.

# THE WINTER OF THE GREAT SNOWS

*Allen Cove, March 27, 1971*

Somebody told me the other day that a seagull won't eat a smelt. Even if the gull takes the smelt by mistake, he will disgorge it. I find this hard to believe, but I haven't had a chance to experiment with a smelt and a live gull. I've always supposed a gull would eat anything. If Herbert Tapley were alive, I would put the question to him and be sure of a straight answer. But Herbert is dead, and I find people quite evasive when I ask them if a gull will eat a smelt. I raised a gull chick once, and it never refused anything I handed it. And once, years ago, when I worked in a ship, I used to empty garbage into a chute that discharged overboard. Gulls attended this rite in great numbers, screaming their appreciation. I can't recall ever seeing a gull reject anything that came out of that chute. There were never any smelts in the garbage, though, and this leaves the question wide open. A smelt has rather a sweet taste—there seems to be nothing of the salt sea in its flesh. Perhaps that's why a gull won't eat a smelt, if indeed it is true.

This has not been an ideal winter for pure experimentation here in the East—to see if a gull will eat a smelt. It has been more a time of simple survival, to see if a man can stay alive in the cold. The snows arrived early, before the ground froze. Storm followed storm, each depositing its load and rousing the plowman in the night. And then the cold set in, steady and hard. The ponds froze, then the saltwater coves and harbors, then the bay itself. As far as I know, the ground, despite the deep cold, remains unfrozen: snow is a buffer against the frost, an almost perfect insulating material. A fellow recently reported driving a stake into a snowbank, and when the point of the stake reached ground level it kept right on going. I haven't tested this—it's like the gull and the smelt, a matter of hearsay. But I would have to have a pretty long stake, so remote is the ground.

When snow accumulates week after week, month after month, it works curious miracles. Familiar objects simply disappear, like my pig house and the welltop near the barn door, and one tends to forget that they are there. Our cedar hedge (about five feet high) disappeared months ago, along with the pink snow fences that are set to hold the drifts. My two small guard dogs, Jones and Susy, enjoy the change in elevation and the excitement of patrol duty along the crusted top of the hedge, where they had never been before. They have lookout posts made of snow that the plow has thrown high in the air, giving them a chance to take the long view of things. For a while, the barnyard fence was buried under a magnificent drift. This delighted the geese, who promptly walked to freedom on their orange-colored snowshoes. They then took off into the air, snowshoes and all, freedom having gone to their heads, and visited the trout pond, where they spent an enjoyable morning on the ice. On several occasions this winter, we had to shovel a path for the geese, to make it possible for them to get from their pen in the barn to their favorite loitering spot in the barn cellar. Imagine a man's shoveling a path for a goose! So the goose can loiter!

The door of the woodshed hasn't been open since early in December, the snows having sealed it shut. The house, which always gets banked with spruce brush against the winter, never got banked. The flower beds never got covered. We were simply caught short: the snow arrived ahead of schedule and in large amounts. (I think we've had something like one hundred inches, all told.) We did manage to give the rosebushes decent burial; they are not only out of sight but almost out of mind. It takes an effort of the imagination to conjure up a rose. Only an inch or two of the tall stakes that mark the grave is visible. For most of the winter, the highway has resembled an enormous bobsled run: the passage of the plow builds towering walls of snow higher than the roof of your car, so that you travel through a great white trough, sealed against disaster. (Last summer, my car went off the road and I hit a pole and broke it. The accident was six months too soon—I should have waited till January, when a soft cushion of snow surrounded all poles. I passed my pole the other day and noticed that it had recovered fully from the blow, but I haven't.)

Maine towns take winter seriously. They are ready with money and trucks and men and sand and salt. Derring-do is in good supply, and the roads stay open, no matter what. The things that do *not* stay open are the driveways of the people. Every new swipe of the plow hurls a gift of snow into the mouth of a driveway, so that, in effect, the plowmen, often working while we sleep snug in our beds, create a magnificent smooth, broad highway to which nobody can gain access with his automobile until he has passed a private miracle of snow removal. It is tantalizing to see a fine stretch of well-plowed public road just the other side of a six-foot barricade of private snow. My scheme for town plowing would be to have each big plow attended by a small plow, as a big fish is sometimes attended by a small fish. There would be a pause at each driveway while the little plow removes the snow that the big plow has deposited. But I am just a dreamer. I have two plows of my own—a big V on the pickup and a lift-blade on the little Cub tractor. Even with this equipment, we were licked a lot of the time this winter and had to call for help. It got so there was no place to put the snow even if you were able to push it around. On the day before Christmas, the storm was so great, the wind so high, people were marooned in my house and had to spend the night. And a couple of days later I had to hire a loader to lift the snow from the mouth of the driveway, scurry across the road with it, and drop it into the swamp.

Except for winter's causing me to become housebound, I like the cold. I like snow. I like the descent to the dark, cold kitchen at six in the morning, to put a fire in the wood stove and listen to weather from Boston. My movements at that hour are ritualistic—they vary hardly at all from morning to morning. I steal down in my wrapper carrying a pair of corduroy pants under one arm and balancing a small tray (by de Miskey) that holds the empty glasses from the night before. The night nurse has preceded me into the living room and has hooked up the thermostat—too high. I nudge it down. As I enter the kitchen, my left hand shoots out and snaps on the largest burner on the electric stove. Then I set the glasses in the sink, snap on the pantry light, start the cold water in the tap, and fill the kettle with fresh spring water, which I then set atop the now red burner. Then comes the real warmup: with a poker I clear the grate in the big black Home Crawford 8-20, roll up two sheets of yesterday's Bangor *Daily News*, and lay them in the firebox along with a few sticks of cedar kindling and two sticks of stovewood on top of that. (I always put on my glasses before stuffing the *News* in, to see who is dead and to find out what's been going on in the world, because I seldom have time in these twilight years to read newspapers—too many other things to tend to. I always check on "Dear Abby" at this dawn hour, finding it a comfort to read about people whose problems are even greater than mine, like the man yesterday who sought Abby's advice because his wife would sleep with him only on Thursday nights, which was all right until his bowling club changed *its* night to Thursday, and by the time the man got home his wife was far gone in shut-eye.) I drop the match, open the flue to "Kindle," open the bottom draft, and wait a few seconds to catch the first reassuring sound of snap-and-crackle. (That's the phrase around here for a wood fire—always "snap-and-crackle.") As the first light of day filters into the kitchen, I set out the juicer, set out the coffeepot and coffee, set out the pitchers for milk and cream, and, if it's a Tuesday or a Thursday or a Saturday, solemnly mark the milk order blank and tuck it in the milk box in the entryway while the subzero draft creeps in around my ankles. A good beginning for the day. Then I pull my trousers on over my pajama bottoms, pull on my barn boots, drape myself in a wool shirt and a down jacket, and pay a call in the barn, where the geese give me a tumultuous reception, one of them imitating Bert Lahr's vibrato gargle.

The guard changes here at seven: the night nurse goes off (if her car will start) and the housekeeper comes on (if her brother-in-law's truck has started). I observe all this from an upstairs window. It is less splendid than the change at Buckingham Palace but somehow more impressive, the palace guard never having been dependent on the vagaries of the internal-combustion engine in a subzero wintertime.

The chief topics of conversation this winter have been the weather, the schools, and the shadow of oil. Quarreling over the schools has split the town wide open, as it has neighboring towns here on the mainland and over on Deer Isle. Feeling ran so high some people stopped speaking to each other—which is one form of discourse. Forty years ago, when I landed here, we had five one-room or two-room schoolhouses scattered at strategic points. The scholars walked to school. We also had our high school, which was a cultural monument in the town along with the two stores, the Baptist church, the Beth-Eden chapel, and the Rockbound chapel. Times have changed. All through New England, the little red schoolhouse is on the skids, and the small high school that graduates only four or five seniors in June, in a gymnasium decked with lilac and apple blossoms, is doomed. The State Board of Education withholds its blessing from high schools that enroll fewer than three hundred students. Under mounting pressure from the state, the towns organized a school administrative district, usually referred to as SAD. Sad is the word for it. A plan was drawn for an area schoolhouse at a central point near the Deer Isle Bridge, but it was voted down. Too much money and too many frills. Another plan was drawn and failed. Meanwhile, schoolchildren were shuttled around, here and there, in an attempt to close the gap. We no longer have a high school in town; the building is used for the junior-high grades. Most of the children in the ninth, tenth, eleventh, and twelfth grades are carried by bus across to the high school in the town of Deer Isle. A few travel in the opposite direction to a nearby academy. Sending their children over to an island irritated a lot of parents; some disapproved of the building, some had a deep feeling that when you leave the mainland and head for an island in the sea you are headed in the wrong direction —back toward primitivism. Other parents were violently opposed to dispatching their offspring to the academy town, on the score that the place was a citadel of evil, just one step short of Gomorrah. (There was also an ancient athletic rivalry, which left scars that have never healed.) The closing of our high school caused an acute pain in the hearts of most of the townsfolk, to whom the building was a symbol of their own cultural life and a place where one's loyalty was real, lasting, and sustaining. All in all, the schools are a mess.

Feeling about oil is now running high, but it lacks the acute pain of nostalgia that characterizes the school controversy. Oil is the pain of the future. A company called Maine Clean Fuels wants to build a refinery on Sears Island, at the head of Penobscot Bay, bringing barges and 200,000-ton tankers slithering through the fog-draped, ledge-encrusted, tide-ripped waters of one of the most beautiful bodies of water in Maine or anywhere. The proposal sticks in all our crops. Battle lines have been drawn, public meetings have been held. On one side, or in one corner, are Maine's Department of Economic Development, the executives of the oil company (full of joyous promises and glad tidings of a better life and a cheaper fuel), and some people in Searsport who hope that oil will bring jobs and elevate the economy of the town. On the other side, or in the other corner, are Ossie Beal and his Maine Lobstermen's Association, the Audubon Society, the Sierra Club, various conservation groups, the *Maine Times*, several action groups hastily formed for the purpose of beating oil, and thousands of property owners (usually described as "rich" property owners) who just have a feeling in their bones that oil is bad news any way you look at it. A 200,000-ton tanker makes an aircraft carrier look like a dory, and if there were to be a bad spill, it could mean the end of marine life and bird life in the bay.

Searsport was host to a public meeting last week to give the oilmen a chance to present their case. It must have been a barrel of fun. The constabulary was out in full force, CBS News turned up with its cameras, and a carefully selected group of concerned citizens was admitted. The meeting was set up in such a way as to prevent the anti-oil people from releasing their wrath when they rose to speak. It was a powder-keg meeting that failed to explode. Week after next, a hearing is scheduled at which the state's Environmental Improvement Commission will listen to testimony. This body, I believe, now has kingmaking authority and can turn thumbs down on an industrial newcomer if he looks and smells like a pollutant.

Pollution stirred our town a couple of years ago when our harbor became filthy as a result of sewage discharged from a school of theology that had magically turned up in our midst. The school had inherited a big old pipe when it bought the property; at low water the pipe lay on the stinking flats, exposed, broken in three places, and discharging. The town was powerless to act, having no ordinance on the books covering any nuisance of the sort. So the Environmental people were called and came over from Augusta. Testimony was offered by clamdiggers, boat owners, the health officer of the town, and concerned citizens. It took a long while, but the nuisance was finally abated and theology acquired a long-overdue septic tank. (The waste had been backing up into the school's swimming pool, it turned out, making the pool probably the largest and most spectacular tank in the whole county—a real tomato surprise.) Anyway, the water of the harbor is clear again, a classic case of cleanliness next to godliness. Clamming is still restricted.

Town Meeting came early this year—March 1st. I wasn't able to attend but have studied the report. One birth was reported in 1970, and twelve deaths. It would appear from this that although the population explosion is still an issue worldwide, we have it licked locally. The town appropriated $7,000 for snow removal and sanding, in addition to $3,000 from unappropriated surplus—a total of $10,000 to get the snow removed. There was no argument. If there's one thing people are agreed on, it's this: the snow must get removed. A century ago in New England, the approach to snow was quite different. When snow began to fly, people switched to runners. Roads were not plowed out, they were rolled down. A giant roller pulled by horses packed the surface to a fine, smooth glaze. Then the sleighs came out, with their bells. And sleds, to haul wood out from the woodlots. Wheels were laid away for the season. The old pleasure in runners hasn't died, though. The snowmobile is the big new thing—life on runners. It pollutes in two ways: with its exhaust fumes and with its noise.

The town voted to enact an ordinance regulating the taking of shellfish. It is now illegal for a nonresident to dig clams, except that he may dig not more than a peck in any one day for the use of himself and his family. A year ago, the town voted to enact an ordinance regulating the use of the town dump. At that meeting, I suggested an ordinance prohibiting the discharge of human waste into ponds and salt water, but it got laid to rest. The selectmen investigated the matter and reported that such an ordinance would be "very complex, extremely difficult to enforce, and possibly declared to be unconstitutional." It seems sad that the town can regulate the taking of shellfish but can't regulate the discharge of the waste that makes the shellfish inedible. But that's the way it is. Years ago, I was sized up as a man who was amiable, honest, and impractical, and I've always agreed with that estimate. Now, I'm not just impractical, I'm unconstitutional.

And I still don't know whether a gull will eat a smelt.

# RIPOSTE

❧§❧

*Allen Cove, December 1971*

To come upon an article in the *Times* called "The Meaning of Brown Eggs" was an unexpected pleasure. To find that it was by an Englishman, J. B. Priestley, gave it an extra fillip. And to happen on it while returning from the barn carrying the day's catch of nine brown eggs seemed almost too pat.

Why is it, do you suppose, that an Englishman is unhappy until he has explained America? Mr. Priestley finds the key to this country in its preference for white eggs—a discovery, he says, that will move him into the "vast invisible realm where our lives are shaped." It's a great idea, but one seldom meets an American who is all tensed up because he has yet to explain England.

Mr. Priestley writes that "the weakness of American civilization . . . is that it is so curiously abstract." In America, he says, "brown eggs are despised, sold off cheaply, perhaps sometimes thrown away." Well, now. In New England, where I live and which is part of America, the brown egg, far from being despised, is king. The Boston market is a brown-egg market. I note in my morning paper, in the Boston produce report, that a dozen large white eggs yesterday brought the jobber forty-two cents, whereas a dozen large brown eggs fetched forty-five cents. Despised? Sold off cheaply? The brown egg beat the white egg by three cents.

"The Americans, well outside the ghettos," writes Mr. Priestley, "despise brown eggs just because they do seem closer to nature. White eggs are much better, especially if they are to be given to precious children, because their very whiteness suggests hygiene and purity." My goodness. Granting that an Englishman is entitled to his reflective moments, and being myself well outside the ghettos, I suspect there is a more plausible explanation for the popularity of the white egg in America. I ascribe the whole business to a busy little female—the White Leghorn hen. She is nervous, she is flighty, she is the greatest egg-machine on two legs, and it just happens that she lays a white egg. She's never too distracted to do her job. A Leghorn hen, if she were on her way to a fire, would pause long enough to lay an egg. This endears her to the poultrymen of America, who are out to produce the greatest number of eggs for the least money paid out for feed. Result: much of America, apart from New England, is flooded with white eggs.

When a housewife, in New York or in Florida, comes home from market with a dozen eggs and opens her package, she finds twelve pure white eggs. This, to her, is not only what an egg should be, it is what an egg is. An egg is a white object. If this same housewife were to stray into New England and encounter a brown egg from the store, the egg would look somehow incorrect, wrong. It would look like something laid by a bird that didn't know what it was about. To a New Englander, the opposite is true. Brought up as we are on the familiar beauty of a richly colored brown egg (gift of a Rhode Island Red or a Barred Plymouth Rock or a New Hampshire) when we visit New York and open a carton of chalk-white eggs, we are momentarily startled. Something is awry. The hen has missed fire. The eggs are white, therefore wrong.

"The English prefer the brown egg," writes Mr. Priestley, "because it belongs to the enduring dream of the English, who always hope sooner or later to move into the country." Here I understand what he's talking about: the brown egg is, indeed, because of its pigmentation, more suggestive of country living—a more "natural" egg, if you wish, although there is no such thing as an *un*natural egg. (My geese lay white eggs, and God knows they are natural enough.) But I find the brown egg esthetically satisfying. For most of my life I have kept hens, brooded chicks, and raised eggs for my own use. I buy chicks from a hatchery in Connecticut; by experimenting, I have found that the most beautiful brown egg of all is the egg of the Silver Cross, a bird arrived at by mating a Rhode Island Red with a White Plymouth Rock. Her egg is so richly brown, so wondrously beautiful as to defy description. Every fall, when the first pullet egg turns up on the range, I bring it into the living room and enshrine it in a black duckshead pottery ashtray, where it remains until Halloween, a symbol of fertility, admired by all. Then I take it outdoors and, in Mr. Priestley's memorable phrase, I throw it away.

A neighbor of mine, a couple of miles up the road, is planning to go the brown egg one better. He dreams of a green egg. And what's more, he knows of a hen who will lay one.

# THE GEESE

❦

*Allen Cove, July 9, 1971*

To give a clear account of what took place in the barnyard early in the morning on that last Sunday in June, I will have to go back more than a year in time, but a year is nothing to me these days. Besides, I intend to be quick about it, and not dawdle.

I have had a pair of elderly gray geese—a goose and a gander—living on this place for a number of years, and they have been my friends. "Companions" would be a better word; geese are friends with no one, they badmouth everybody and everything. But they are companionable once you get used to their ingratitude and their false accusations. Early in the spring, a year ago, as soon as the ice went out of the pond, my goose started to lay. She laid three eggs in about a week's time and then died. I found her halfway down the lane that connects the barnyard with the pasture. There were no marks on her—she lay with wings partly outspread, and with her neck forward in the grass, pointing downhill. Geese are rarely sick, and I think this goose's time had come and she had simply died of old age. I had noticed that her step had slowed on her trips back from the pond to the barn where her nest was. I had never known her age, and so had nothing else to go on. We buried her in our private graveyard, and I felt sad at losing an acquaintance of such long standing—long standing and loud shouting.

Her legacy, of course, was the three eggs. I knew they were good eggs and did not like to pitch them out. It seemed to me that the least I could do for my departed companion was to see that the eggs she had left in my care were hatched. I checked my hen pen to find out whether we had a broody, but there was none. During the next few days, I scoured the neighborhood for a broody hen, with no success. Years ago, if you needed a broody hen, almost any barn or henhouse would yield one. But today broodiness is considered unacceptable in a hen; the modern hen is an egg-laying machine, and her natural tendency to sit on eggs in springtime has been bred out of her. Besides, not many people keep hens anymore—when they want a dozen eggs, they don't go to the barn, they go to the First National.

Days went by. My gander, the widower, lived a solitary life—nobody to swap gossip with, nobody to protect. He seemed dazed. The three eggs were not getting any younger, and I myself felt dazed—restless and unfulfilled. I had stored the eggs down cellar in the arch where it is cool, and every time I went down there for something they seemed silently to reproach me. My plight had become known around town, and one day a friend phoned and said he would lend me an incubator designed for hatching the eggs of waterfowl. I brought the thing home, cleaned it up, plugged it in, and sat down to read the directions. After studying them, I realized that if I were to tend eggs in that incubator, I would have to withdraw from the world for thirty days—give up everything, just as a broody goose does. Obsessed though I was with the notion of bringing life into three eggs, I wasn't quite prepared to pay the price.

Instead, I abandoned the idea of incubation and decided to settle the matter by acquiring three ready-made goslings, as a memorial to the goose and a gift for the lonely gander. I drove up the road about five miles and dropped in on Irving Closson. I knew Irving had geese; he has everything even a sawmill. I found him shoeing a very old horse in the doorway of his barn, and I stood and watched for a while. Hens and geese wandered about the yard, and a turkey tom circled me, wings adroop, strutting. The horse, with one forefoot between the man's knees, seemed to have difficulty balancing himself on three legs but was quiet and sober, almost asleep. When I asked Irving if he planned to put shoes on the horse's hind feet, too, he said, "No, it's hard work for me, and he doesn't use those hind legs much anyway." Then I brought up the question of goslings, and he took me into the barn and showed me a sitting goose. He said he thought she was covering more than twenty eggs and should bring off her goslings in a couple of weeks and I could buy a few if I wanted. I said I would like three.

I took to calling at Irving's every few days—it is about the pleasantest place to visit anywhere around. At last, I was rewarded: I pulled into the driveway one morning and saw a goose surrounded by green goslings. She had been staked out, like a cow. Irving had simply tied a piece of string to one leg and fastened the other end to a peg in the ground. She was a pretty goose—not as large as my old one had been, and with a more slender neck. She appeared to be a cross-bred bird, two-toned gray, with white markings—a sort of particolored goose. The goslings had the cheerful, bright, innocent look that all baby geese have. We scooped up three and tossed them into a box, and I paid Irving and carried them home.

My next concern was how to introduce these small creatures to their foster father, my old gander. I thought about this all the way home. I've had just enough experience with domesticated animals and birds to know that they are a bundle of eccentricities and crotchets, and I was not at all sure what sort of reception three strange youngsters would get from a gander who was full of sorrows and suspicions. (I once saw a gander, taken by surprise, seize a newly hatched gosling and hurl it the length of the barn floor.) I had an uneasy feeling that my three little charges might be dead within the hour, victims of a grief-crazed old fool. I decided to go slow. I fixed a makeshift pen for the goslings in the barn, arranged so that they would be separated from the gander but visible to him, and he would be visible to them. The old fellow, when he heard youthful voices, hustled right in to find out what was going on. He studied the scene in silence and with the greatest attention. I could not tell whether the look in his eye was one of malice or affection—a goose's eye is a small round enigma. After observing this introductory scene for a while, I left and went into the house.

Half an hour later, I heard a commotion in the barnyard: the gander was in full cry. I hustled out. The goslings, impatient with life indoors, had escaped from their hastily constructed enclosure in the barn and had joined their foster father in the barnyard. The cries I had heard were his screams of welcome—the old bird was delighted with the turn that events had taken. His period of mourning was over, he now had interesting and useful work to do, and he threw himself into the role of father with immense satisfaction and zeal, hissing at me with renewed malevolence, shepherding the three children here and there, and running interference against real and imaginary enemies. My fears were laid to rest. In the rush of emotion that seized him at finding himself the head of a family, his thoughts turned immediately to the pond, and I watched admiringly as he guided the goslings down the long, tortuous course through the weedy lane and on down across the rough pasture between blueberry knolls and granite boulders. It was a sight to see him hold the heifers at bay so the procession could pass safely. Summer was upon us, the pond was alive again. I brought the three eggs up from the cellar and dispatched them to the town dump.

At first, I did not know the sex of my three goslings. But nothing on two legs grows any faster than a young goose, and by early fall it was obvious that I had drawn one male and two females. You tell the sex of a goose by its demeanor and its stance—the way it holds itself, its general approach to life. A gander carries his head high and affects a threatening attitude. Females go about with necks in a graceful arch and are less aggressive. My two young females looked like their mother, particolored. The young male was quite different. He feathered out white all over except for his wings, which were a very light, pearly gray. Afloat on the pond, he looked almost like a swan, with his tall, thin white neck and his cocked-up white tail—a real dandy, full of pompous thoughts and surly gestures.

Winter is a time of waiting, for man and goose. Last winter was a long wait, the pasture deep in drifts, the lane barricaded, the pond inaccessible and frozen. Life centered in the barn and the barnyard. When the time for mating came, conditions were unfavorable, and this was upsetting to the old gander. Geese like a body of water for their coupling; it doesn't have to be a large body of water—just any wet place in which a goose can become partly submerged. My old gander, studying the calendar, inflamed by passion, unable to get to the pond, showed signs of desperation. On several occasions, he tried to manage with a ten-quart pail of water that stood in the barnyard. He would chivvy one of his young foster daughters over to the pail, seize her by the nape, and hold her head under water while he made his attempt. It was never a success and usually ended up looking more like a comedy tumbling act than like coitus. One got the feeling during the water-pail routine that the gander had been consulting one of the modern sex manuals describing peculiar positions. Anyway, I noticed two things: the old fellow confined his attentions to one of the two young geese and let the other alone, and he never allowed his foster son to approach either of the girls—he was very strict about that, and the handsome young male lived all spring in a state of ostracism.

Eventually, the pond opened up, the happy band wended its way down across the melting snows, and the breeding season was officially opened. My pond is visible from the house, but it is at quite a distance. I am not a voyeur and do not spend my time watching the sex antics of geese or anything else. But I try to keep reasonably well posted on all the creatures around the place, and it was apparent that the young gander was not allowed by his foster father to enjoy the privileges of the pond and that the old gander's attentions continued to be directed to just one of the young geese. I shall call her Liz to make this tale easier to tell.

Both geese were soon laying. Liz made her nest in the barn cellar;

her sister, Apathy, made hers in the tie-ups on the main floor of the barn. It was the end of April or the beginning of May. Still awfully cold—a reluctant spring.

Apathy laid three eggs, then quit. I marked them with a pencil and left them for the time being in the nest she had constructed. I made a mental note that they were infertile. Liz, unlike her sister, went right on laying, and became a laying fool. She dallied each morning at the pond with her foster father, and she laid and laid and laid, like a commercial hen. I dutifully marked the eggs as they arrived—1, 2, 3, and so on. When she had accumulated a clutch of fifteen, I decided she had all she could cover. From then on, I took to removing the oldest egg from the nest each time a new egg was deposited. I also removed Apathy's three eggs from *her* nest, discarded them, and began substituting the purloined eggs from the barn cellar—the ones that rightfully belonged to Liz. Thus I gradually contrived to assemble a nest of fertile eggs for each bird, all of them laid by the fanatical Liz.

During the last week in May, Apathy, having produced only three eggs of her own but having acquired ten through the kind offices of her sister and me, became broody and began to sit. Liz, with a tally of twenty-five eggs, ten of them stolen, showed not the slightest desire to sit. Laying was her thing. She laid and laid, while the other goose sat and sat. The old gander, marveling at what he had wrought, showed a great deal of interest in both nests. The young gander was impressed but subdued. I continued to remove the early eggs from Liz's nest, holding her to a clutch of fifteen and discarding the extras. In late June, having produced forty-one eggs, ten of which were under Apathy, she at last sat down.

I had marked Apathy's hatching date on my desk calendar. On the night before the goslings were due to arrive, when I made my rounds before going to bed, I looked in on her. She hissed, as usual, and ran her neck out. When I shone my light at her, two tiny green heads were visible, thrusting their way through her feathers. The goslings were here—a few hours ahead of schedule. My heart leapt up. Outside, in the barnyard, both ganders stood vigil. They knew very well what was up: ganders take an enormous interest in family affairs and are deeply impressed by the miracle of the egg-that-becomes-goose. I shut the door against them and went to bed.

Next morning, Sunday, I rose early and went straight to the barn to see what the night had brought. Apathy was sitting quietly while five goslings teetered about on the slopes of the nest. One of them, as I watched, strayed from the others, and, not being able to find his way back, began sending out cries for help. They were the kind of distress signal any anxious father would instantly respond to. Suddenly, I heard sounds of a rumble outside in the barnyard where the ganders were—loud sounds of scuffling. I ran out. A fierce fight was in progress —it was no mere skirmish, it was the real thing. The young gander had grabbed the old one by the stern, his white head buried in feathers right where it would hurt the most, and was running him around the yard, punishing him at every turn—thrusting him on ahead and beating him unmercifully with his wings. It was an awesome sight, these two great male birds locked in combat, slugging it out—not for the favors of a female but for the dubious privilege of assuming the responsibilities of parenthood. The young male had suffered all spring the indignities of a restricted life at the pond; now he had turned, at last, against the old one, as though to get even. Round and round, over rocks and through weeds, they raced, struggling and tripping, the old one in full retreat and in apparent pain. It was a beautiful late–June morning, with fair-weather clouds and a light wind going, the grasses long in the orchard—the kind of morning that always carries for me overtones of summer sadness, I don't know why. Overhead, three swallows circled at low altitude, pursuing one white feather, the coveted trophy of nesting time. They were like three tiny fighter planes giving air support to the battle that raged below. For a moment, I thought of climbing the fence and trying to separate the combatants, but instead I just watched. The engagement was soon over. Plunging desperately down the lane, the old gander sank to the ground. The young one let go, turned, and walked back, screaming in triumph, to the door behind which his newly won family were waiting: a strange family indeed—the sister who was not even the mother of the babies, and the babies who were not even his own get.

When I was sure the fight was over, I climbed the fence and closed the barnyard gate, effectively separating victor from vanquished. The old gander had risen to his feet. He was in almost the same spot in the lane where his first wife had died mysteriously more than a year ago. I watched as he threaded his way slowly down the narrow path between clumps of thistles and daisies. His head was barely visible above the grasses, but his broken spirit was plain to any eye. When he reached the pasture bars, he hesitated, then painfully squatted and eased himself under the bottom bar and into the pasture, where he sat down on the cropped sward in the bright sun. I felt very deeply his sorrow and his defeat. As things go in the animal kingdom, he is about my age, and when he lowered himself to creep under the bar, I could feel in my own bones his pain at bending down so far. Two hours later, he was still sitting there, the sun by this time quite hot. I had seen his likes often enough on the benches of the treeless main street of a Florida city —spent old males, motionless in the glare of the day.

Toward the end of the morning, he walked back up the lane as far as the gate, and there he stood all afternoon, his head and orange bill looking like the head of a great snake. The goose and her goslings had emerged into the barnyard. Through the space between the boards of the gate, the old fellow watched the enchanting scene: the goslings taking their frequent drinks of water, climbing in and out of the shallow pan for their first swim, closely guarded by the handsome young gander, shepherded by the pretty young goose.

After supper, I went into the tie-ups and pulled the five remaining, unhatched eggs from the nest and thought about the five lifeless chicks inside the eggs—the unlucky ones, the ones that lacked what it takes to break out of an egg into the light of a fine June morning. I put the eggs in a basket and set the basket with some other miscellany consigned to the dump. I don't know anything sadder than a summer's day.

# II

### ❧❧

# THE PLANET

# LETTER FROM THE EAST

**ᚱᚻᚷᚻᚹ**

*Allen Cove, February 8, 1975*

On an afternoon in the spring of 1938, foreseeing a change in my life, I rode the subway down to Cortlandt Street, visited Peter Henderson's seed store, and came away with a mixed order of flower and vegetable seeds. The bill was $19. Peter Henderson is long gone, and times have changed—but not the warm, receptive earth, yielding to the advances of the sun. Today, with so much wrong with the planet, with everyone discouraged and uneasy and some desperate, almost the only things that can dispel the gloom for me are the bright and fraudulent pictures in a seed catalogue and the glad cry that issues from a box of day-old chicks arriving on an April morning from the hatchery. Our 1975 orders went off in the mail three weeks ago. The seeds came to $67, up from $19. A baby chick this spring will cost me thirty-three cents, up five cents from the 1974 chick. Even so, there is hardly a better buy around: the seed, the exploded egg, the perennial promise that they hold. In the years that have intervened since 1938, we have not missed a springtime of this wild dreaming and scheming. We are hooked and are making no attempt to kick the habit.

I'm behind on my correspondence, and this letter is overdue. Quite aside from the mess my desk is in, everything else here in the East is in a mess, just as it is in other parts of the nation, and in all parts of the world. The strain has begun to show in people's faces. Events and portents swirl around all our heads in dazzling array and in great numbers. Oil. Unemployment. Nuclear power plants. The spruce budworm. The SST. Land use and zoning. The plight of the small hospital. Pollution. The supertanker. Windmills. Lead poisoning in the pottery.

[ 71 ]

Passamaquoddy. Food stamps. The price of gas at the pump. The price of doughnuts in the store. The power of the Federal Government. The long shadow of the state. The fuel-adjustment additive. Breaking and entering. Drug abuse. Centralization. The disappearance of haddock. Russian trawlers. Arab sheikhs. It is all very confusing, makes one's head swim. Last November, the voters became so confused they forgot to elect a Republican or a Democrat for governor and elected instead an independent insurance man, James Longley, who is said to sleep only four hours a night, jogs at daylight, and summons people to his office at seven o'clock in the morning to start putting the state on a sound business basis. I met my pharmacist on the street the other day —he is a freshman member of the legislature. And when I asked him how he liked being up in Augusta he replied, "Love it." Then, in a sentence that followed along naturally, he used the phrase "viable alternative," and I marveled at how quickly he had learned the language of government. Longley likes the word "input" and on taking office accepted a $15,000 input to his salary. He has since declared his willingness to cancel it. It is all quite confusing, and sometimes scary.

But in many ways things are the same as they've always been, hereabouts. The February days lengthen, the light strengthens, the plow goes by in the night. Our woodpile, thanks to Henry Allen, who keeps disappearing into the woods mounted on a Cub tractor and towing a small trailer, has built to nine cords—mostly birch this year. When one of my hens prepares to lay an egg, she picks up a few shreds of nesting material and tosses them onto her back, as hens have been doing ever since the egg was invented. On subzero mornings, the vapor rises from the bay, obscuring Herriman Point. If the day is quiet and the sea calm, the scallop draggers move out to the fishing grounds to make their sweeps. The price of scallops is down from what it was a year ago. We get ours direct from Lawrence Cole, right off his boat. We buy a gallon, eat a mess, and freeze the rest. I'm not supposed to eat scallops, but I love the taste of cholesterol and can't leave them alone. Lawrence told me this is his forty-sixth year at it.

There was a wedding in town this winter. Walter Crockett, our master carpenter and cabinetmaker, got married at the age of ninety-three. He met his bride—a younger woman—in the nursing home where they had both gone to die: and, such is the power of love, they sprang from the home and are happily settled in Penobscot, keeping house. This, it seems to me, pretty well takes the wind out of Barbara Walters' sails. I heard her say on television that marriage, as we know it, is on the way out and will be gone by the year 2000. I didn't take much stock in that. Many of the remarks you hear on television are questionable, except on the Tarzan hour, which I never miss if I can help it. In the jungle world men have managed to create for themselves, with its gloomy wars, its smashed atom, its hair sprays that threaten the ozone layer, its balance of power, and its absence of any sensible and orderly way (except Kissinger) to settle the myriad things that need to be settled, Tarzan in his loincloth is the one person who seems at home in the environment, as he utters his wild cry and swings along on those old moss-covered docking lines. His speech nowadays is immaculate, and his rapport with animals has always been good. There is a little five-year-old girl in our town who can't tell time by the clock but knows instinctively when the hour of Tarzan is at hand. She runs to her grandmother and insists that the set be turned on so she can partake of the Weintraub delicatessen.

All sorts of queer and unexpected events have taken place since my last report from the East. In the nearby town of Blue Hill, ordinarily a quiet village, heavy machinery arrived three summers ago and began ripping the town to pieces, to make room for a new steel-and-concrete wing for the hospital and a sewage-treatment plant for the town, at the head of the harbor. The noise was awful. Month after month, a giant crane swept the sky, and ten-wheel trucks bearing the legend WE MOVE THE EARTH banged through the streets, hauling gravel and rubble from one spot and dumping them into another spot. The hospital was in a survival situation: unless its bed patients were moved from the original wooden building into fireproof quarters, Medicare payments would be cut off, and this would spell certain doom. The operation cost more than $2 million—a tremendous tab for so small a community. People baked pies, knit sweaters, put on auction sales, staged variety shows in the town hall, and dug into sagging pocketbooks. It was a near thing for a while, but it's over now: the wing is occupied. We have wall-to-wall carpeting in the corridors, parking space outside for a hundred cars, telephones by every bed, air conditioning, and a nurses' station that goes beep beep. Patients have a view of the harbor and a view of the sewage-treatment facility.

Meantime, over at Harborside on Cape Rosier, just above the beautiful little reversing falls of Goose Cove, a mining company called Callahan was busy. They dammed the falls, shutting out the tide, and dug a pit so deep you could look down and see China. This excavation greatly altered the appearance of Goose Cove without greatly enriching the community. The mining company soon milked the place dry of copper and zinc and got out, the way mining companies do. But nothing ever stands still around here: someone at Callahan must have taken a long last look at the salt water entering the abandoned pit from the open gate in the dam and thought, What a place to raise fish! In no time at all, the company banished minerals from its thoughts and stocked the pool with salmon. This enterprise promises to be a success. A young fellow named Bob Mant bought out Callahan in 1973, procured 800,000 Coho salmon eggs from the State of Washington, hatched the eggs in freshwater tanks, and then transferred the fingerlings into the pool, where they are now confined in large nylon nets, feeding on shrimp. Mant began to harvest his first crop last fall—100,000 Coho salmon. He cleans them and, with the help of another fellow, sells them for about a dollar and a quarter apiece to restaurants and markets around the state and as far west as Boston. One would assume that a salmon raised in a mine pit might easily contain as much mercury as a small thermometer. But the Goose Cove salmon have been studied by the University of Maine and by the State Department of Marine Resources and have been given a clean bill—"all metals negligible." I ate two of the fish when I dined at a friend's house recently and they were delicious—delicate, like a brook trout. I'm a believer in mercury, anyway, and am curing my arthritis on a diet of fish and rice, on the advice of a Chinese doctor named Dong, who wrote a cookbook for arthritics. Many fish contain mercury, and I am proceeding on the assumption that it is the mercury, not the fish, that knocks the arthritis. A man has to have a few firm beliefs to cling to in these chancy times. A New York waiter once told me I should eat the skins of fishes in order to stay healthy, and he may have been right. (You eat grapes to ward off cancer.)

Another experiment in aquaculture is being conducted in the Salt Pond just north of here, a handsome small inland sea between Blue Hill Bay and the Benjamin River. A neighbor of ours, Mark Richmond, is busy raising European oysters in trays submerged in the pond. At this writing, he has something like a half-million oysters under cultivation. Instead of being bedded on bottom, in the life style of most oysters, these pampered mollusks live in ballasted trays made of wire and wood, about the size of a small coffee table. In winter, when the pond is frozen, the trays are sunk below the ice. When the oysters are big enough to eat, they are sold to restaurants and individual gourmets. Thus, an owner of shorefront property can buy a couple of trays of oysters, moor them off his beach or tie them to his float, and when he is hungry wander down and bring home a first course for dinner—assuming he knows how to open an oyster. Richmond's operation, like Mant's, has the threat of mining hanging over it. The Salt Pond lies in tranquil beauty a few miles below the Kerramerican Mine, of Blue Hill, which discharges thousands of gallons of effluent every day into a handy little stream that drains, conveniently, into the pond and thence into the bay—a threat to shellfish. Everywhere trouble lurks. But the oysters are in no trouble right now, and may never be.

For a number of years, the largest structure in this neighborhood was a four-story henhouse, about four miles up the road from where I live. It was our Empire State Building, visible a long way off, a landmark for boats coming up the bay. Lights burned at night for the hens, and food came to them by a conveyor belt. But the egg business fell on hard times and the henhouse went dark. For a while, it was just a deserted palace. Suddenly, one day, there were signs of life about the place. Cars were drawn up. And I learned at the store that the building had been bought by Noel Paul Stookey, the "Paul" of the musical group Peter, Paul, and Mary. A spicy item of local news. Stookey, undaunted by the lingering smell of departed hens, went quietly to work and converted one of the upper stories into a recording studio. He lives in a house nearby with his wife and three small daughters, rents the studio by the hour, plans to complete an album of his own in March, and hopes eventually to create a studio for animation, where he will put young artists to work. A queer and unexpected event.

There has been a rash of thievery in our area. (I remember when you didn't even bother to lock your door at night.) Boys have broken into stores and taken cigarettes and beer. Sophisticated burglars have entered the deserted houses of the summer people and stolen Hitchcock chairs. The most picturesque heist occurred a short distance up the road at Arcady, the Italianate villa built years ago by the widow of Ethelbert Nevin from the proceeds of "The Rosary" and "Mighty Lak a Rose." The alleged thieves, enjoying the concealment of a twenty-foot-high cedar hedge, backed a U-Haul truck up to the door last November, extracted a seventeenth-century harpsichord valued at more than $40,-000, and drove away. I like to think of them drawn up for a coffee break in some dismal picnic area, running a few scales and trying the instrument out for "Chopsticks." In good time, they transferred the harpsichord to another rental truck and set out for California, arriving in San Francisco a few days later after a truly baroque journey—the harpsichord in the U-Haul, Arcady to the Golden Gate. The instrument was eventually recovered and identified through the combined efforts of an alert sheriff, a harpsichord maker, a grandson of the composer, and the Smithsonian Institution.

Not long ago, the supersonic transport Concorde paid us a visit, dropping into the Bangor International Airport out of a clear sky. It flew away to the West Coast and later was back again, this time detained overnight in Bangor because of having to send to England for a part. Even in the midst of all the trouble we are now in, even though no one knows which way to turn and which way to go, there still persists the notion that we must get there with ever greater speed. My oldest grandson made his first trip abroad in January. He flew to Switzerland to visit a friend, and on arrival phoned home. When asked about his trip, he reported that "it was cramped" and he "didn't like the movie." Thus has travel degenerated in the age of speed. If the SST takes hold, we will soon be whisked from continent to continent, from zone to zone, and there won't even be time enough not to like the movie. We will all be Kissingers, darting from flower to flower, without ever savoring the day.

Energy, of course, is the leading topic and the toughest nut to crack. The Maine House of Representatives quickly jumped on President Ford's oil-import tariff and austerity program. One of the legislators came back strong with a counterproposal—an open season on moose. Whenever we Maine men feel something threatening our way of life from as far away as Washington, our thoughts turn unerringly to the gun on the rack and the rich flavor of wild meat.

Our snowmobilers met the energy crunch with their customary directness and verve: they got up a two-day race meet in Bangor, the Paul Bunyan Snowmobile Championship, and tore round and round and round, drawing throngs to Bass Park from far and near. The Bangor *Daily News* reported the number of legs broken and backs sprained but neglected to report the number of gallons of gas it took to accomplish it. A year ago, with gasoline already showing signs of petering out, a snowmobile gymkhana was staged at the Blue Hill Fair Grounds. There was no snow on the track, so dump trucks were hired to transport snow all the way from Ellsworth to provide the surface for the racing. You don't hear much complaint about snowmobilers, though. If a man were to lose the snowmobile vote in Maine, his political life would be at an end.

Just the day-to-day activity of the concerned citizens bent on solving the energy crisis is itself a great drain on fuel: lights burn far into the night in the halls where the planners do their planning and the debaters hold their debates. I drove over to South Brooksville not long ago to attend an evening forum on nuclear power, sponsored by the public library. To get over and back, I had to travel twenty-five miles, which must have burned up a gallon and a half of gas. And the hall had to be lighted. And the representative from the Central Maine Power Company had to burn up a great deal more gas than I did, because he came a long distance for the powwow. People in this age are adjusted to the free use of power; they do not readily change their habits, even for a power shortage. On my way home over the road after the meeting, I noticed that most of the houses I passed were brightly lit— people sitting up late to watch television, with the oil-burner grinding away in the basement and the water pump leaping into action at the bidding of the pressure tank and the hot-water heater eating up the kilowatts in answer to the thermostat. A hundred years ago, the denizens of those same houses would have been abed long since. They would have had neither power nor a power shortage—merely a long night's sleep. We don't really know yet whether we can have energy all day and Johnny Carson all night. It just isn't clear.

The Central Maine Power Company feels very good about nuclear generating plants, is not worried about radiation or accidents, and is proposing to construct a plant on Sears Island in Penobscot Bay. (It has also acquired an option on four hundred acres of land on Cape Rosier, just in case.) A group calling itself Safe Power for Maine takes the opposite position and is disturbed that nuclear plants should be built while scientists are still in disagreement and before anyone has found a way to dispose of the nuclear waste safely. A Brooksville man who keeps goats got up in meeting and asked why, if nuclear plants were so safe, he had received a letter from a research firm employed by the power company inquiring as to the whereabouts of his goats. Mr. Randazza, the C.M.P. man, replied that it was a routine inquiry. "We must know where the goats are," he said, "so corrective measures could be taken if something went wrong." Iodine can contaminate milk, he acknowledged. But he was cheerful about the prospect. You would simply put the animals on a controlled diet, he said, and after about forty days the radioactivity would be gone.

At this writing, no one knows what is going to happen at Eastport, if indeed anything ever does happen. Eastport is a small, down-at-heel town, nestled against the Canadian border and washed by the fabulous tides of Passamaquoddy Bay. Oilmen can never get Eastport out of their minds, because it has a deepwater harbor. Power companies find Eastport troubling their dreams at night because the place has probably the greatest natural-power potential of any town in Maine and perhaps of any town anywhere in the world. It is very disturbing, Eastport. For the last two years an oil company called Pittston has been trying to get a toe in the door—they propose to build a $350-million refinery there, and they have been pleading their case before the Maine Board of Environmental Protection. The hearings came to an end a few days ago, and the board's decision will be rendered any minute now. To an oilman, Passamaquoddy is not just an Indian word, it is a dirty word:

it suggests unlimited power that will go on forever or as long as the tides come surging in and go boiling out. At the Pittston Company hearings, Robert Monks, director of the state's Office of Energy Resources, opposed granting the application. So did Horace Hildreth, Jr., lawyer for the Coastal Resources Action Committee. So did many others. Monks argued that the Pittston plan as now drafted would "forever foreclose" on the possibility of harnessing the tides of Passamaquoddy. And, of course, there is always the specter of an oil spill.

I have never experienced the great tides and swift currents of the waters around Eastport, have never ventured that far east in a small boat. But I've examined the charts of those legendary seas, and my opinion is that the only person who could successfully guide a super-tanker around East Quoddy Head and into the hairpin turn from the Bay of Fundy to Head Harbour Passage would be Harold Lloyd—on a good day. Lloyd could do it, but the thought of a run-of-the-mill Liberian flagship captain attempting it gives me goose pimples the size of sea urchins. The captain might easily blow it, particularly if the fog were to shut in, as it does about half the time. Brooks Hamilton, a professor at the University of Maine who navigated an LST in the Second World War, has calculated that in one slackwater period there is just barely time enough to get a ship from East Quoddy Head to a berth in East-port before the current starts the other way.

Governor Longley wants to explore tidal power; Muskie does, Hathaway does, President Ford does. But Quoddy still has a bad name from the old boondoggling days. Canada is at work on a scheme for developing tidal power. Even if Pittston's application is granted, there's a good chance no oil refinery will be built there, because Canada controls a piece of the sea through which the tankers would have to pass. Energy, energy, energy!

The government itself forces a citizen to burn fuel. I sat up most of one night in January, making out W-2 statements for the employees who were in and out of our house at one time or another during 1974. I'm not good at filling out forms: all those long Social Security numbers, all those enigmatic little cubicles, all those unwieldy sheets of carbon paper. Lights blazed, while the furnace plugged away in the cellar to keep me from freezing to death. The very next morning, a letter arrived from the I.R.S. advising me, in a pleasant and chatty fashion, that our returns for 1972 and 1973 were up for audit and would I please have the following documents ready for the inspector's visit. Then followed a list as long as your arm. If I'm to produce all those curios, the lights will burn late enough to satisfy even the insatiable electric company.

I believe, from the sessions I've attended in my kitchen, which is where I get my most reliable information, that what most deeply disturbs the people in the small towns of Maine these days is not gasoline, not the cost of living, not unemployment. I think people are disturbed by the discovery that no longer is a small town autonomous—it is a creature of the state and of the Federal Government. We have accepted money for our schools, our libraries, our hospitals, our winter roads. Now we face the inevitable consequence: the benefactor wants to call the turns. The Blue Hill Hospital's $2-million wing had hardly opened its doors when the citizens of the town awoke one morning to find, in the Portland *Sunday Telegram*, a story based on an interview with Mark Knowles, director of the State Comprehensive Health Planning Agency, suggesting that small hospitals "under thirty-five beds" might soon be marked for oblivion. People who have just gone through the agonies of raising a great deal of money for a well-loved local institution don't take it lightly when they hear that perhaps their work has been for nothing. People were mad as hops. Yankees don't want a planner in Augusta or in Washington telling them where to put a hospital or a school or how many beds or desks to install. They are accustomed to making decisions like that for themselves. They feel it is their right. (They also take the grants, and once the habit has been formed it is not likely to be broken.) Knowles made the big mistake of using the word "parameter" in a letter to the president of the Maine Hospital Association. Most of us are familiar with a "perimeter," but a "parameter" was a little too much, considering the raw state of our nerves. It's bad enough to hear that your hospital is the wrong size, without having a parameter thrown at you.

With so much that is disturbing our lives and clouding our future, beginning right here in my own little principality, with its private pools of energy (the woodpile, the black stove, the germ in the seed, the chick in the egg), and extending outward to our unhappy land and our plundered planet, it is hard to foretell what is going to happen. I know one thing that *has* happened: the willow by the brook has slipped into her yellow dress, lending, along with the faded pink of the snow fences, a spot of color to the vast gray-and-white world. I know, too, that on some not too distant night, somewhere in pond or ditch or low place, a frog will awake, raise his voice in praise, and be joined by others. I will feel a whole lot better when I hear the frogs.

# BEDFELLOWS

❦

Turtle Bay, February 6, 1956

I am lying here in my private sick bay on the east side of town between Second and Third avenues, watching starlings from the vantage point of bed. Three Democrats are in bed with me: Harry Truman (in a stale copy of the *Times*), Adlai Stevenson (in *Harper's*), and Dean Acheson (in a book called *A Democrat Looks at His Party*). I take Democrats to bed with me for lack of a dachshund, although as a matter of fact on occasions like this I am almost certain to be visited by the ghost of Fred, my dash-hound everlasting, dead these many years. In life, Fred always attended the sick, climbing right into bed with the patient like some lecherous old physician, and making a bad situation worse. All this dark morning I have reluctantly entertained him upon the rumpled blanket, felt his oppressive weight, and heard his fraudulent report. He was an uncomfortable bedmate when alive; death has worked little improvement—I still feel crowded, still wonder why I put up with his natural rudeness and his pretensions.

The only thing I used to find agreeable about him in bed was his smell, which for some reason was nonirritating to my nose and evocative to my mind, somewhat in the way that a sudden whiff of the cow barn or of bone meal on a lawn in springtime carries sensations of the richness of earth and of experience. Fred's aroma has not deserted him; it wafts over me now, as though I had just removed the stopper from a vial of cheap perfume. His aroma has not deserted the last collar he wore, either. I ran across this great, studded strap not long ago when I was rummaging in a cabinet. I raised it cautiously toward my nose, fearing a quill stab from his last porcupine. The collar was extremely high—had lost hardly 10 percent of its potency.

Fred was sold to me for a dachshund, but I was in a buying mood and would have bought the puppy if the storekeeper had said he was an Irish Wolfschmidt. He was only a few weeks old when I closed the deal, and he was in real trouble. In no time at all, his troubles cleared up and mine began. Thirteen years later he died, and by rights *my* troubles should have cleared up. But I can't say they have. Here I am, seven years after his death, still sharing a fever bed with him and, what is infinitely more burdensome, still feeling the compulsion to write about him. I sometimes suspect that subconsciously I'm trying to revenge myself by turning him to account, and thus recompensing myself for the time and money he cost me.

He was red and low-posted and long-bodied like a dachshund, and when you glanced casually at him he certainly gave the quick impression of being a dachshund. But if you went at him with a tape measure, and forced him onto scales, the dachshund theory collapsed. The papers that came with him were produced hurriedly and in an illicit atmosphere in a back room of the pet shop, and are most unconvincing. However, I have no reason to unsettle the Kennel Club; the fraud, if indeed it was a fraud, was ended in 1948, at the time of his death. So much of his life was given to shady practices, it is only fitting that his pedigree should have been (as I believe it was) a forgery.

I have been languishing here, looking out at the lovely branches of the plane tree in the sky above our city back yard. Only starlings and house sparrows are in view at this season, but soon other birds will show up. (Why, by the way, doesn't the *Times* publish an "Arrival of Birds" column, similar to its famous "Arrival of Buyers"?) Fred was a window gazer and bird watcher, particularly during his later years, when hardened arteries slowed him up and made it necessary for him to substitute sedentary pleasures for active sport. I think of him as he used to look on our bed in Maine—an old four-poster, too high from the floor for him to reach unassisted. Whenever the bed was occupied during the daylight hours, whether because one of us was sick or was napping, Fred would appear in the doorway and enter without knocking. On his big gray face would be a look of quiet amusement (at having caught somebody in bed during the daytime) coupled with his usual look of fake respectability. Whoever occupied the bed would reach down, seize him by the loose folds of his thick neck, and haul him painfully up. He dreaded this maneuver, and so did the occupant of the bed. There was far too much dead weight involved for anybody's comfort. But Fred was always willing to put up with being hoisted in order to gain the happy heights, as, indeed, he was willing to put up with far greater discomforts—such as a mouthful of porcupine quills—when there was some prize at the end.

Once up, he settled into his pose of bird watching, propped luxuriously against a pillow, as close as he could get to the window, his great soft brown eyes alight with expectation and scientific knowledge. He seemed never to tire of his work. He watched steadily and managed to give the impression that he was a secret agent of the Department of Justice. Spotting a flicker or a starling on the wing, he would turn and make a quick report.

"I just saw an eagle go by," he would say. "It was carrying a baby."

This was not precisely a lie. Fred was like a child in many ways, and sought always to blow things up to proportions that satisfied his imagination and his love of adventure. He was the Cecil B. deMille of dogs. He was a zealot, and I have just been reminded of him by a quote from one of the Democrats sharing my bed—Acheson quoting Brandeis. "The greatest dangers to liberty," said Mr. Brandeis, "lurk in insidious encroachment by men of zeal, well-meaning but without understanding." Fred saw in every bird, every squirrel, every housefly, every rat, every skunk, every porcupine, a security risk and a present danger to his republic. He had a dossier on almost every living creature, as well as on several inanimate objects, including my son's football.

Although birds fascinated him, his real hope as he watched the big shade trees outside the window was that a red squirrel would show up. When he sighted a squirrel, Fred would straighten up from his pillow, tense his frame, and then, in a moment or two, begin to tremble. The knuckles of his big forelegs, unstable from old age, would seem to go into spasm, and he would sit there with his eyes glued on the squirrel and his front legs alternately collapsing under him and bearing his weight again.

I find it difficult to convey the peculiar character of this ignoble old vigilante, my late and sometimes lamented companion. What was there about him so different from the many other dogs I've owned that he keeps recurring and does not, in fact, seem really dead at all? My wife used to claim that Fred was deeply devoted to me, and in a certain sense he was, but his was the devotion of an opportunist. He knew that on the farm I took the overall view and traveled pluckily from one trouble spot to the next. He dearly loved this type of work. It was not his habit to tag along faithfully behind me, as a collie might, giving moral support and sometimes real support. He ran a trouble-shooting business of his own and was usually at the scene ahead of me, compounding the trouble and shooting in the air. The word "faithful" is an adjective I simply never thought of in connection with Fred. He differed from most dogs in that he tended to knock down, rather than build up, the master's ego. Once he had outgrown the capers of puppy-hood, he never again caressed me or anybody else during his life. The only time he was ever discovered in an attitude that suggested affection was when I was in the driver's seat of our car and he would lay his heavy head on my right knee. This, I soon perceived, was not affection, it was nausea. Drooling always followed, and the whole thing was extremely inconvenient, because the weight of his head made me press too hard on the accelerator.

Fred devoted his life to deflating me and succeeded admirably. His attachment to our establishment, though untinged with affection, was strong nevertheless, and vibrant. It was simply that he found in our persons, in our activities, the sort of complex, disorderly society that fired his imagination and satisfied his need for tumult and his quest for truth. After he had subdued six or seven porcupines, we realized that his private war against porcupines was an expensive bore, so we took to tying him, making him fast to any tree or wheel or post or log that was at hand, to keep him from sneaking off into the woods. I think of him as always at the end of some outsize piece of rope. Fred's disgust at these confinements was great, but he improved his time, nonetheless, in a thousand small diversions. He never just lay and rested. Within the range of his tether, he continued to explore, dissect, botanize, conduct post-mortems, excavate, experiment, expropriate, savor, masticate, regurgitate. He had no contemplative life, but he held as a steady gleam the belief that under the commonplace stone and behind the unlikely piece of driftwood lay the stuff of high adventure and the opportunity to save the nation.

But to return to my other bedfellows, these quick Democrats. They are big, solid men, every one of them, and they have been busy writing and speaking, and sniffing out the truth. I did not deliberately pack my counterpane with members of a single political faith; they converged on me by the slick device of getting into print. All three turn up saying things that interest me, so I make bed space for them.

Mr. Truman, reminiscing in a recent issue of the *Times*, says the press sold out in 1948 to "the special interests," was 90 percent hostile to his candidacy, distorted facts, caused his low popularity rating at that period, and tried to prevent him from reaching the people with his message in the campaign. This bold, implausible statement engages my fancy because it is a half-truth, and all half-truths excite me. An attractive half-truth in bed with a man can disturb him as deeply as a cracker crumb. Being a second-string member of the press myself, and working, as I do, for the special interests, I tend to think there is a large dollop of pure irascibility in Mr. Truman's gloomy report. In 1948, Mr. Truman made a spirited whistle-stop trip and worked five times as hard as his rival. The "Republican-controlled press and radio" reported practically everything he said, and also gave vent to frequent horse-laughs in their editorials and commentaries. Millions of studious, worried Americans heard and read what he said; then they checked it against the editorials; then they walked silently into the voting booths and returned him to office. Then they listened to Kaltenborn. Then they listened to Truman doing Kaltenborn. The criticism of the opposition in 1948 was neither a bad thing nor a destructive thing. It was healthy and (in our sort of society) necessary. Without the press, radio, and TV, President Truman couldn't have got through to the people in anything like the volume he achieved. Some of the published news was distorted, but distortion is inherent in partisan journalism, the same as it is in political rallies. I have yet to see a piece of writing, political or non-political, that doesn't have a slant. All writing slants the way a writer leans, and no man is born perpendicular, although many men are born upright. The beauty of the American free press is that the slants and the twists and the distortions come from so many directions, and the special interests are so numerous, the reader must sift and sort and check and countercheck in order to find out what the score is. This he does. It is only when a press gets its twist from a single source, as in the case of government-controlled press systems, that the reader is licked.

Democrats do a lot of bellyaching about the press's being preponderantly Republican, which it is. But they don't do the one thing that could correct the situation: they don't go into the publishing business. Democrats say they haven't got that kind of money, but I'm afraid they haven't got that kind of temperament or, perhaps, nerve.

Adlai Stevenson takes a view of criticism almost opposite to Harry Truman's. Writing in *Harper's*, Stevenson says, ". . . I very well know that in many minds 'criticism' has today become an ugly word. It has become almost *lèse majesté*. It conjures up pictures of insidious radicals hacking away at the very foundations of the American way of life. It suggests nonconformity and nonconformity suggests disloyalty and disloyalty suggests treason, and before we know where we are, this process has all but identified the critic with the saboteur and turned political criticism into an un-American activity instead of democracy's greatest safeguard."

The above interests me because I agree with it and everyone is fascinated by what he agrees with. Especially when he is sick in bed.

Mr. Acheson, in his passionately partisan yet temperate book, writes at some length about the loyalty-security procedures that were started under the Democrats in 1947 and have modified our lives ever since. This theme interests me because I believe, with the author, that security declines as security machinery expands. The machinery calls for a secret police. At first, this device is used solely to protect us from unsuitable servants in sensitive positions. Then it broadens rapidly and permeates nonsensitive areas, and, finally, business and industry. It is in the portfolios of the secret police that nonconformity makes the subtle change into disloyalty. A secret-police system first unsettles, then desiccates, then calcifies a free society. I think the recent loyalty investigation of the press by the Eastland subcommittee was a disquieting event. It seemed to assume for Congress the right to poke about in newspaper offices and instruct the management as to which employees were okay and which were not. That sort of procedure opens wonderfully attractive vistas to legislators. If it becomes an accepted practice, it will lead to great abuses. Under extreme conditions, it could destroy the free press.

The loyalty theme also relates to Fred, who presses ever more heavily against me this morning. Fred was intensely loyal to himself, as every strong individualist must be. He held unshakable convictions, like Harry Truman. He was absolutely sure that he was in possession of the truth. Because he was loyal to himself, I found his eccentricities supportable. Actually, he contributed greatly to the general health and security of the household. Nothing has been quite the same since he departed. His views were largely of a dissenting nature. Yet in tearing us apart he somehow held us together. In obstructing, he strengthened us. In criticizing, he informed. In his rich, aromatic heresy, he nourished our faith. He was also a plain damned nuisance, I must not forget that.

The matter of "faith" has been in the papers again lately. President Eisenhower (I will now move over and welcome a Republican into bed, along with my other visitors) has come out for prayer and has emphasized that most Americans are motivated (as they surely are) by religious faith. The *Herald Tribune* headed the story, PRESIDENT SAYS PRAYER IS PART OF DEMOCRACY. The implication in such a pronouncement, emanating from the seat of government, is that religious faith is a *condition*, or even a *precondition*, of the democratic life. This is just wrong. A President should pray whenever and wherever he feels like it (most Presidents have prayed hard and long, and some of them in desperation and in agony), but I don't think a President should advertise prayer. That is a different thing. Democracy, if I understand it at all, is a society in which the unbeliever feels undisturbed and at home. If there were only half a dozen unbelievers in America, their well-being would be a test of our democracy, their tranquillity would be its proof. The repeated suggestion by the present administration that religious faith is a precondition of the American way of life is disturbing to me and, I am willing to bet, to a good many other citizens. President Eisenhower spoke of the tremendous favorable mail he received in response to his inaugural prayer in 1953. What he perhaps did not realize is that the persons who felt fidgety or disquieted about the matter were not likely to write in about it, lest they appear irreverent, irreligious, unfaithful, or even un-American. I remember the prayer very well. I didn't mind it, although I have never been able to pray electronically and doubt that I ever will be. Still, I was able to perceive that the President was sincere and was doing what came naturally, and anybody who is acting in a natural way is all right by me. I believe that our political leaders should live by faith and should, by deeds and sometimes by prayer, demonstrate faith, but I doubt that they should *advocate* faith, if only because such advocacy renders a few people uncomfortable. The concern of a democracy is that no honest man shall feel uncomfortable, I don't care who he is, or how nutty he is.

I hope that belief never is made to appear mandatory. One of our founders, in 1787, said, "Even the diseases of the people should be represented." Those were strange, noble words, and they have endured. They were on television yesterday. I distrust the slightest hint of a standard for political rectitude, knowing that it will open the way for persons in authority to set arbitrary standards of human behavior.

Fred was an unbeliever. He worshiped no personal God, no Supreme Being. He certainly did not worship *me*. If he had suddenly taken to worshiping me, I think I would have felt as queer as God must have felt the other day when a minister in California, pronouncing the invocation for a meeting of Democrats, said, "We believe Adlai Stevenson to be Thy choice for President of the United States. Amen."

I respected this quirk in Fred, this inability to conform to conventional canine standards of religious feeling. And in the miniature democracy that was, and is, our household he lived undisturbed and at peace with his conscience. I hope my country will never become an uncomfortable place for the unbeliever, as it could easily become if prayer was made one of the requirements of the accredited citizen. My wife, a spiritual but not a prayerful woman, read Mr. Eisenhower's call to prayer in the *Tribune* and said something I shall never forget. "Maybe it's all right," she said. "But for the first time in my life I'm beginning to feel like an outsider in my own land."

Democracy is itself a religious faith. For some it comes close to being the only formal religion they have. And so when I see the first faint shadow of orthodoxy sweep across the sky, feel the first cold whiff of its blinding fog steal in from sea, I tremble all over, as though I had just seen an eagle go by, carrying a baby.

Anyway, it's pleasant here in bed with all these friendly Democrats and Republicans, every one of them a dedicated man, with all these magazine and newspaper clippings, with Fred, watching the starlings against the wintry sky, and the prospect of another presidential year, with all its passions and its distortions and its dissents and its excesses and special interests. Fred died from a life of excesses, and I don't mind if I do, too. I love to read all these words—most of them sober, thoughtful words—from the steadily growing book of democracy: Acheson on security, Truman on the press, Eisenhower on faith, Stevenson on criticism, all writing away like sixty, all working to improve and save and maintain in good repair what was so marvelously constructed to begin with. This is the real thing. This is bedlam in bed. As Mr. Stevenson puts it: ". . . no civilization has ever had so haunting a sense of an ultimate order of goodness and rationality which can be known and achieved." It makes me eager to rise and meet the new day, as Fred used to rise to his, with the complete conviction that through vigilance and good works all porcupines, all cats, all skunks, all squirrels, all houseflies, all footballs, all evil birds in the sky could be successfully brought to account and the scene made safe and pleasant for the sensible individual—namely, him. However distorted was his crazy vision of the beautiful world, however perverse his scheme for establishing an order of goodness by murdering every creature that seemed to him bad, I had to hand him this: he really worked at it.

P.S. (June 1962).    This piece about prayer and about Fred drew a heavy mail when it appeared—heavy for me, anyway. (I call six letters a heavy mail.) Some of the letters were from persons who felt as I did about the advocacy of prayer but who had been reluctant to say anything about it. And there were other letters from readers who complained that my delineation of Fred's character (half vigilante, half dissenter) was contradictory, or at least fuzzy. I guess there is some justification for this complaint: the thing didn't come out as clear as I would have liked, but nothing I write ever does.

In the 1960 presidential campaign, faith and prayer took a back seat and the big question was whether the White House could be occupied by a Catholic or whether that would be just too much. Again the voters studied the *Racing Form*, the *Wall Street Journal*, the *Christian Science Monitor*; they sifted the winds that blew through the Republican-controlled press; they gazed into television's crystal ball; they went to church and asked guidance; and finally they came up with the opinion that a Catholic *can* be President. It was a memorable time, a photo finish, and a healthful exercise generally.

The McCarthy era, so lately dead, has been followed by the Birch Society era (eras are growing shorter and shorter in America—some of them seem to last only a few days), and again we find ourselves with a group of people that proposes to establish a standard for political rectitude, again we have vigilantes busy compiling lists and deciding who is anti-Communist and who fails in that regard. Now in 1962, conservatism is the big, new correct thing, and the term "liberal" is a term of opprobrium. In the newspaper that arrives on my breakfast table every morning, liberals are usually referred to as "so-called" liberals, the implication being that they are probably something a whole lot worse than the name "liberal" would indicate, something really shady. The Birchers, luckily, are not in as good a position to create sensational newspaper headlines as was Senator McCarthy, who, because he was chairman of a Senate committee, managed to turn page one into a gibbet, and hung a new fellow each day, with the help of a press that sometimes seemed to me unnecessarily cooperative in donating its space for the celebration of those grim rites.

Prayer broke into the news again with the Supreme Court's decision in the New York school prayer case. From the violence of the reaction you would have thought the Court was in the business of stifling America's religious life and that the country was going to the dogs. But I think the Court again heard clearly the simple theme that ennobles our Constitution: that no one shall be made to feel uncomfortable or unsafe because of nonconformity. New York State, with the best intentions in the world, created a moment of gentle orthodoxy in public school life, and here and there a child was left out in the cold, bearing the stigma of being different. It is this one child that our Constitution is concerned about—his tranquillity, his health, his safety, his conscience. What a kindly old document it is, and how brightly it shines, through interpretation after interpretation!

One day last fall I wandered down through the orchard and into the woods to pay a call at Fred's grave. The trees were bare; wild apples hung shamelessly from the grapevine that long ago took over the tree. The old dump, which is no longer used and which goes out of sight during the leafy months, lay exposed and candid—rusted pots and tin cans and sundries. The briers had lost some of their effectiveness, the air was good, and the little dingle, usually so mean and inconsiderable, seemed to have acquired stature. Fred's headstone, ordinarily in collapse, was bolt upright, and I wondered whether he had quieted down at last. I felt uneasy suddenly, as the quick do sometimes feel when in the presence of the dead, and my uneasiness went to my bladder. Instead of laying a wreath, I watered an alder and came away.

This grave is the only grave I visit with any regularity—in fact, it is the only grave I visit at all. I have relatives lying in cemeteries here and there around the country, but I do not feel any urge to return to them, and it strikes me as odd that I should return to the place where an old dog lies in a shabby bit of woodland next to a private dump. Besides being an easy trip (one for which I need make no preparation) it is a natural journey—I really go down there to see what's doing. (Fred himself used to scout the place every day when he was alive.) I do not experience grief when I am down there, nor do I pay tribute to the dead. I feel a sort of overall sadness that has nothing to do with the grave or its occupant. Often I feel extremely well in that rough cemetery, and sometimes flush a partridge. But I feel sadness at All Last Things, too, which is probably a purely selfish, or turned-in, emotion —sorrow not at my dog's death but at my own, which hasn't even occurred yet but which saddens me just to think about in such pleasant surroundings.

# SOOTFALL AND FALLOUT

*Turtle Bay, October 18, 1956*

This is a dark morning in the apartment, but the block is gay with yellow moving vans disgorging Mary Martin's belongings in front of a house a couple of doors east of here, into which (I should say from the looks of things) she is moving. People's lives are so exposed at moments like this, their possessions lying naked in the street, the light of day searching out every bruise and mark of indoor living. It is an unfair exposé—end tables with nothing to be at the end of, standing lamps with their cords tied up in curlers, bottles of vermouth craning their long necks from cartons of personal papers, and every waste-basket carrying its small cargo of miscellany. The vans cause a stir in the block. Heads appear in the windows of No. 230, across the way. Passers-by stop on the sidewalk and stare brazenly into the new home through the open door. I have a mezzanine seat for the performance; like a Peeping Tom, I lounge here in my bathrobe and look down, held in the embrace of a common cold, before which scientists stand in awe although they have managed to split the atom, infect the topsoil with strontium 90, break the barrier of sound, and build the Lincoln Tunnel.

What a tremendous lot of stuff makes up the cumulus called "the home"! The trivet, the tiny washboard, the fire tools, the big copper caldron large enough to scald a hog in, the metal filing cabinets, the cardboard filing cabinets, the record player, the glass and the china invisible in their barrels, the carpet sweeper. (I wonder whether Miss Martin knows that she owns an old-fashioned carpet sweeper in a modern shade of green.) And here comes a bright little hacksaw, probably the apple of Mr. Halliday's eye. When a writing desk appears, the movers take the drawers out, to lighten the load, and I am free to observe what a tangle Mary Martin's stationery and supplies are in— like my wife's, everything at sixes and sevens. And now the bed, under the open sky above Forty-eighth Street. And now the mattress. A wave of decency overtakes me. I avert my gaze.

The movers experience the worst trouble with two large house plants, six-footers, in their great jars. The jars, on being sounded, prove to be a third full of water and have to be emptied into the gutter. Living things are always harder to lift, somehow, than inanimate objects, and I think any mover would rather walk up three flights with a heavy bureau than go into a waltz with a rubber plant. There is really no way for a man to put his arms around a big house plant and still remain a gentleman.

Out in back, away from the street, the prospect is more pleasing. The yellow cat mounts the wisteria vine and tries to enter my bedroom, stirred by dreams of a bullfinch in a cage. The air is hazy, smoke and fumes being pressed downward in what the smog reporter of the *Times* calls "a wigwam effect." I don't know what new gadget the factories of Long Island are making today to produce such a foul vapor—probably a new jet applicator for the relief of nasal congestion. But whatever it is, I would swap it for a breath of fresh air. On every slight stirring of the breeze, the willow behind Mary Martin's wigwam lets drop two or three stylish yellow leaves, and they swim lazily down like golden fish to where Paul, the handyman, waits with his broom. In the ivy border along the wall, watchful of the cat, three thrushes hunt about among the dry leaves. I can't pronounce "three thrushes," but I can see three thrushes from this window, and this is the first autumn I have ever seen three at once. An October miracle. I think they are hermits, but the visibility is so poor I can't be sure.

This section of Manhattan boasts the heaviest sootfall in town, and the United States of America boasts the heaviest fallout in the world, and when you take the sootfall and the fallout and bring smog in on top of them, I feel I am in a perfect position to discuss the problem of universal pollution. The papers, of course, are full of the subject these days, as they follow the presidential campaigners around the nation from one contaminated area to another.

I have no recent figures on sootfall in the vicinity of Third Avenue, but the *Times* last Saturday published some figures on fallout from Dr. Willard F. Libby, who said the reservoir of radioactive materials now floating in the stratosphere from the tests of all nations was roughly twenty-four billion tons. That was Saturday. Sunday's *Times* quoted Dr. Laurence H. Snyder as saying, "In assessing the potential harm [of weapons-testing], statements are always qualified by a phrase such as 'if the testing of weapons continues at the present rate . . .' This qualification is usually obsolete by the time the statement is printed." I have an idea the figure twenty-four billion tons may have been obsolete when it appeared in the paper. It may not have included, for instance, the radioactive stuff from the bomb the British set off in Australia a week or two ago. Maybe it did, maybe it didn't. The point of Dr. Snyder's remark is clear; a thermonuclear arms race is, as he puts it, self-accelerating. Bomb begets bomb. A begets H. Anything you can build, I can build bigger.

"Unhappily," said Governor Harriman the other night, "we are still thinking in small, conventional terms, and with unwarranted complacency."

The habit of thinking in small, conventional terms is, of course, not limited to us Americans. You could drop a leaflet or a Hubbard squash on the head of any person in any land and you would almost certainly hit a brain that was whirling in small, conventional circles. There is something about the human mind that keeps it well within the confines of the parish, and only one outlook in a million is nonparochial. The impression one gets from campaign oratory is that the sun revolves around the earth, the earth revolves around the United States, and the United States revolves around whichever city the speaker happens to be in at the moment. This is what a friend of mine used to call the Un-Copernican system. During a presidential race, candidates sometimes manage to create the impression that their thoughts are ranging widely and that they have abandoned conventional thinking. I love to listen to them when they are in the throes of these quadrennial seizures. But I haven't heard much from either candidate that sounded unconventional—although I have heard some things that sounded sensible and sincere. A candidate could easily commit political suicide if he were to come up with an unconventional thought during a presidential tour.

I think man's gradual, creeping contamination of the planet, his sending up of dust into the air, his strontium additive in our bones, his discharge of industrial poisons into rivers that once flowed clear, his mixing of chemicals with fog on the east wind add up to a fantasy of such grotesque proportions as to make everything said on the subject seem pale and anemic by contrast. I hold one share in the corporate earth and am uneasy about the management. Dr. Libby said there is new evidence that the amount of strontium reaching the body from topsoil impregnated by fallout is "considerably less than the 70 percent of the topsoil concentration originally estimated." Perhaps we should all feel elated at this, but I don't. The correct amount of strontium with which to impregnate the topsoil is *no* strontium. To rely on "tolerances" when you get into the matter of strontium 90, with three sovereign bomb testers already testing, independently of one another, and about fifty potential bomb testers ready to enter the stratosphere with their contraptions, is to talk with unwarranted complacency. I belong to a small, unconventional school that believes that *no* rat poison is the correct amount to spread in the kitchen where children and puppies can get at it. I believe that *no* chemical waste is the correct amount to discharge into the fresh rivers of the world, and I believe that if there is a way to trap the fumes from factory chimneys, it should be against the law to set these deadly fumes adrift where they can mingle with fog and, given the right conditions, suddenly turn an area into another Donora, Pa.

"I have seen the smoky fury of our factories—rising to the skies," said President Eisenhower pridefully as he addressed the people of Seattle last night. Well, I can see the smoky fury of our factories drifting right into this room this very minute; the fury sits in my throat like a bundle of needles, it explores my nose, chokes off my breath, and makes my eyes burn. The room smells like a slaughterhouse. And the phenomenon gets a brief mention in the morning press.

One simple, unrefuted fact about radioactive substances is that scientists do not agree about the "safe" amount. All radiation is harmful, all of it shortens life, all is cumulative, nobody keeps track of how much he gets in the form of X rays and radio therapy, and all of it affects not only the recipient but his heirs. Both President Eisenhower and Governor Stevenson have discussed H-bomb testing and the thermonuclear scene, and their views differ. Neither of them, it seems to me, has quite told the changing facts of life on earth. Both tend to speak of national security as though it were still capable of being dissociated from universal well-being; in fact, sometimes in these political addresses it sounds as though this nation, or any nation, through force of character or force of arms, could damn well rise *above* planetary considerations, as though we were greater than our environment, as though the national verve somehow transcended the natural world.

"Strong we shall stay free," said President Eisenhower in Pittsburgh. And Governor Stevenson echoed the statement in Chicago: ". . . only the strong can be free."

This doctrine of freedom through strength deserves a second look. It would have served nicely in 1936, but nobody thought of it then. Today, with the H-bomb deterring war, we are free and we are militarily

strong, but the doctrine is subject to a queer, embarrassing amend-
ment. Today it reads, "Strong we shall stay free, *provided we do not
have to use our strength.*" That's not quite the same thing. What was
true in 1936, if not actually false today, is at best a mere partial, or
half truth. A nation wearing atomic armor is like a knight whose armor
has grown so heavy he is immobilized; he can hardly walk, hardly sit
his horse, hardly think, hardly breathe. The H-bomb is an extremely
effective deterrent to war, but it has little virtue as a *weapon* of war,
because it would leave the world uninhabitable.

For a short while following the release of atomic energy, a strong
nation was a secure nation. Today, no nation, whatever its thermonuclear power, is a strong nation in the sense that it is a fully independent nation. All are weak, and all are weak from the same cause: each
depends on the others for salvation, yet none likes to admit this dependence, and there is no machinery for interdependence. The big nations are weak because the strength has gone out of their arms—which
are too terrifyng to use, too poisonous to explode. The little nations are
weak because they have always been relatively weak and now they have
to breathe the same bad air as the big ones. Ours is a balance, as Mr.
Stevenson put it, not of power but of terror. If anything, the H-bomb
rather favors small nations that don't as yet possess it; they feel slightly
more free to jostle other nations, having discovered that a country
can stick its tongue out quite far these days without provoking war, so
horrible are war's consequences.

The atom, then, is a proper oddity. It has qualified the meaning
of national security, it has very likely saved us from a third world war,
it has given a new twist to the meaning of power, and it has already
entered our bones with a cancer-producing isotope. Furthermore,
it has altered the concept of personal sacrifice for moral principle. Human beings have always been willing to shed their blood for what they
believed in. Yesterday this was clear and simple; we would pay in blood
because, after the price was exacted, there was still a chance to make
good the gain. But the modern price tag is not blood. Today our leaders
and the leaders of other nations are, in effect, saying, "We will defend
our beliefs not alone with our blood—by God, we'll defend them, if we
have to, with our genes." This is bold, resolute talk, and one can't
help admiring the spirit of it. I admire the spirit of it, but the logic of
it eludes me. I doubt whether any noble principle—or any ignoble
principle, either, for that matter—can be preserved at the price of
genetic disintegration.

The thing I watch for in the speeches of the candidates is some
hint that the thermonuclear arms race may be bringing people nearer

together, rather than forcing them farther apart. I suspect that because of fallout we may achieve a sort of universality sooner than we bargained for. Fallout may compel us to fall in. The magic-carpet ride on the mushroom cloud has left us dazed—we have come so far so fast. There is a passage in Anne Lindbergh's book *North to the Orient* that captures the curious lag between the mind and the body during a plane journey, between the slow unfolding of remembered images and the swift blur of modern flight. Mrs. Lindbergh started her flight to the Orient by way of North Haven, her childhood summer home. "The trip to Maine," she wrote, "used to be a long and slow one. There was plenty of time in the night, spattered away in the sleeper, in the morning spent ferrying across the river at Bath, in the afternoon syncopated into a series of calls on one coast town after another—there was plenty of time to make the mental change coinciding with our physical change. . . . But on this swift flight to North Haven in the *Sirius* my mind was so far behind my body that when we flew over Rockland Harbor the familiar landmarks below me had no reality."

Like the girl in the plane, we have arrived, but the familiar scene lacks reality. We cling to old remembered forms, old definitions, old comfortable conceptions of national coziness, national self-sufficiency. The Security Council meets solemnly and takes up Suez, eleven sovereign fellows kicking a sovereign ditch around while England threatens war to defend her "lifelines," when modern war itself means universal contamination, universal deathlines, and the end of ditches. I would feel more hopeful, more *secure*, if the councilmen suddenly changed their tune and began arguing the case for mud turtles and other ancient denizens of ponds and ditches. That is the thing at stake now, and it is what will finally open the canal to the world's ships in perfect concord.

Candidates for political office steer clear of what Mrs. Luce used to call "globaloney," for fear they may lose the entire American Legion vote and pick up only Norman Cousins. Yet there are indications that supranational ideas are alive in the back of a few men's minds. Through the tangle of verbiage, the idea of "common cause" skitters like a shy bird. Mr. Dulles uses the word "interdependent" in one sentence, then returns promptly to the more customary, safer word "independent." We give aid to Yugoslavia to assure her "independence," and the very fact of the gift is proof that neither donor nor recipient enjoys absolute independence anymore, the two are locked in mortal interdependence. Mr. Tito says he is for "new forms and new laws." I haven't the vaguest notion of what he means by that, and I doubt whether he has, either. Certainly there are no *old* laws, if by "laws" he means enforceable rules of conduct by which the world community is governed. But I'm for new forms, all right. Governor Stevenson, in one of his talks, said, "Nations have become so accustomed to living in the dark that they find it hard to learn to live in the light." What light? The light of government? If so, why not say so? President Eisenhower ended a speech the other day with the phrase "a peace of justice in a world of law." Everything else in his speech dealt with a peace of justice in a world of anarchy.

The riddle of disarmament, the riddle of peace, seems to me to hang on the interpretation of these conflicting and contradictory phrases —and on whether or not the men who use them really mean business. Are we independent or interdependent? We can't possibly be both. Do we indeed seek a peace of justice in a world of law, as the President intimates? If so, when do we start, and how? Are we for "new forms," or will the old ones do? In 1945, after the worst blood bath in history, the nations settled immediately back into old forms. In its structure, the United Nations reaffirms everything that caused the Second World War. At the end of a war fought to defeat dictators, the U.N. welcomed Stalin and Perón to full membership, and the Iron Curtain quickly descended to put the seal of authority on this inconsistent act. The drafters of the Charter assembled in San Francisco and defended their mild, inadequate format with the catchy phrase "Diplomacy is the art of the possible." Meanwhile, a little band of physicists met in a squash court and said, "The hell with the art of the possible. Watch this!"

The world organization debates disarmament in one room and, in the next room, moves the knights and pawns that make national arms imperative. This is not justice and law, and this is not light. It is not new forms. The U.N. is modern in intent, old-fashioned in shape. In San Francisco in 1945, the victor nations failed to create a constitution that placed a higher value on principle than on sovereignty, on common cause than on special cause. The world of 1945 was still 100 percent parochial. The world of 1956 is still almost 100 percent parochial. But at last we have a problem that is clearly a community problem, devoid of nationality—the problem of the total pollution of the planet.

We have, in fact, a situation in which the deadliest of all weapons, the H-bomb, together with its little brother, the A-bomb, is the latent source of great agreement among peoples. The bomb is universally hated, and it is universally feared. We cannot escape it with collective security; we shall have to face it with united action. It has given us a few years of grace without war, and now it offers us a few millenniums of oblivion. In a paradox of unbelievable jocundity, the shield of national sovereignty suddenly becomes the challenge of national sovereignty. And, largely because of events beyond our control, we are able to sniff the faint stirring of a community ferment—something every man can enjoy.

The President speaks often of "the peaceful uses of atomic energy," and they are greatly on his mind. I believe the peaceful use of atomic energy that should take precedence over all other uses in this: stop it from contaminating the soil and the sea, the rain and the sky, and the bones of man. This is elementary. It comes ahead of "good-will" ships and it comes ahead of cheap power. What good is cheap power if your child already has an incurable cancer?

The hydrogen-garbage disposal program unites the people of the earth in a common antilitterbug drive for salvation. Radioactive dust has no nationality, is not deflected by boundaries; it falls on Turk and Texan impartially. The radio-strontium isotope finds its way into the milk of Soviet cow and English cow with equal ease. This simple fact profoundly alters the political scene and calls for political leaders to echo the physicists and say, "Never mind the art of the possible. Watch this!"

To me, living in the light means an honest attempt to discover the germ of common cause in a world of special cause, even against the almost insuperable odds of parochialism and national fervor, even in the face of the dangers that always attend political growth. Actually, nations are already enjoying little pockets of unity. The European coal-steel authority is apparently a success. The U.N., which is usually impotent in political disputes, has nevertheless managed to elevate the world's children and the world's health to a community level. The trick is to encourage and hasten this magical growth, this benign condition—encourage it and get it on paper, while children still have healthy bones and before we have all reached the point of no return. It will not mean the end of nations; it will mean the true beginning of nations.

Paul-Henri Spaak, addressing himself to the Egyptian government the other day, said, "We are no longer at the time of the absolute sovereignty of states." We are not, and we ought by this time to know we are not. I just hope we learn it in time. In the beautiful phrase of Mrs. Lindbergh's, there used to be "plenty of time in the night." Now there is hardly any time at all.

Well, this started out as a letter and has turned into a discourse. But I don't mind. If a candidate were to appear on the scene and come out for the dignity of mud turtles, I suppose people would hesitate to support him, for fear he had lost his reason. But he would have my vote, on the theory that in losing his reason he had kept his head. It is time men allowed their imagination to infect their intellect, time we all rushed headlong into the wilder regions of thought where the earth again revolves around the sun instead of around the Suez, regions where no individual and no group can blithely assume the right to sow the sky with seeds of mischief, and where the sovereign nation at last begins to function as the true friend and guardian of sovereign man.

P.S. (May 1962).     The dirty state of affairs on earth is getting worse, not better. Our soil, our rivers, our seas, our air carry an ever-increasing load of industrial wastes, agricultural poisons, and military debris. The seeds of mischief are in the wind—in the warm sweet airs of spring. Contamination continues in greater force and new ways, and with new excuses: the Soviet tests last autumn had a double-barreled purpose—to experiment and to intimidate. This was the first appearance of the diplomacy of dust; the breaking of the moratorium by Russia was a high crime, murder in the first degree. President Kennedy countered with the announcement that he would reply in kind unless a test-ban agreement could be reached by the end of April. None was reached, and our tests are being conducted. One more nation, France, has joined the company of testers. If Red China learns the trick, we will probably see the greatest pyrotechnic display yet, for the Chinese love fireworks of all kinds.

I asked myself what I would have done, had I been in the President's shoes, and was forced to admit I would have taken the same course—test. The shattering of the moratorium was for the time being the shattering of our hopes of good nuclear conduct. In a darkening and dirt-ridden world the course of freedom must be maintained even by desperate means, while there is a time of grace, and the only thing worse than being in an arms race is to be in one and not compete. The President's decision to resume testing in the atmosphere was, I believe, a correct decision, and I think the people who protest by lying down in the street have not come up with an alternative course that is sensible and workable. But the time of grace will run out, sooner or later, for all nations. We are in a vast riddle, all of us— dependence on a strength that is inimical to life—and what we are really doing is fighting a war that uses the lives of future individuals, rather than the lives of existing young men. The President did his best to lighten the blow by pointing out that fallout isn't as bad as it used to be, that our tests would raise the background radiation by only one percent. But this is like saying that it isn't dangerous to go in the cage with the tiger because the tiger is taking a nap. I am not calmed by the news of fallout's mildness, or deceived by drowsy tigers. The percentages will increase, the damage will mount steadily unless a turn is made somehow. Because our adversary tests, we test; because we test, they test. Where is the end of this dirty habit? I think there is no military solution, no economic solution, only a political solution, and this is the area to which we should give the closest attention and in which we should show the greatest imaginative powers.

These nuclear springtimes have a pervasive sadness about them, the virgin earth having been the victim of rape attacks. This is a smiling morning; I am writing where I can look out at our garden piece, which has been newly harrowed, ready for planting. The rich brown patch of ground used to bring delight to eye and mind at this fresh season of promise. For me the scene has been spoiled by the maggots that work in the mind. Tomorrow we will have rain, and the rain falling on the garden will carry its cargo of debris from old explosions in distant places. Whether the amount of this freight is great or small, whether it is measurable by the farmer or can only be guessed at, one thing is certain: the character of rain has changed, the joy of watching it soak the waiting earth has been diminished, and the whole meaning and worth of gardens has been brought into question.

# UNITY

◦⟩§⟨◦

*Avenue of the Americas, June 4, 1960*

In 1899, the year I was born, a peace conference was held at The Hague. I don't remember how it came out, but there have been two memorable wars since then, and I am now sixty, and peace parleys, some of them tackling the subject of disarmament, have been held at intervals all my life. At this writing, five nations of the East and five of the West are studying disarmament, hopeful of achieving peace. When last heard from, they were deadlocked, which is the natural condition of nations engaged in arms negotiations. The Soviet Union has suggested that they "start all over again."

The West has a real genius for doing approximately what the East wants it to do. We go to Paris and sit in stunned surprise while Khrushchev bangs a cat against a wall. We go to Geneva and listen solemnly while Russia presents herself as the author of total disarmament and peace. We hasten to the Security Council room at the United Nations and earnestly defend ourselves against a charge that we have "aggressed." We join England for Princess Margaret's wedding, and next day we separate from England again, to return our trust to last-minute diplomatic conformity. We use the word "peace" the way the East likes to see it used—in the last paragraph of the President's formal speeches, and preceded by the adjectives "just" and "lasting," as though peace were some sort of precious stone that, once discovered, would put an end to trouble for all time. After the recent events in Paris, and the bruises of the night, it is not at all certain that the West should indulge itself longer in the pleasures of perfect political disunity.

Soviet arms, terrible as they are, seem less fearsome to me than the Soviet's dedication to its political faith, which includes the clear goal of political unity. Russia openly proclaims her intention of communizing the world and announces that she is on the march. Not all her cronies present the face of unity—Mao's China, Tito's Yugoslavia, Gomulka's Poland—but at least the idea of unity is implicit in the religion of Communism. Must we in the West leave all the marching to our opponent? I hope not. Not until free men get up in the morning with the feeling that they, too, are on the march will the danger to Western society begin to subside. But marching is futile unless there is a destination, and the West's destination is fuzzy. Perhaps I should merely say that it is not clear to *me*. I do not think that it is discernible in the utterances of our statesmen.

*Life* magazine, I see, has raised the question of the free world's destiny with a series of pieces on "National Purpose." The title of the series is revealing. America's purpose, everyone's purpose in the West, is still painted in the national frame. When we aid a friend, it is "foreign" aid. And when the aided country emerges, it gains "independence," thus adding one more sovereign political unit to the ever-growing list of destiny seekers. When we establish a military base in some indispensable location outside our borders, we call it a base on "foreign" soil, and so it is. The U-2 plane incident disclosed an American pilot taking off from an American nook in Turkey and heading for an American nook in Norway. This famous flight illustrated the queer conditions we and our Western associates are compelled to face—a world grown so small that other people's airfields are essential to our own safety, and ours to theirs, yet a world that has made no progress in bringing free men together in a political community and under a common roof. The West's only roof these days is the wild sky, with its flights, its overflights, and the boom of broken barriers. Our scientists long ago broke all known boundaries, yet the rest of us work sedulously to maintain them, in our pursuits, in our prayers, in our minds, and in our constitutions. We dwell in a house one wall of which has been removed, all the while pretending that we are still protected against the wind and the rain.

Most people think of peace as a state of Nothing Bad Happening, or Nothing Much Happening. Yet if peace is to overtake us and make us the gift of serenity and well-being, it will have to be the state of Something Good Happening. What is this good thing? I think it is the evolution of community, community slowly and surely invested with the robes of government by the consent of the governed. We cannot conceivably achieve a peaceful life merely by relaxing the tensions of sovereign nations; there is an unending supply of them. We may gain a breather by relaxing a tension here and there, but I think it a fallacy that a mere easement, or diplomacy triumphant, can ever be the whole base for peace. You could relax every last tension tonight and wake tomorrow morning with all the makings of war, all the familiar promise of trouble.

A popular belief these days is that the clue to peace is in disarmament. Pick a statesman of any stature in any nation and he will almost certainly tell you that a reduction in arms is the gateway to peace. Unfortunately, disarmament doesn't have much to do with peace. I sometimes wish it had, it enjoys such an excellent reputation and commands such a lot of attention. Keeping itself strong is always a nation's first concern whenever arms are up for discussion, and disarmament is simply one of the devices by which a nation tries to increase its strength relative to the strength of others. On this naked earth, a nation that approaches disarmament as though it were a humanitarian ideal is either suffering from delusions or planning a deception.

Chairman Khrushchev recently asked, "Is there any . . . way which would remove the threat of war without prejudicing the interests of states?" and then answered his own question: "We see it in the general and complete disarmament of states." Now, even if one were to believe that Mr. Khrushchev is averse to prejudicing the interests of states, one might still wonder whether any state relieved of its weapons was thereby relieved of the threat of war. I am afraid that blaming armaments for war is like blaming fever for disease. Khrushchev's total-disarmament bid was made for the same reason he makes other bids; namely, to advance the cause of international Communism. Total disarmament would not leave anyone free of the threat of war, it would simply leave everyone temporarily without the help of arms in the event of war. Disarmament talks divert our gaze from the root of the matter, which is not the control of weapons, or weapons themselves, but the creation of machinery for the solution of the problems that give rise to the use of weapons.

Disarmament, I think, is a mirage. I don't mean it is indistinct or delusive, I mean it isn't there. Every ship, every plane could be scrapped, every stockpile destroyed, every soldier mustered out, and if the original reasons for holding arms were still present, the world would not have been disarmed. Arms would simply be in a momentary state of suspension, preparatory to new and greater arms. The eyes of all of us are fixed on a shape we seem to see up ahead—a vision of a world relaxed, orderly, secure, friendly. Disarmament looks good because it sounds good, but unhappily one does not get rid of disorder by getting rid of munitions, and disarmament is not solid land containing a harbor, it is an illusion caused by political phenomena, just as a mirage is an illusion caused by atmospheric phenomena, a land mass that doesn't exist.

Weapons are worrisome and expensive; they make everyone edgy. But weapons are not and never have been the cause of the trouble. The only weapon in this decade that is intrinsically harmful is the nuclear weapon during its test period, and that is a new and separate problem, which must be dealt with separately. I think it can and will be dealt with, for although it is related to the balance of power, and therefore is capable of being used for national advantage, it carries a threat that is the same for all nations, Eastern and Western, atomic and non-atomic—the threat that the earth will eventually bear too great a residue of poison and will no longer support life. All nations know this, though some are reluctant to admit it. At any rate, a test ban, though full of danger for whoever signs it, has at least a reasonable chance of success, provided the nations signing it do not disarm. A nation signing an agreement to quit exploding nuclear devices has a selfish interest in honoring the agreement. The debris from tests falls on home ground as well as on enemy territory; it covers the earth like the dew. And although the nation might find many attractive reasons for breaking the agreement, the selfish reason would still be present, as a deterrent to violation. That is why we may profitably talk about stopping nuclear tests: national self-interest happens in this case to coincide with universal interest, and the whole business is a simple matter of human survival on a shaky planet. Usually, in negotiations, that isn't true. It isn't true of a disarmament agreement, which is no sooner signed than a thousand selfish reasons crop up for wanting to violate it.

We hold arms so that, in the event of another nation's breaking its word, we will have something to fall back on, something by which we can command respect, enforce our position, and have our way. Modern arms are complicated by their very destructiveness, their ability to turn and bite whoever unleashes them. That is why everyone is pleased by the prospect of disarming and why there is a great hue and cry raised against arms. And how are we to disarm? By signing a treaty. And what is a treaty? A treaty is a document that is generally regarded as so untrustworthy we feel we must hold arms in order to make sure we're not disadvantaged by its being broken. In other words, we are seriously proposing to sign an agreement to abandon the very thing we will need in the event that the agreement itself fails to stick. This seems a queer program to me.

In drawing up plans for disarming, the nations are making it clear that their distrust of one another and of treaties is as strong as ever. They're insisting that there be "controls"—they are called "adequate" controls—and that there be "inspection." President Eisenhower has suggested an "open-sky" system. And everyone agrees that the treaty must be "enforceable"—some say by an international disarmament organization free of the veto and affiliated with the United Nations. As for control, there is no way to control any aspect of a sovereign nation's internal life. The U.N. designers sensibly bowed to this sticky fact when they installed the veto and provided that the internal affairs of a member should be nobody else's business. (The Hungarian revolt demonstrated how sad are the facts of international life.) It is possible to *influence* a sovereign nation, through public opinion and through pressures of one sort or another, but it is not possible to control it, short of domination by force. In the case of arms, which are among the most intimate of a nation's garments, and which a nation instinctively conceals from view, we do not even know at any given moment what we would be hoping to control the next moment, so speedy is the evolution of weapons and counterweapons. National life is secret life. It has always been secret, and I think it is necessarily secret. To live openly, one must first have a framework of open living—a political framework very different from anything that now exists on the international level. A disarmament arrangement backed by controls and inspection is not such a framework, it is simply a veiled invitation to more and greater secrecy.

Can we inspect the Soviet Union? Can it inspect us? In this jungle world, inspection would be an attempt to license an international legion of Peeping Toms. I cannot believe that it would work. It would probably spawn a legion of counter-Toms, fellows to peep at the peepers. An "open-sky" system in which the inspectors carried operator's licenses would itself be under the surveillance of the open-*spy* system that all nations feel obliged to maintain at all times. And the open-sky system, although a new idea, has already been overtaken by events: the sovereign sky is no longer top-level—space hangs above it, from which East and West are taking pictures of each other with flying cameras.

As for "enforcement," an arms pact is by its nature unenforceable. It would be enforceable only if there were an authority higher and more powerful than that of the parties involved in the deal. The principal characteristic of life on earth today is that no such authority exists. An international disarmament organization, created by treaty and representing the East and the West and equipped with police powers, would not constitute such an authority. This does not mean that nations do not take their treaty obligations seriously; it simply means that no nation takes *any* obligation seriously if it begins to threaten the national safety or obstruct the national will. In the case of a disarmament "authority," any attempt to invoke it might easily result in a riot or a war. National arms would quickly resume their ascendancy over pooled arms, because national forces are responsive to the will of the nation, and this is a fluid, living thing; whereas international arms would be the servant of the signatory powers and of a *status quo*—the conditions that prevailed on the day the treaty was signed. The Soviet Union wants this police force to be under the Security Council, where it would be subject to the veto—in short, a cop who would swing his club or fail to swing it according to the whim of one of the parties.

Many statesmen feel that weapons are in themselves evil, and that they should be eliminated, as you would crush a snake. They feel that vast stores of arms create tension and threaten the peace by the mere fact of their existence. This is perfectly true. I doubt, though, whether the tension created by the existence of arms is as great as the tension that would arise if there were no arms, or too few arms. President Eisenhower has said that war in this day and age would yield "only a great emptiness." So, I think, would disarmament in this day and age. An arms race is a frightening thing, but eighty sovereign nations suddenly turning up without arms is truly terrifying. One may even presume that Russia came forward with the most sensational of the disarmament proposals—total disarmament in four years—just because it *is* terrifying. A dictator dearly loves a vacuum, and he loves to rattle people. Disarmament in this day would increase, not diminish, the danger of war. Today's weapons are too destructive to use, so they stand poised and quiet; this is our strange climate, when arms are safer than no arms. If modern weapons make war unlikely, had we not better keep them until we have found the political means of making war unnecessary?

To hold quixotic views about disarmament is my lot, and it is not a happy one. What happens to arms in the next few years may save all of us, or destroy all of us. In these circumstances a man feels uneasy at expressing any opinion at all, since it might in some slight way affect adversely the course of events.

In a letter to Dag Hammarskjöld, Khrushchev said, "General and complete disarmament cannot result in advantage to any side." This is nonsense. The side that enjoys numerical superiority stands to gain by disarmament, the side that does not have any intention of remaining unarmed for more than a few minutes stands to gain, and the side that uses the lie as an instrument of national policy stands to gain. If disarmament carried no chance of advantage, Mr. Khrushchev would not be wasting his breath on it. He likes it because of its propaganda value and because it gives him a chance to oust us from our advanced military bases—which is the Soviet's precondition of an arms agreement.

Perhaps the most valuable clues to peace nowadays are to be found in the Soviet Union's own fears, and these are many. Russia's greatest fear, apparently, is that Western democracies will act in a united and constructive way. Russia is constantly on the alert to divide us and drive the wedge that we read about every day in the papers. Mr. Khrushchev's March visit to Paris was designed primarily to arouse France against West Germany. His conniptions at the summit and his vilification of President Eisenhower were designed to stir up irritation and allow him to threaten the countries that had accidentally got involved in the spy-plane affair. If it's so very important to Russia that the West be a house divided against itself, then it should be equally important to the free nations that they stand together, not simply as old friends who have a common interest but as a going political concern. A successful attempt to open discussions on this subject has yet to be made, and the matter is seldom referred to in exact terms.* The Western nations are still content to put their trust in what they know— the techniques of diplomacy, of alliance, of collective security, of bargaining, of last-ditch solidarity. A few months ago, when the United States and Great Britain were faced with a decision about nuclear-test arrangements, Macmillan had to duck over here at the eleventh hour for a quick talk. This kind of hasty tucking up should be unnecessary. It is appalling that at this late date the two great English-speaking countries, both equipped with atomic weapons, both desirous of presenting a solid front to the world, each wholly dependent on the other for survival and neither sure that it will survive, should have no political machinery for translating the wishes of their peoples and should still be obliged to go philandering to gain a decision on some vital point. England and America in this fateful decade remind me of a fabulous two-headed sheep I encountered in a book by Laurie Lee: "It could sing harmoniously in a double voice and cross-question itself for hours."

Well, politicians are busy men. Primarily they are not paid to indulge in the pastime of shaping the world in an ideal mold, out of pure theory and pure reason; they are paid to get us through the day as best they can. A public servant has a thousand pressing obligations

---

* In 1962, two years after this piece was written, Nelson Rockefeller managed to discuss unity in exact terms in his Harvard lectures. He proposed the federal design as the correct *theoretical* solution to mankind's urgent problem. This is the first and hardest step. Until a design is welcomed *in theory* by persons high in public life, not much progress can be made among the people toward the political goal of liberty-in-unity.

as well as a strong distaste for theoretical ideas that are bound to irritate voters. But I believe that if a public man speaks of the rule of law at all, he should stay with the subject long enough to say what he has in mind: Who are the authors of this law? Who are the enforcers? From whom do they derive their authority? What are the geographical conditions? What is the framework within which it lives? The simple truth is, we in the West have not yet attempted a political inventiveness, we do not seek a political framework, the centrifugal forces causing friendly nations to fly apart are still operating, we are in disarray, and "the rule of law" is a cloudy phrase in a closing paragraph, not a clear gleam in somebody's eye.

Perhaps this is not the proper time to explore the foundations of unity of the West. Many people would say that although the vision of a federal union of free democratic capitalist states is a pleasing prospect for dreamers, actual work on it would be too upsetting, would shake us at a ticklish time. We might become so absorbed in establishing order on a higher level that we'd lose what little order we now enjoy, and thus play into the hands of our enemies. Others would say that if the political unity of free powers were to become an accomplished fact, it would merely increase the challenge and the fury of the East. Others would argue that most people find unity repugnant; it spoils the fun.

These are all good arguments against trying to bring greater order into Western society. As an American citizen, though, I would welcome the stirrings of political union with the United Kingdom, with Scandinavia, with the Western European nations—with any nation, in fact, that practices government by the consent of the governed. For I would feel that although I was being placed temporarily in a more dangerous position, I was nevertheless occupying higher ground, where the view was better.

The Communists have a shape they pursue; they propose an Eastern union that will eventually erode the West and occupy the globe. In a day when imperialism is despised and languishing, they brazenly construct an empire. To do this they engage us in a Cold War. I believe this war would be easier to fight if we, too, could find a shape to pursue, a proposal to make. Let us pursue the shape of English liberty— what Santayana once described as "this slow cooperation of free men, this liberty in democracy." English liberty in a federal hall—there's a shape to conjure with! "Far from being neutralized by American dash and bravura," wrote Santayana, "or lost in the opposite instincts of so many alien races, it seems to be adopted at once in the most mixed circles and in the most novel predicaments." A federation of free states, with its national units undisturbed and its people elevated to a new and greater sovereignty, is a long way off, by anybody's guess; but if we could once settle on it among ourselves, and embrace it unashamedly, then we would begin to advance in a clear direction and enjoy the pleasures and disciplines of a political destination. Liberty is never out of bounds or off limits; it spreads wherever it can capture the imagination of men.

In the long debate on disarmament, I encountered a statement that has proved memorable; it was in a piece in the *Times* magazine last October, by Salvador de Madariaga, who for a number of years watched disarmament from the vantage point of the League of Nations. Señor de Madariaga ended his article with an observation that should inform and enliven every free nation.

"The trouble today," he wrote, "is that the Communist world understands unity but not liberty, while the free world understands liberty but not unity. Eventual victory may be won by the first of the two sides to achieve the synthesis of both liberty and unity."

I have never seen the matter stated more succinctly, nor have I ever read a prediction I felt greater confidence in. President Eisenhower often talks of "peace with justice," but fails to supply a sketch. Diplomacy, treaties, national aspirations, peace parley hot, peace parley cold, good-will tours, secrecy, spying, foreign aid, foreign trade, foreign relations—these seem to be the only building blocks we are trustful of. From them justice cannot be expected to arise, although occasionally some benefits do come from them, more by good luck than by good management. Our national strategy goes something like this: Keep your chin up, keep your powder dry, be willing to negotiate, keep your friends happy, be popular, be strong, get to outer space, stall for time, justice is bound to come eventually, and the rule of law.

I doubt whether justice, which is the forerunner of peace, will ever be pulled out of a hat, as some suppose. Justice will find a home where there is a synthesis of liberty and unity in a framework of government. And when justice appears on any scene, on any level of society, men's problems enjoy a sort of automatic solution, because they enjoy the means of solution. Unity is no mirage. It is the distant shore. I believe we should at least head for that good shore, though most of us will not reach it in this life.

III

❧❦❧

# THE CITY

# THE WORLD OF TOMORROW

*May 1939*

I wasn't really prepared for the World's Fair last week, and it certainly wasn't prepared for me. Between the two of us there was considerable of a mixup.

The truth is that my ethmoid sinuses broke down on the eve of Fair Day, and this meant I had to visit the Fair carrying a box of Kleenex concealed in a copy of the *Herald Tribune*. When you can't breathe through your nose, Tomorrow seems strangely like the day before yesterday. The Fair, on its part, was having trouble too. It couldn't find its collar button. Our mutual discomfort established a rich bond of friendship between us, and I realize that the World's Fair and myself actually both need the same thing—a nice warm day.

The road to Tomorrow leads through the chimney pots of Queens. It is a long, familiar journey, through Mulsified Shampoo and Mobilgas, through Bliss Street, Kix, Astring-O-Sol, and the Majestic Auto Seat Covers. It winds through Textene, Blue Jay Corn Plasters; through Musterole and the delicate pink blossoms on the fruit trees in the ever-hopeful back yards of a populous borough, past Zemo, Alka-Seltzer, Baby Ruth, past Iodent and the Fidelity National Bank, by trusses, belts, and the clothes that fly bravely on the line under the trees with the new little green leaves in Queens' incomparable springtime. Suddenly you see the first intimation of the future, of man's dream—the white ball and spire—and there are the ramp and the banners flying from the pavilions and the brave hope of a glimpsed destination. Except for the Kleenex, I might have been approaching the lists at Camelot, for I felt that perhaps here would be the tournament all men wait for, the field of honor, the knights and the ladies under these bright banners, beyond these great walls. A closer inspection, however, on the other side of the turnstile, revealed that it was merely Heinz jousting with Beech-Nut—the same old contest on a somewhat larger field, with accommodations for more spectators, and rather better facilities all round.

The place is honeycombed with streets—broad, gusty streets, with tulips bending to the gale and in the air the sound of distant choirs. There are benches all along for the weary and the halt, but though science's failure to cope with the common cold had embittered my heart and slowed my step, the ball and spire still beckoned me on. It was not particularly surprising, somehow, when at last after so many months of anticipation and after so much of actual travail and suffering, when at last I arrived, paper handkerchiefs in hand, at the very threshold of Tomorrow, when I finally presented myself there at the base of the white phallus, face to face with the girl in the booth behind the little bars behind the glass window with the small round hole, expectant, ready, to see at last what none had ever seen, Tomorrow—it was not, somehow, particularly surprising to see the window close in my face and hear a bald contemporary voice say, "There will be a short wait of a few minutes, please."

That's the way it is with the future. Even after Grover Whalen has touched it with his peculiar magic, there is still a short wait.

The lady behind me was not surprised either, but she seemed apprehensive.

"Anything wrong in there?" she asked testily.

"No, madam," said the guard. "Just some minor difficulty in the Perisphere."

The lady was not satisfied. "Is there anything in there to scare you?" she asked, looking at the Perisphere rolling motionless in the gray vapors that have hung for centuries above the Flushing Meadows.

"No, madam," he replied. "The longest escalator in the world moves very slowly."

I clocked the wait. It was twenty minutes. Not bad, for a man who's waited all his life.

Much depends, when you ascend into the interior of the Perisphere, on the moment at which you happen to arrive at the top of the escalator and teeter off in a sidewise direction onto one of the two great moving rings that turn endlessly above the City of Man. If you arrive just as day has faded into night, and without any advance information about being shunted from an upward moving stairway onto a sideways moving balcony, the experience is something that stays with you. I was lucky. The City of Man, when it first broke on my expectant sight, was as dark as a hall bedroom, and for a second or two I didn't catch on that I myself was in motion—except celestially. If I hadn't recognized Mr. Kaltenborn's electric voice, I would have felt lonelier than perhaps the situation warranted.

"As day fades into night," he said, with the majestic huskiness which science has given speech, "each man seeks home, for here are children, comfort, neighbors, recreation—the good life of the well-planned city."

Trembling in violet light beneath me, there it was—the towers, now to the adjusted eye dimly visible—"a brave new world [such a big voice you have, Grandpa!] built by united hands and hearts. Here brain and brawn, faith and courage, are linked in high endeavor as men march on toward unity and peace. Listen! From office, farm, and factory they come with joyous song."

I don't know how long it takes in there. Ten minutes, maybe. But when I emerged from the great ball, to begin the descent of the Helicline, it had come on to rain.

To be informative about the Fair is a task for someone with a steadier nose than mine. I saw all as in a dream, and I cherish the dream and have put it away in lavender. The great size of the place has been a temporary disadvantage these first few days, when the draftiness, the chill, the disorder, the murky bath of canned reverence in which many of the commercial exhibits are steeped have conspired to give the place the clammy quality of a seaside resort in mid-November. But this same great size, come the first warm, expansive days, will suddenly become the most valuable asset of the Fair. The refurbished ash heap, rising from its own smolder, is by far the biggest show that has ever been assembled on God's earth, and it is going to be a great place to go on a fine summer night, a great place to go on a sunny spring morning. After all, nobody can embrace Culture in a topcoat.

The architecture is amusing enough, the buildings are big enough, to give the visitor that temporary and exalted feeling of being in the presence of something pretty special, something full of aspiration, something which at times is even exciting. And the exhibition is cock-eyed enough to fall, as it naturally does, in line with all carnivals, circuses, and wonderlands. The buildings (there are two hundred of them) have color and a certain dash, here and there a certain beauty. They are of the type that shows up best in strong light. Like any Miami Beach cottage, they look incredibly lovely in sunlight, adorned with a necklace of vine shadow against a clear white skin, incredibly banal and gloom-infested on cloudy days, when every pimple of plaster shows up in all its ugly pretension. The designers of this twentieth-century bazaar have been resourceful and have kept the comfort of the people in mind. Experience has taught them much. The modern technique of sightseeing is this: you sit in a chair (wired for sound) or stand on a platform (movable, glass-embowered) and while sitting, standing, you are brought mysteriously and reverently into easy view of what you want to see. There is no shoving in the exhibit hall of Tomorrow. There is no loitering and there is usually no smoking. Even in the girl show in the amusement area, the sailor is placed in a rather astringent attitude, behind glass, for the adoration of the female form. It is all rather serious-minded, this World of Tomorrow, and extremely impersonal. A ride on the Futurama of General Motors induces approximately the same emotional response as a trip through the Cathedral of St. John the Divine. The countryside unfolds before you in $5-million micro-loveliness, conceived in motion and executed by Norman Bel Geddes. The voice is a voice of utmost respect, of complete religious faith in the eternal benefaction of faster travel. The highways unroll in ribbons of perfection through the fertile and rejuvenated America of 1960—a vision of the day to come, the unobstructed left turn, the vanished grade crossing, the town which beckons but does not impede, the millennium of passionless motion. When night falls in the General Motors exhibit and you lean back in the cushioned chair (yourself in motion and the world so still) and hear (from the depths of the chair) the soft electric assurance of a better life—the life which rests on wheels alone--there is a strong, sweet poison which infects the blood. I didn't want to wake up. I liked 1960 in purple light, going a hundred miles an hour around impossible turns ever onward toward the certified cities of the flawless future. It wasn't till I passed an apple orchard and saw the trees, each blooming under its own canopy of glass, that I perceived that even the General Motors dream, as dreams so often do, left some questions unanswered about the future. The apple tree of Tomorrow, abloom under its inviolate hood, makes you stop and wonder. How will the little boy climb it? Where will the little bird build its nest?

I made a few notes at the Fair, a few hints of what you may expect of Tomorrow, its appointments, its characteristics.

In Tomorrow, people and objects are lit not from above but from below. Trees are lit from below. Even the cow on the rotolactor appears to be lit from below—the buried flood lamp illuminates the distended udder.

In Tomorrow one voice does for all. But it is a little unsure of itself; it keeps testing itself; it says, "Hello One, two, three, four. Hello! One, two, three, four."

Rugs do not slip in Tomorrow, and the bassinets of newborn infants are wired against kidnappers.

There is no talking back in Tomorrow. You are expected to take it or leave it alone. There are sailors there (which makes you feel less lonely) and the sound of music.

The living room of Tomorrow contains the following objects: a broadloom carpet, artificial carnations, a television radio victrola incessantly producing an image of someone or something which is somewhere else, a glass bird, a chrome steel lamp, a terracotta zebra, some veneered book cabinets containing no visible books, another cabinet out of which a small newspaper slowly pours in a never-ending ribbon, and a small plush love seat in the shape of a new moon.

In Tomorrow, most sounds are not the sounds themselves but a memory of sounds, or an electrification. In the case of a cow, the moo will come to you not from the cow but from a small aperture above your head.

Tomorrow is a little on the expensive side. I checked this with my cabdriver in Manhattan to make sure. He was full of praise about the Fair, but said he hadn't seen it and might, in fact, never see it. "I hack out there, but I got it figured that for me and the wife to go all through and do it right—no cheapskate stuff—it would break the hell out of a five-dollar bill. In my racket, I can't afford it."

Tomorrow does not smell. The World's Fair of 1939 has taken the body odor out of man, among other things. It is all rather impersonal, this dream. The country fair manages better, where you can hang over the rail at the ox-pulling and smell the ox. It's not only that the sailors can't get at the girls through the glass, but even so wholesome an exhibit as Swift's Premium Bacon produces twenty lovesick maidens in a glass pit hermetically sealed from the ultimate consumer.

The voice of Mr. Kaltenborn in the City of Man says, "They come with joyous song," but the truth is there is very little joyous song in the Fair grounds. There is a great deal of electrically transmitted joy, but very little spontaneous joy. Tomorrow's music, I noticed, came mostly from Yesterday's singer. In fact, if Mr. Whalen wants a suggestion from me as to how to improve his show (and I am reasonably confident he doesn't), it would be to snip a few wires, hire a couple of bands, and hand out ticklers. Gaiety is not the keynote in Tomorrow. I finally found it at the tag end of a chilly evening, far along in the amusement area, in a tent with some black people. There was laughing and shouting there, and a beautiful brown belly-dancer.

Another gay spot, to my surprise, was the American Telephone & Telegraph Exhibit. It took the old Telephone Company to put on the best show of all. To anyone who draws a lucky number, the company grants the privilege of making a long-distance call. This call can be to any point in the United States, and the bystanders have the exquisite privilege of listening in through earphones and of laughing unashamed. To understand the full wonder of this, you must reflect that there are millions of people who have never either made or received a long-distance call, and that when Eddie Pancha, a waiter in a restaurant in El Paso, Texas, hears the magic words "New York is calling . . . go ahead, please," he is transfixed in holy dread and excitement. I listened for two hours and ten minutes to this show, and I'd be there this minute if I were capable of standing up. I had the good luck to be listening at the earphone when a little boy named David Wagstaff won the toss and put in a call to tell his father in Springfield, Mass., what a good time he was having at the World's Fair. David walked resolutely to the glass booth before the assembled kibitzers and in a tiny, timid voice gave the operator his call, his little new cloth hat set all nicely on his head. But his father wasn't there, and David was suddenly confronted with the necessity of telling his story to a man named Mr. Henry, who happened to answer the phone and who, on hearing little David Wagstaff's voice calling from New York, must surely have thought that David's mother had been run down in the BMT and that David was doing the manly thing.

"Yes, David," he said, tensely.

"Tell my father this," began David, slowly, carefully, determined to go through with the halcyon experience of winning a lucky call at the largest fair the world had yet produced.

"Yes, David."

"We got on the train, and . . . and . . . had a nice trip, and at New Haven, when they were taking off the car and putting another car on, it was *awfully* funny because the car gave a great—big—BUMP!"

Then followed David's three-minute appreciation of the World of Tomorrow and the Citadel of Light, phrased in the crumbling remnants of speech that little boys are left with when a lot of people are watching, and when their thoughts begin to run down, and when Perispheres begin to swim mistily in time. Mr. Henry—the invisible and infinitely surprised Mr. Henry—maintained a respectful and indulgent silence. I don't know what he was thinking, but I would swap the Helicline for a copy of his attempted transcription of David's message to his father.

My own memory of the Fair, like David's, has begun to dim. From so much culture, from so much concentrated beauty and progress, one can retain only a fragment. I remember the trees at night, shivering in their burlap undershirts, the eerie shadows clinging to the wrong side of their branches. I remember the fountains playing in the light, I remember the girl who sat so still, so clean, so tangible, producing with the tips of her fingers the synthetic speech—but the words were not the words she wanted to say, they were not the words that were in her mind. I remember the little old Stourbridge Lion, puffing in under its own steam to start the railroads bursting across America. But mostly the Fair has vanished, leaving only the voice of little David Wagstaff and the rambling ecstasy of his first big trip away from home; so many million dollars spent on the idea that our trains and our motorcars should go fast and smoothly, and the child remembering, not the smoothness, but the great—big—BUMP.

So (as the voice says) man dreams on. And the dream is still a contradiction and an enigma—the biologist peeping at bacteria through his microscope, the sailor peeping at the strip queen through binoculars, the eyes so watchful, and the hopes so high. Out in the honky-tonk section, in front of the Amazon show, where the ladies exposed one breast in deference to the fleet, kept one concealed in deference to Mr. Whalen, there was an automaton—a giant man in white tie and tails, with enormous rubber hands. At the start of each show, while the barker was drumming up trade, a couple of the girls would come outside and sit in the robot's lap. The effect was peculiarly lascivious—the extra-size man, exploring with his gigantic rubber hands the breasts of the little girls, the girls with their own small hands (by comparison so small, by comparison so terribly real) restrainingly on his, to check the unthinkable impact of his mechanical passion. Here was the Fair, all fairs, in pantomime; and here the strange mixed dream that made the Fair: the heroic man, bloodless and perfect and enormous, created in his own image, and in his hand (rubber, aseptic) the literal desire, the warm and living breast.

# HERE IS NEW YORK

❦

On any person who desires such queer prizes, New York will bestow the gift of loneliness and the gift of privacy. It is this largess that accounts for the presence within the city's walls of a considerable section of the population; for the residents of Manhattan are to a large extent strangers who have pulled up stakes somewhere and come to town, seeking sanctuary or fulfillment or some greater or lesser grail. The capacity to make such dubious gifts is a mysterious quality of New York. It can destroy an individual, or it can fulfill him, depending a good deal on luck. No one should come to New York to live unless he is willing to be lucky.

New York is the concentrate of art and commerce and sport and religion and entertainment and finance, bringing to a single compact arena the gladiator, the evangelist, the promoter, the actor, the trader, and the merchant. It carries on its lapel the unexpungeable odor of the long past, so that no matter where you sit in New York you feel the vibrations of great times and tall deeds, of queer people and events and undertakings. I am sitting at the moment in a stifling hotel room in 90-degree heat, halfway down an air shaft, in midtown. No air moves in or out of the room, yet I am curiously affected by emanations from the immediate surroundings. I am twenty-two blocks from where Rudolph Valentino lay in state, eight blocks from where Nathan Hale was executed, five blocks from the publisher's office where Ernest Hemingway hit Max Eastman on the nose, four miles from where Walt Whitman sat sweating out editorials for the Brooklyn *Eagle*, thirty-four blocks from the street Willa Cather lived in when she came to New York to write books about Nebraska, one block from where Marceline used to clown on the boards of the Hippodrome, thirty-six blocks from the spot where the historian Joe Gould kicked a radio to pieces in full view of the public, thirteen blocks from where Harry Thaw shot Stanford White, five blocks from where I used to usher at the Metropolitan Opera and only 112 blocks from the spot where Clarence Day the Elder was washed of his sins in the Church of the Epiphany (I could continue this list indefinitely); and for that matter I am probably occupying the very room that any number of exalted and somewise memorable characters sat in, some of them on hot, breathless afternoons, lonely and private and full of their own sense of emanations from without.

When I went down to lunch a few minutes ago I noticed that the man sitting next to me (about eighteen inches away along the wall) was Fred Stone. The eighteen inches were both the connection and the separation that New York provides for its inhabitants. My only connection with Fred Stone was that I saw him in *The Wizard of Oz* around the beginning of the century. But our waiter felt the same stimulus from being close to a man from Oz, and after Mr. Stone left the room the waiter told me that when he (the waiter) was a young man just arrived in this country and before he could understand a word of English, he had taken his girl for their first theater date to *The Wizard of Oz*. It was a wonderful show, the waiter recalled—a man of straw, a man of tin. Wonderful! (And still only eighteen inches away.) "Mr. Stone is a very hearty eater," said the waiter thoughtfully, content with this fragile participation in destiny, this link with Oz.

New York blends the gift of privacy with the excitement of participation; and better than most dense communities it succeeds in insulating the individual (if he wants it, and almost everybody wants or needs it) against all enormous and violent and wonderful events that are taking place every minute. Since I have been sitting in this miasmic air shaft, a good many rather splashy events have occurred in town. A man shot and killed his wife in a fit of jealousy. It caused no stir outside his block and got only small mention in the papers. I did not attend. Since my arrival, the greatest air show ever staged in all the world took place in town. I didn't attend and neither did most of the eight million other inhabitants, although they say there was quite a crowd. I didn't even hear any planes except a couple of westbound commercial airliners that habitually use this air shaft to fly over. The biggest oceangoing ships on the North Atlantic arrived and departed. I didn't notice them and neither did most other New Yorkers. I am told this is the greatest seaport in the world, with 650 miles of waterfront, and ships calling here from many exotic lands, but the only boat I've happened to notice since my arrival was a small sloop tacking out of the East River night before last on the ebb tide when I was walking across the Brooklyn Bridge. I heard the *Queen Mary* blow one midnight, though, and the sound carried the whole history of departure and longing and loss. The Lions have been in convention. I've seen not one Lion. A friend of mine saw one and told me about him. (He was lame, and was wearing a bolero.) At the ballgrounds and horse parks the greatest sporting spectacles have been enacted. I saw no ballplayer, no race horse. The governor came to town. I heard the siren scream, but that was all there was to that—an eighteen-inch margin again. A man was killed by a falling cornice. I was not a party to the tragedy, and again the inches counted heavily.

I mention these merely to show that New York is peculiarly constructed to absorb almost anything that comes along (whether a thousand-foot liner out of the East or a twenty-thousand-man convention out of the West) without inflicting the event on its inhabitants, so that every event is, in a sense, optional, and the inhabitant is in the happy position of being able to choose his spectacle and so conserve his soul. In most metropolises, small and large, the choice is often not with the individual at all. He is thrown to the Lions. The Lions are overwhelming; the event is unavoidable. A cornice falls, and it hits every citizen on the head, every last man in town. I sometimes think that the only event that hits every New Yorker on the head is the annual St. Patrick's Day parade, which is fairly penetrating—the Irish are a hard race to tune out, there are 500,000 of them in residence, and they have the police force right in the family.

The quality in New York that insulates its inhabitants from life may simply weaken them as individuals. Perhaps it is healthier to live in a community where, when a cornice falls, you feel the blow; where, when the governor passes, you see at any rate his hat.

I am not defending New York in this regard. Many of its settlers are probably here merely to escape, not face, reality. But whatever it means, it is a rather rare gift, and I believe it has a positive effect on the creative capacities of New Yorkers—for creation is in part merely the business of forgoing the great and small distractions.

Although New York often imparts a feeling of great forlornness or forsakenness, it seldom seems dead or unresourceful; and you always feel that either by shifting your location ten blocks or by reducing your fortune by five dollars you can experience rejuvenation. Many people who have no real independence of spirit depend on the city's tremendous variety and sources of excitement for spiritual sustenance and maintenance of morale. In the country there are a few chances of sudden rejuvenation—a shift in weather, perhaps, or something arriving in the mail. But in New York the chances are endless. I think that although many persons are here from some excess of spirit (which caused them to break away from their small town), some, too, are here from a deficiency of spirit, who find in New York a protection, or an easy substitution.

There are roughly three New Yorks. There is, first, the New York of the man or woman who was born here, who takes the city for granted and accepts its size and its turbulence as natural and inevitable. Second, there is the New York of the commuter—the city that is devoured by locusts each day and spat out each night. Third, there is the New York of the person who was born somewhere else and came to New York in quest of something. Of these three trembling cities the greatest is the last—the city of final destination, the city that is a goal. It is this third city that accounts for New York's high-strung disposition, its poetical deportment, its dedication to the arts, and its incomparable achievements. Commuters give the city its tidal restlessness, natives give it solidity and continuity, but the settlers give it passion. And whether it is a farmer arriving from Italy to set up a small grocery store in a slum, or a young girl arriving from a small town in Mississippi to escape the indignity of being observed by her neighbors, or a boy arriving from the Corn Belt with a manuscript in his suitcase and a pain in his heart, it makes no difference: each embraces New York with the intense excitement of first love, each absorbs New York with the fresh eyes of an adventurer, each generates heat and light to dwarf the Consolidated Edison Company.

The commuter is the queerest bird of all. The suburb he inhabits has no essential vitality of its own and is a mere roost where he comes at day's end to go to sleep. Except in rare cases, the man who lives in Mamaroneck or Little Neck or Teaneck and works in New York, discovers nothing much about the city except the time of arrival and departure of trains and buses, and the path to a quick lunch. He is desk-bound, and has never, idly roaming in the gloaming, stumbled suddenly on Belvedere Tower in the Park, seen the ramparts rise sheer from the water of the pond, and the boys along the shore fishing for minnows, girls stretched out negligently on the shelves of the rocks; he has never come suddenly on anything at all in New York as a loiterer, because he has had no time between trains. He has fished in Manhattan's wallet and dug out coins but has never listened to Manhattan's breathing, never awakened to its morning, never dropped off to sleep in its night. About 400,000 men and women come charging onto the island each weekday morning, out of the mouths of tubes and tun-

nels. Not many among them have ever spent a drowsy afternoon in the
great rustling oaken silence of the reading room of the Public Library,
with the book elevator (like an old water wheel) spewing out books onto
the trays. They tend their furnaces in Westchester and in Jersey but
have never seen the furnaces of the Bowery, the fires that burn in oil
drums on zero winter nights. They may work in the financial district
downtown and never see the extravagant plantings of Rockefeller
Center—the daffodils and grape hyacinths and birches and the flags
trimmed to the wind on a fine morning in spring. Or they may work in
a midtown office and may let a whole year swing round without sighting
Governors Island from the sea wall. The commuter dies with tremendous
mileage to his credit, but he is no rover. His entrances and exits are
more devious than those in a prairie-dog village, and he calmly plays
bridge while buried in the mud at the bottom of the East River. The
Long Island Rail Road alone carried forty million commuters last year,
but many of them were the same fellow retracing his steps.

The terrain of New York is such that a resident sometimes travels
farther, in the end, than a commuter. Irving Berlin's journey from
Cherry Street in the Lower East Side to an apartment uptown was
through an alley and was only three or four miles in length, but it
was like going three times around the world.

A poem compresses much in a small space and adds music, thus
heightening its meaning. The city is like poetry: it compresses all life,
all races and breeds, into a small island and adds music and the accompaniment of internal engines. The island of Manhattan is without
any doubt the greatest human concentrate on earth, the poem whose
magic is comprehensible to millions of permanent residents but whose
full meaning will always remain elusive. At the feet of the tallest and
plushiest offices lie the crummiest slums. The genteel mysteries housed
in the Riverside Church are only a few blocks from the voodoo charms
of Harlem. The merchant princes, riding to Wall Street in their limou-
sines down the East River Drive, pass within a few hundred yards of
the gypsy kings; but the princes do not know they are passing kings,
and the kings are not up yet anyway—they live a more leisurely life
than the princes and get drunk more consistently.

New York is nothing like Paris; it is nothing like London; and it
is not Spokane multiplied by sixty, or Detroit multiplied by four. It is
by all odds the loftiest of cities. It even managed to reach the highest
point in the sky at the lowest moment of the Depression. The Empire
State Building shot 1250 feet into the air when it was madness to put
out as much as six inches of new growth. (The building has a mooring

mast that no dirigible has ever tied to; it employs a man to flush toilets in slack times; it has been hit by an airplane in a fog, struck countless times by lightning, and been jumped off of by so many unhappy people that pedestrians instinctively quicken step when passing Fifth Avenue and Thirty-fourth Street.)

Manhattan has been compelled to expand skyward because of the absence of any other direction in which to grow. This, more than any other thing, is responsible for its physical majesty. It is to the nation what the white church spire is to the village—the visible symbol of aspiration and faith, the white plume saying that the way is up. The summer traveler swings in over Hell Gate Bridge and from the window of his sleeping car as it glides above the pigeon lofts and back yards of Queens looks southwest to where the morning light first strikes the steel peaks of midtown, and he sees its upward thrust unmistakable: the great walls and towers rising, the smoke rising, the heat not yet rising, the hopes and ferments of so many awakening millions rising—this vigorous spear that presses heaven hard.

It is a miracle that New York works at all. The whole thing is implausible. Every time the residents brush their teeth, millions of gallons of water must be drawn from the Catskills and the hills of Westchester. When a young man in Manhattan writes a letter to his girl in Brooklyn, the love message gets blown to her through a pneumatic tube—*pfft*— just like that. The subterranean system of telephone cables, power lines, steam pipes, gas mains, and sewer pipes is reason enough to abandon the island to the gods and the weevils. Every time an incision is made in the pavement, the noisy surgeons expose ganglia that are tangled beyond belief. By rights New York should have destroyed itself long ago, from panic or fire or rioting or failure of some vital supply line in its circulatory system or from some deep labyrinthine short circuit. Long ago the city should have experienced an insoluble traffic snarl at some impossible bottleneck. It should have perished of hunger when food lines failed for a few days. It should have been wiped out by a plague starting in its slums or carried in by ships' rats. It should have been overwhelmed by the sea that licks at it on every side. The workers in its myriad cells should have succumbed to nerves, from the fearful pall of smoke-fog that drifts over every few days from Jersey, blotting out all light at noon and leaving the high offices suspended, men groping and depressed, and the sense of world's end. It should have been touched in the head by the August heat and gone off its rocker.

Mass hysteria is a terrible force, yet New Yorkers seem always to escape it by some tiny margin: they sit in stalled subways without claustrophobia, they extricate themselves from panic situations by some lucky wisecrack, they meet confusion and congestion with patience and grit—a sort of perpetual muddling through. Every facility is inadequate—the hospitals and schools and the playgrounds are overcrowded, the express highways are feverish, the unimproved highways and bridges are bottlenecks, there is not enough air and not enough light, and there is usually either too much heat or too little. But the city makes up for its hazards and its deficiencies by supplying its citizens with massive doses of a supplementary vitamin: the sense of belonging to something unique, cosmopolitan, mighty, and unparalleled.

To an outlander a stay in New York can be and often is a series of small embarrassments and discomforts and disappointments: not understanding the waiter, not being able to distinguish between a sucker joint and a friendly saloon, riding the wrong subway, being slapped down by a bus driver for asking an innocent question, enduring sleepless nights when the street noises fill the bedroom. Tourists make for New York, particularly in summertime—they swarm all over the Statue of Liberty (where many a resident of the town has never set foot), they invade the Automat, visit radio studios, St. Patrick's Cathedral, and they window shop. Mostly they have a pretty good time. But sometimes in New York you run across the disillusioned—a young couple who are obviously visitors, newlyweds perhaps, for whom the bright dream has vanished. The place has been too much for them; they sit languishing in a cheap restaurant over a speechless meal.

The oft-quoted thumbnail sketch of New York is, of course: "It's a wonderful place, but I'd hate to live there." I have an idea that people from villages and small towns, people accustomed to the convenience and the friendliness of neighborhood over-the-fence living, are unaware that life in New York follows the neighborhood pattern. The city is literally a composite of tens of thousands of tiny neighborhood units. There are, of course, the big districts and big units: Chelsea and Murray Hill and Gramercy (which are residential units), Harlem (a racial unit), Greenwich Village (a unit dedicated to the arts and other matters), and there is Radio City (a commercial development), Peter Cooper Village (a housing unit), the Medical Center (a sickness unit) and many other sections each of which has some distinguishing characteristic. But the curious thing about New York is that each large geographical unit is composed of countless small neighborhoods. Each neighborhood is virtually self-sufficient. Usually it is no more than two or three blocks long and a couple of blocks wide. Each area is a city within a city within a city. Thus, no matter where you live in New York, you will find within a block or two a grocery store, a barbershop, a newsstand and shoeshine shack, an ice-coal-and-wood cellar (where you write your order on a pad outside as you walk by), a dry cleaner, a laundry, a delicatessen (beer and sandwiches delivered at any hour to your door), a flower shop, an undertaker's parlor, a movie house, a radio-repair shop, a stationer, a haberdasher, a tailor, a drugstore, a garage, a tearoom, a saloon, a hardware store, a liquor store, a shoe-repair shop. Every block or two, in most residential sections of New York, is a little main street. A man starts for work in the morning and before he has gone two hundred yards he has completed half a dozen missions: bought a paper, left a pair of shoes to be soled, picked up a pack of cigarettes, ordered a bottle of whiskey to be dispatched in the opposite direction against his home-coming, written a message to the unseen forces of the wood cellar, and notified the dry cleaner that a pair of trousers awaits call. Homeward-bound eight hours later, he buys a bunch of pussy willows, a Mazda bulb, a drink, a shine—all between the corner where he steps off the bus and his apartment. So complete is each neighborhood, and so strong the sense of neighborhood, that many a New Yorker spends a lifetime within the confines of an area smaller than a country village. Let him walk two blocks from his corner and he is in a strange land and will feel uneasy till he gets back.

Storekeepers are particularly conscious of neighborhood boundary lines. A woman friend of mine moved recently from one apartment to another, a distance of three blocks. When she turned up, the day after the move, at the same grocer's that she had patronized for years, the proprietor was in ecstasy—almost in tears—at seeing her. "I was afraid," he said, "now that you've moved away I wouldn't be seeing you anymore." To him, *away* was three blocks, or about 750 feet.

I am, at the moment of writing this, living not as a neighborhood man in New York but as a transient, or vagrant, in from the country for a few days. Summertime is a good time to reexamine New York and to receive again the gift of privacy, the jewel of loneliness. In summer the city contains (except for tourists) only die-hards and authentic characters. No casual, spotty dwellers are around, only the real article. And the town has a somewhat relaxed air, and one can lie in a loincloth, gasping and remembering things.

I've been remembering what it felt like as a young man to live in the same town with giants. When I first arrived in New York, my personal giants were a dozen or so columnists and critics and poets whose names appeared regularly in the papers. I burned with a low steady fever just because I was on the same island with Don Marquis, Heywood Broun, Christopher Morley, Franklin P. Adams, Robert C.

Benchley, Frank Sullivan, Dorothy Parker, Alexander Woollcott, Ring Lardner, and Stephen Vincent Benét. I would hang around the corner of Chambers Street and Broadway, thinking: "Somewhere in that building is the typewriter that archy the cockroach jumps on at night." New York hardly gave me a living at that period, but it sustained me. I used to walk quickly past the house in West Thirteenth Street between Sixth and Seventh where F.P.A. lived, and the block seemed to tremble under my feet—the way Park Avenue trembles when a train leaves Grand Central. This excitation (nearness of giants) is a continuing thing. The city is always full of young worshipful beginners—young actors, young aspiring poets, ballerinas, painters, reporters, singers—each depending on his own brand of tonic to stay alive, each with his own stable of giants.

New York provides not only a continuing excitation but also a spectacle that is continuing. I wander around, reexamining this spectacle, hoping that I can put it on paper. It is Saturday, toward the end of the afternoon. I turn through West Forty-eighth Street. From the open windows of the drum and saxophone parlors come the listless sounds of musical instruction, monstrous insect noises in the brooding field of summer. The Cort Theater is disgorging its matinee audience. Suddenly the whole block is filled with the mighty voice of a street singer. He approaches, looking for an audience, a large, cheerful Negro with grand-opera contours, strolling with head thrown back, filling the canyon with uninhibited song. He carries a long cane as his sole prop, and is tidily but casually dressed—slacks, seersucker jacket, a book showing in his pocket.

This is perfect artistic timing; the audience from the Cort, where *The Respectful Prostitute* is playing, has just received a lesson in race relations and is in a mood to improve the condition of the black race as speedily as possible. Coins (mostly quarters) rattle to the street, and a few minutes of minstrelsy improves the condition of one Negro by about eight dollars. If he does as well as this at every performance, he has a living right there. New York is the city of opportunity, they say. Even the mounted cop, clumping along on his nag a few minutes later, scans the gutter carefully for dropped silver, like a bird watching for spilt grain.

It is seven o'clock and I reexamine an ex-speakeasy in East Fifty-third Street, with dinner in mind. A thin crowd, a summer-night buzz of fans interrupted by an occasional drink being shaken at the small bar. It is dark in here (the proprietor sees no reason for boosting his light bill just because liquor laws have changed). How dark, how pleasing; and how miraculously beautiful the murals showing Italian lake scenes—probably executed by a cousin of the owner. The owner himself mixes. The fans intone the prayer for cool salvation. From the next booth drifts the conversation of radio executives; from the green salad comes the little taste of garlic. Behind me (eighteen inches again) a young intellectual is trying to persuade a girl to come live with him and be his love. She has her guard up, but he is extremely reasonable, careful not to overplay his hand. A combination of intellectual companionship and sexuality is what they have to offer each other, he feels. In the mirror over the bar I can see the ritual of the second drink. Then he has to go to the men's room and she has to go to the ladies' room, and when they return, the argument has lost its tone. And the fan takes over again, and the heat and the relaxed air and the memory of so many good little dinners in so many good little illegal places, with the theme of love, the sound of ventilation, the brief medicinal illusion of gin.

Another hot night I stop off at the Goldman Band concert in the Mall in Central Park. The people seated on the benches fanned out in front of the band shell are attentive, appreciative. In the trees the night wind stirs, bringing the leaves to life, endowing them with speech; the electric lights illuminate the green branches from the under side, translating them into a new language. Overhead a plane passes dreamily, its running lights winking. On the bench directly in front of me, a boy sits with his arm around his girl; they are proud of each other and are swathed in music. The cornetist steps forward for a solo, begins, "Drink to me only with thine eyes. . . ." In the wide, warm night the horn is startlingly pure and magical. Then from the North River another horn solo begins—the *Queen Mary* announcing her intentions. She is not on key; she is a half tone off. The trumpeter in the bandstand never flinches. The horns quarrel savagely, but no one minds having the intimation of travel injected into the pledge of love. "I leave," sobs Mary. "And I will pledge with mine," sighs the trumpeter. Along the asphalt paths strollers pass to and fro; they behave considerately, respecting the musical atmosphere. Popsicles are moving well. In the warm grass beyond the fence, forms wriggle in the shadows, and the skirts of the girls approaching on the Mall are ballooned by the breeze, and their bare shoulders catch the lamplight. "Drink to me only with thine eyes." It is a magical occasion, and it's all free.

On weekends in summer the town empties. I visit my office on a Saturday afternoon. No phone rings, no one feeds the hungry IN-baskets, no one disturbs the papers; it is a building of the dead, a time of awesome suspension. The whole city is honeycombed with abandoned cells—a jail that has been effectively broken. Occasionally from somewhere in the building a night bell rings, summoning the elevator—a special fire-alarm ring. This is the pit of loneliness, in an office on a summer Saturday. I stand at the window and look down at the batteries and batteries of offices across the way, recalling how the thing looks in winter twilight when everything is going full blast, every cell lighted, and how you can see in pantomime the puppets fumbling with their slips of paper (but you don't hear the rustle), see them pick up their phone (but you don't hear the ring), see the noiseless, ceaseless moving about of so many passers of pieces of paper: New York, the capital of memoranda, in touch with Calcutta, in touch with Reykjavik, and always fooling with something.

In the café of the Lafayette, the regulars sit and talk. It is busy yet peaceful. Nursing a drink, I stare through the west windows at the Manufacturers Trust Company and at the red brick fronts on the north side of Ninth Street, watching the red turning slowly to purple as the light dwindles. Brick buildings have a way of turning color at the end of the day, the way a red rose turns bluish as it wilts. The café is a sanctuary. The waiters are ageless and they change not. Nothing has been modernized. Notre Dame stands guard in its travel poster. The coffee is strong and full of chicory, and good.

Walk the Bowery under the El at night and all you feel is a sort of cold guilt. Touched for a dime, you try to drop the coin and not touch the hand, because the hand is dirty; you try to avoid the glance, because the glance accuses. This is not so much personal menace as universal—the cold menace of unresolved human suffering and poverty and the advanced stages of the disease alcoholism. On a summer night the drunks sleep in the open. The sidewalk is a free bed, and there are no lice. Pedestrians step along and over and around the still forms as though walking on a battlefield among the dead. In doorways, on the steps of the savings bank, the bums lie sleeping it off. Standing sentinel at each sleeper's head is the empty bottle from which he drained his release. Wedged in the crook of his arm is the paper bag containing his things. The glib barker on the sightseeing bus tells his passengers that this is the "street of lost souls," but the Bowery does not think of itself as lost; it meets its peculiar problem in its own way—plenty of gin mills, plenty of flophouses, plenty of indifference, and always, at the end of the line, Bellevue.

A block or two east and the atmosphere changes sharply. In the slums are poverty and bad housing, but with them the reassuring sobriety and safety of family life. I head east along Rivington. All is cheerful and filthy and crowded. Small shops overflow onto the sidewalk, leaving only half the normal width for passers-by. In the candid

light from unshaded bulbs gleam watermelons and lingerie. Families
have fled the hot rooms upstairs and have found relief on the pavement.
They sit on orange crates, smoking, relaxed, congenial. This is the
nightly garden party of the vast Lower East Side—and on the whole
they are more agreeable-looking hot-weather groups than some you see
in bright canvas deck chairs on green lawns in country circumstances.
It is folksy here with the smell of warm flesh and squashed fruit and
fly-bitten filth in the gutter, and cooking.

At the corner of Lewis, in the playground behind the wire fence,
an open-air dance is going on—some sort of neighborhood affair, probably designed to combat delinquency. Women push baby carriages in
and out among the dancers, as though to exhibit what dancing leads
to at last. Overhead, like banners decorating a cotillion hall, stream
the pants and bras from the pulley lines. The music stops, and a
beautiful Italian girl takes a brush from her handbag and stands under
the street lamp brushing her long blue-black hair till it shines. The
cop in the patrol car watches sullenly.

The Consolidated Edison Company says there are eight million
people in the five boroughs of New York, and the company is in a
position to know. As in every dense community, virtually all races, all
religions, all nationalities are represented. Population figures are shifty
—they change almost as fast as one can break them down. It is safe to
say that about two million of New York's eight million are Jews—
roughly one in four. Among this two million who are Jewish are, of
course, a great many nationalities: Russian, German, Polish, Rumanian,
Austrian, a long list. The Urban League of Greater New York estimates
that the number of Negroes in New York is about 700,000. Of these,
about 500,000 live in Harlem, a district that extends northward from
110th Street. The Negro population has increased rapidly in the last
few years. There are half again as many Negroes in New York today
as there were in 1940. There are about 230,000 Puerto Ricans living
in New York. There are half a million Irish, half a million Germans.
There are 900,000 Russians, 150,000 English, 400,000 Poles, and there
are quantities of Finns and Czechs and Swedes and Danes and Nor-
wegians and Latvians and Belgians and Welsh and Greeks, and even
Dutch, who have been here from away back. It is very hard to say
how many Chinese there are. Officially there are twelve thousand, but
there are many Chinese who are in New York illegally and who don't
like census takers.

The collision and the intermingling of these millions of foreign-
born people representing so many races, creeds, and nationalities make

New York a permanent exhibit of the phenomenon of one world. The citizens of New York are tolerant not only from disposition but from necessity. The city has to be tolerant, otherwise it would explode in a radioactive cloud of hate and rancor and bigotry. If the people were to depart even briefly from the peace of cosmopolitan intercourse, the town would blow up higher than a kite. In New York smolders every race problem there is, but the noticeable thing is not the problem but the inviolate truce. Harlem is a city in itself, and being a city Harlem symbolizes segregation; yet Negro life in New York lacks the more conspicuous elements of Jim Crowism. Negroes ride subways and buses on terms of equality with whites, but they have not yet found that same equality in hotels and restaurants. Professionally, Negroes get on well in the theater, in music, in art, and in literature; but in many fields of employment the going is tough. The Jim Crow principle lives chiefly in the housing rules and customs. Private owners of dwellings legally can, and do, exclude Negroes. Under a recent city ordinance, however, apartment buildings that are financed with public moneys or that receive any tax exemption must accept tenants without regard to race, color, or religion.

To a New Yorker the city is both changeless and changing. In many respects it neither looks nor feels the way it did twenty-five years ago. The elevated railways have been pulled down, all but the Third Avenue. An old-timer walking up Sixth past the Jefferson Market jail misses the railroad, misses its sound, its spotted shade, its little aerial stations, and the tremor of the thing. Broadway has changed in aspect. It used to have a discernible bony structure beneath its loud bright surface; but the signs are so enormous now, the buildings and shops and hotels have largely disappeared under the neon lights and letters and the frozen-custard façade. Broadway is a custard street with no frame supporting it. In Greenwich Village the light is thinning: big apartments have come in, bordering the square, and the bars are mirrored and chromed. But there are still in the Village the lingering traces of poesy, Mexican glass, hammered brass, batik, lamps made of whiskey bottles, first novels made of fresh memories—the old Village with its alleys and ratty one-room rents catering to the erratic needs of those whose hearts are young and gay.

Grand Central has become honky-tonk, with its extra-dimensional advertising displays and its tendency to adopt the tactics of a travel broker. I practically lived in Grand Central Terminal at one period (it has all the conveniences and I had no other place to stay) and the great hall seemed to me one of the more inspiring interiors in New York, until Lastex and Coca-Cola got into the temple.

All over town the great mansions are in decline. Schwab's house facing the Hudson on Riverside is gone. Gould's house on Fifth Avenue is an antique shop. Morgan's house on Madison Avenue is a church administration office. What was once the Fahnestock house is now Random House. Rich men nowadays don't live in houses; they live in the attics of big apartment buildings and plant trees on the setbacks, hundreds of feet above the street.

There are fewer newspapers than there used to be, thanks somewhat to the late Frank Munsey. One misses the *Globe*, the *Mail*, the *Herald*; and to many a New Yorker life has never seemed the same since the *World* took the count.

Police now ride in radio prowl cars instead of gumshoeing around the block swinging their sticks. A ride in the subway costs ten cents, and the seats are apt to be dark green instead of straw yellow. Men go to saloons to gaze at televised events instead of to think long thoughts. It is all very disconcerting. Even parades have changed some. The last triumphal military procession in Manhattan simply filled the city with an ominous and terrible rumble of heavy tanks.

The slums are gradually giving way to the lofty housing projects —high in stature, high in purpose, low in rent. There are a couple of dozens of these new developments scattered around; each is a city in itself (one of them in the Bronx accommodates twelve thousand families), sky acreage hitherto untilled, lifting people far above the street, standardizing their sanitary life, giving them some place to sit other than an orange crate. Federal money, state money, city money, and private money have flowed into these projects. Banks and insurance companies are in back of some of them. Architects have turned the buildings slightly on their bases, to catch more light. In some of them, rents are as low as $8 a room. Thousands of new units are still needed and will eventually be built, but New York never quite catches up with itself, is never in equilibrium. In flush times the population mushrooms and the new dwellings sprout from the rock. Come bad times and the population scatters and the lofts are abandoned and the landlord withers and dies.

New York has changed in tempo and in temper during the years I have known it. There is greater tension, increased irritability. You encounter it in many places, in many faces. The normal frustrations of modern life are here multiplied and amplified—a single run of a crosstown bus contains, for the driver, enough frustration and annoyance to carry him over the edge of sanity: the light that changes always an instant too soon, the passenger that bangs on the shut door, the truck that blocks the only opening, the coin that slips to the floor, the question asked at the wrong moment. There is greater tension and there is greater speed. Taxis roll faster than they rolled ten years ago —and they were rolling fast then. Hackmen used to drive with verve; now they sometimes seem to drive with desperation, toward the ultimate tip. On the West Side Highway, approaching the city, the motorist is swept along in a trance—a sort of fever of inescapable motion, goaded from behind, hemmed in on either side, a mere chip in a millrace.

The city has never been so uncomfortable, so crowded, so tense. Money has been plentiful and New York has responded. Restaurants are hard to get into; businessmen stand in line for a Schrafft's luncheon as meekly as idle men used to stand in soup lines. (Prosperity creates its bread lines, the same as depression.) The lunch hour in Manhattan has been shoved ahead half an hour, to twelve or twelve-thirty in the hopes of beating the crowd to a table. Everyone is a little emptier at quitting time than he used to be. Apartments are festooned with No Vacancy signs. There is standing-room-only in Fifth Avenue buses, which once reserved a seat for every paying customer. The old double-deckers are disappearing—people don't ride just for the fun of it anymore.

At certain hours on certain days it is almost impossible to find an empty taxi and there is a great deal of chasing around after them. You grab a handle and open the door, and find that some other citizen is entering from the other side. Doormen grow rich blowing their whistles for cabs; and some doormen belong to no door at all—merely wander about through the streets, opening cabs for people as they happen to find them. By comparison with other less hectic days, the city is uncomfortable and inconvenient; but New Yorkers temperamentally do not crave comfort and convenience—if they did they would live elsewhere.

The subtlest change in New York is something people don't speak much about but that is in everyone's mind. The city, for the first time in its long history, is destructible. A single flight of planes no bigger than a wedge of geese can quickly end this island fantasy, burn the towers, crumble the bridges, turn the underground passages into lethal chambers, cremate the millions. The intimation of mortality is part of New York now: in the sound of jets overhead, in the black headlines of the latest edition.

All dwellers in cities must live with the stubborn fact of annihilation; in New York the fact is somewhat more concentrated because of the concentration of the city itself, and because, of all targets, New York has a certain clear priority. In the mind of whatever perverted dreamer who might loose the lightning, New York must hold a steady, irresistible charm.

It used to be that the Statue of Liberty was the signpost that proclaimed New York and translated it for all the world. Today Liberty shares the role with Death. Along the East River, from the razed slaughterhouses of Turtle Bay, as though in a race with the spectral flight of planes, men are carving out the permanent headquarters of the United Nations—the greatest housing project of them all. In its stride, New York takes on one more interior city, to shelter, this time, all governments, and to clear the slum called war. New York is not a capital city—it is not a national capital or a state capital. But it is by way of becoming the capital of the world. The buildings, as conceived by architects, will be cigar boxes set on end. Traffic will flow in a new tunnel under First Avenue. Forty seventh Street will be widened (and if my guess is any good, trucks will appear late at night to plant tall trees surreptitiously, their roots to mingle with the intestines of the town). Once again the city will absorb, almost without showing any sign of it, a congress of visitors. It has already shown itself capable of stashing away the United Nations—a great many of the delegates have been around town during the past couple of years, and the citizenry has hardly caught a glimpse of their coattails or their black Homburgs.

This race—this race between the destroying planes and the struggling Parliament of Man—it sticks in all our heads. The city at last perfectly illustrates both the universal dilemma and the general solution, this riddle in steel and stone is at once the perfect target and the perfect demonstration of nonviolence, of racial brotherhood, this lofty target scraping the skies and meeting the destroying planes halfway, home of all people and all nations, capital of everything, housing the deliberations by which the planes are to be stayed and their errand forestalled.

A block or two west of the new City of Man in Turtle Bay there is an old willow tree that presides over an interior garden. It is a battered tree, long-suffering and much-climbed, held together by strands of wire but beloved of those who know it. In a way it symbolizes the city: life under difficulties, growth against odds, sap-rise in the midst of concrete, and the steady reaching for the sun. Whenever I look at it nowadays, and feel the cold shadow of the planes, I think: "This must be saved, this particular thing, this very tree." If it were to go, all would go—this city, this mischievous and marvelous monument which not to look upon would be like death.

# IV

❧❦❧

# FLORIDA

# ON A FLORIDA KEY

❧

*February 1941*

I am writing this in a beach cottage on a Florida key. It is raining to beat the cars. The rollers from a westerly storm are creaming along the shore, making a steady boiling noise instead of the usual intermittent slap. The Chamber of Commerce has drawn the friendly blind against this ugliness and is busy getting out some advance notices of the style parade which is to be held next Wednesday at the pavilion. The paper says cooler tomorrow.

The walls of my room are of matched boarding, applied horizontally and painted green. On the floor is a straw mat. Under the mat is a layer of sand that has been tracked into the cottage and has sifted through the straw. I have thought some of taking the mat up and sweeping the sand into a pile and removing it, but have decided against it. This is the way keys form, apparently, and I have no particular reason to interfere. On a small wooden base in one corner of the room is a gas heater, supplied from a tank on the premises. This device can raise the temperature of the room with great rapidity by converting the oxygen of the air into heat. In deciding whether to light the heater or leave it alone, one has only to choose whether he wants to congeal in a well-ventilated room or suffocate in comfort. After a little practice, a nice balance can be established—enough oxygen left to sustain life, yet enough heat generated to prevent death from exposure.

On the west wall hangs an Indian rug, and to one edge of the rug is pinned a button which carries the legend: Junior Programs Joop Club. Built into the north wall is a cabinet made of pecky cypress. On the top shelf are three large pine cones, two of them painted emerald-green, the

[ 137 ]

third painted brick-red. Also a gilded candlestick in the shape of a Roman chariot. Another shelf holds some shells which, at the expenditure of considerable effort on somebody's part, have been made to look like birds. On the bottom shelf is a tiny toy collie, made of rabbit fur, with a tongue of red flannel.

In the kitchenette just beyond where I sit is a gas stove and a small electric refrigerator of an ancient vintage. The ice trays show deep claw marks, where people have tried to pry them free, using can openers and knives and screwdrivers and petulance. When the refrigerator snaps on it makes a noise which can be heard all through the cottage and the lights everywhere go dim for a second and then return to their normal brilliancy. This refrigerator contains the milk, the butter, and the eggs for tomorrow's breakfast. More milk will arrive in the morning, but I will save it for use on the morrow, so that every day I shall use the milk of the previous day, never taking advantage of the opportunity to enjoy perfectly fresh milk. This is a situation which could be avoided if I had the guts to throw away a whole bottle of milk, but nobody has that much courage in the world today. It is a sin to throw away milk and we know it.

The water that flows from the faucets in the kitchen sink and in the bathroom contains sulphur and is not good to drink. It leaves deep-brown stains around the drains. Applied to the face with a shaving brush, it feels as though fine sandpaper were being drawn across your jowls. It is so hard and sulphurous that ordinary soap will not yield to it, and the breakfast dishes have to be washed with a washing powder known as Dreft.

On the porch of the cottage, each in a special stand, are two carboys of spring water—for drinking, making coffee, and brushing teeth. There is a deposit of two dollars on bottle and stand, and the water itself costs fifty cents. Two rival companies furnish water to the community, and I happened to get mixed up with both of them. Every couple of days a man from one or the other of the companies shows up and hangs around for a while, whining about the presence on my porch of the rival's carboy. I have made an attempt to dismiss one company and retain the other, but to accomplish it would require a dominant personality and I haven't one. I have been surprised to see how long it takes a man to drink up ten gallons of water. I should have thought I could have done it in half the time it has taken me.

This morning I read in the paper of an old Negro, one hundred-and-one years old, and he was boasting of the quantity of whiskey he had drunk in his life. He said he had once worked in a distillery and they used to give him half a gallon of whiskey a day to take home, which kept him going all right during the week, but on weekends, he said, he would have to buy a gallon extry, to tide him over till Monday.

In the kitchen cabinet is a bag of oranges for morning juice. Each orange is stamped "Color Added." The dyeing of an orange, to make it orange, is man's most impudent gesture to date. It is really an appalling piece of effrontery, carrying the clear implication that Nature doesn't know what she is up to. I think an orange, dyed orange, is as repulsive as a pine cone painted green. I think it is about as ugly a thing as I have ever seen, and it seems hard to believe that here, within ten miles, probably, of the trees that bore the fruit, I can't buy an orange that somebody hasn't smeared with paint. But I doubt that there are many who feel that way about it, because fraudulence has become a national virtue and is well thought of in many circles. In the last twenty-four hours, I see by this morning's paper, 136 cars of oranges have been shipped. There are probably millions of children today who have never seen a natural orange—only an artificially colored one. If they should see a natural orange they might think something had gone wrong with it.

There are two moving picture theaters in the town to which my key is attached by a bridge. In one of them colored people are allowed in the balcony. In the other, colored people are not allowed at all. I saw a patriotic newsreel there the other day which ended with a picture of the American flag blowing in the breeze, and the words: one nation indivisible, with liberty and justice for all. Everyone clapped, but I decided I could not clap for liberty and justice (for all) while I was in a theater from which Negroes had been barred. And I felt there were too many people in the world who think liberty and justice for all means liberty and justice for themselves and their friends. I sat there wondering what would happen to me if I were to jump up and say in a loud voice: "If you folks like liberty and justice so much, why do you keep Negroes from this theater?" I am sure it would have surprised everybody very much and it is the kind of thing I dream about doing but never do. If I had done it I suppose the management would have taken me by the arm and marched me out of the theater, on the grounds that it is disturbing the peace to speak up for liberty just as the feature is coming on. When a man is in the South he must do as the Southerners do; but although I am willing to call my wife "sugar" I am not willing to call a colored person a nigger.

Northerners are quite likely to feel that Southerners are bigoted on the race question, and Southerners almost invariably figure that Northerners are without any practical experience and therefore their opinions aren't worth much. The Jim Crow philosophy of color is unsatisfying to a Northerner, but is regarded as sensible and expedient to residents of towns where the Negro population is as large as or larger than the white. Whether one makes a practical answer or an idealistic answer to a question depends partly on whether one is talking in terms of one year, or ten years, or a hundred years. It is, in other words, conceivable that the Negroes of a hundred years from now will enjoy a greater degree of liberty if the present restrictions on today's Negroes are not relaxed too fast. But that doesn't get today's Negroes in to see Hedy Lamarr.

I have to laugh when I think about the sheer inconsistency of the Southern attitude about color: the Negro barred from the movie house because of color, the orange with "color added" for its ultimate triumph. Some of the cities in this part of the State have fête days to commemorate the past and advertise the future, and in my mind I have been designing a float that I would like to enter in the parades. It would contain a beautiful Negro woman riding with the other bathing beauties and stamped with the magical words, Color Added.

In the cottage next door is a lady who is an ardent isolationist and who keeps running in and out with pamphlets, books, and marked-up newspapers, hoping to convince me that America should mind its own business. She tracks sand in, as well as ideas, and I have to sweep up after her two or three times a day.

Floridians are complaining this year that business is below par. They tell you that the boom in industry causes this unwholesome situation. When tycoons are busy in the North they have no time for sunning themselves, or even for sitting in a semitropical cottage in the rain. Miami is appropriating a few extra thousand dollars for its advertising campaign, hoping to lure executives away from the defense program for a few golden moments.

Although I am no archeologist, I love Florida as much for the remains of her unfinished cities as for the bright cabanas on her beaches. I love to prowl the dead sidewalks that run off into the live jungle, under the broiling sun of noon, where the cabbage palms throw their spiny shade across the stillborn streets and the creepers bind old curbstones in a fierce sensual embrace and the mocking birds dwell in song upon the remembered grandeur of real estate's purple hour. A boulevard which has been reclaimed by Nature is an exciting avenue; it breathes a strange prophetic perfume, as of some century still to come, when the birds will remember, and the spiders, and the little quick lizards that toast themselves on the smooth hard surfaces that once held the impossible dreams of men. Here along these bristling walks is a decayed symmetry in a living forest—straight lines softened by a kindly and haphazard Nature, pavements nourishing life with the beginnings of topsoil, the cracks in the walks possessed by root structures, the brilliant blossoms of the domesticated vine run wild, and overhead the turkey buzzard in the clear sky, on quiet wings, awaiting new mammalian death among the hibiscus, the yucca, the Spanish bayonet, and the palm. I remember the wonderful days and the tall dream of rainbow's end; the offices with the wall charts, the pins in the charts, the orchestras playing gently to prepare the soul of the wanderer for the mysteries of subdivision, the free bus service to the rainbow's beginning, the luncheon served on the little tables under the trees, the warm sweet air so full of the deadly contagion, the dotted line, the signature, and the premonitory qualms and the shadow of the buzzard in the wild wide Florida sky.

I love these rudimentary cities that were conceived in haste and greed and never rose to suffer the scarifying effects of human habitation, cities of not quite forgotten hopes, untouched by neon and by filth. And I love the beaches too, out beyond the cottage colony, where they are wild and free still, visited by the sandpipers that retreat before each wave, like children, and by an occasional hip-sprung farmwife hunting shells, or sometimes by a veteran digging for *Donax variabilis* to take back to his hungry mate in the trailer camp.

The sound of the sea is the most time-effacing sound there is. The centuries reroll in a cloud and the earth becomes green again when you listen, with eyes shut, to the sea—a young green time when the water and the land were just getting acquainted and had known each other for only a few billion years and the mollusks were just beginning to dip and creep in the shallows; and now man the invertebrate, under his ribbed umbrella, anoints himself with oil and pulls on his Polaroid glasses to stop the glare and stretches out his long brown body at ease upon a towel on the warm sand and listens.

The sea answers all questions, and always in the same way; for when you read in the papers the interminable discussions and the bickering and the prognostications and the turmoil, the disagreements and the fateful decisions and agreements and the plans and the programs and the threats and the counter threats, then you close your eyes and the sea dispatches one more big roller in the unbroken line since the beginning of the world and it combs and breaks and returns foaming and saying. "So soon?"

# THE RING OF TIME

*Fiddler Bayou, March 22, 1956*

After the lions had returned to their cages, creeping angrily through
the chutes, a little bunch of us drifted away and into an open doorway
nearby, where we stood for a while in semidarkness, watching a big
brown circus horse go harumphing around the practice ring. His
trainer was a woman of about forty, and the two of them, horse and
woman, seemed caught up in one of those desultory treadmills of afternoon from which there is no apparent escape. The day was hot, and
we kibitzers were grateful to be briefly out of the sun's glare. The long
rein, or tape, by which the woman guided her charge counterclockwise
in his dull career formed the radius of their private circle, of which she
was the revolving center; and she, too, stepped a tiny circumference of
her own, in order to accommodate the horse and allow him his maximum
scope. She had on a short-skirted costume and a conical straw hat. Her
legs were bare and she wore high heels, which probed deep into the
loose tanbark and kept her ankles in a state of constant turmoil. The
great size and meekness of the horse, the repetitious exercise, the heat
of the afternoon, all exerted a hypnotic charm that invited boredom;
we spectators were experiencing a languor—we neither expected relief
nor felt entitled to any. We had paid a dollar to get into the grounds, to
be sure, but we had got our dollar's worth a few minutes before, when
the lion trainer's whiplash had got caught around a toe of one of the
lions. What more did we want for a dollar?

Behind me I heard someone say, "Excuse me, please," in a low
voice. She was halfway into the building when I turned and saw her—
a girl of sixteen or seventeen, politely threading her way through us

[ 142 ]

onlookers who blocked the entrance. As she emerged in front of us, I saw that she was barefoot, her dirty little feet fighting the uneven ground. In most respects she was like any of two or three dozen show-girls you encounter if you wander about the winter quarters of Mr. John Ringling North's circus, in Sarasota—cleverly proportioned, deeply browned by the sun, dusty, eager, and almost naked. But her grave face and the naturalness of her manner gave her a sort of quick distinction and brought a new note into the gloomy octagonal building where we had all cast our lot for a few moments. As soon as she had squeezed through the crowd, she spoke a word or two to the older woman, whom I took to be her mother, stepped to the ring, and waited while the horse coasted to a stop in front of her. She gave the animal a couple of affectionate swipes on his enormous neck and then swung herself aboard. The horse immediately resumed his rocking canter, the woman goading him on, chanting something that sounded like "Hop! Hop!"

In attempting to recapture this mild spectacle, I am merely acting as recording secretary for one of the oldest of societies—the society of those who, at one time or another, have surrendered, without even a show of resistance, to the bedazzlement of a circus rider. As a writing man, or secretary, I have always felt charged with the safekeeping of all unexpected items of worldly or unworldly enchantment, as though I might be held personally responsible if even a small one were to be lost. But it is not easy to communicate anything of this nature. The circus comes as close to being the world in microcosm as anything I know, in a way, it puts all the rest of show business in the shade. Its magic is universal and complex. Out of its wild disorder comes order; from its rank smell rises the good aroma of courage and daring; out of its preliminary shabbiness comes the final splendor. And buried in the familiar boasts of its advance agents lies the modesty of most of its people. For me the circus is at its best before it has been put to-gether. It is at its best at certain moments when it comes to a point, as through a burning glass, in the activity and destiny of a single performer out of so many. One ring is always bigger than three. One rider, one aerialist, is always greater than six. In short, a man has to catch the circus unawares to experience its full impact and share its gaudy dream.

The ten-minute ride the girl took achieved—as far as I was con-cerned, who wasn't looking for it, and quite unbeknownst to her, who wasn't even striving for it—the thing that is sought by performers everywhere, on whatever stage, whether struggling in the tidal currents of Shakespeare or bucking the difficult motion of a horse. I somehow got the idea she was just cadging a ride, improving a shining ten min-

utes in the diligent way all serious artists seize free moments to hone
the blade of their talent and keep themselves in trim. Her brief tour
included only elementary postures and tricks, perhaps because they
were all she was capable of, perhaps because her warmup at this hour
was unscheduled and the ring was not rigged for a real practice session.
She swung herself off and on the horse several times, gripping his mane.
She did a few knee-stands—or whatever they are called—dropping to
her knees and quickly bouncing back up on her feet again. Most of the
time she simply rode in a standing position, well aft on the beast, her
hands hanging easily at her sides, her head erect, her straw-colored
ponytail lightly brushing her shoulders, the blood of exertion showing faintly through the tan of her skin. Twice she managed a one-
foot stance—a sort of ballet pose, with arms outstretched. At one point
the neck strap of her bathing suit broke and she went twice around
the ring in the classic attitude of a woman making minor repairs to a
garment. The fact that she was standing on the back of a moving horse
while doing this invested the matter with a clownish significance
that perfectly fitted the spirit of the circus—jocund, yet charming.
She just rolled the strap into a neat ball and stowed it inside her bodice
while the horse rocked and rolled beneath her in dutiful innocence.
The bathing suit proved as self-reliant as its owner and stood up well
enough without benefit of strap.

The richness of the scene was in its plainness, its natural condition—of horse, of ring, of girl, even to the girl's bare feet that gripped
the bare back of her proud and ridiculous mount. The enchantment
grew not out of anything that happened or was performed but out of
something that seemed to go round and around and around with the
girl, attending her, a steady gleam in the shape of a circle—a ring of
ambition, of happiness, of youth. (And the positive pleasures of equil-
ibrium under difficulties.) In a week or two, all would be changed, all
(or almost all) lost: the girl would wear makeup, the horse would wear
gold, the ring would be painted, the bark would be clean for the feet
of the horse, the girl's feet would be clean for the slippers that she'd
wear. All, all would be lost.

As I watched with the others, our jaws adroop, our eyes alight,
I became painfully conscious of the element of time. Everything in the
hideous old building seemed to take the shape of a circle, conforming
to the course of the horse. The rider's gaze, as she peered straight ahead,
seemed to be circular, as though bent by force of circumstance; then
time itself began running in circles, and so the beginning was where
the end was, and the two were the same, and one thing ran into the next
and time went round and around and got nowhere. The girl wasn't so

young that she did not know the delicious satisfaction of having a perfectly behaved body and the fun of using it to do a trick most people can't do, but she was too young to know that time does not really move in a circle at all. I thought: "She will never be as beautiful as this again"—a thought that made me acutely unhappy—and in a flash my mind (which is too much of a busybody to suit me) had projected her twenty-five years ahead, and she was now in the center of the ring, on foot, wearing a conical hat and high-heeled shoes, the image of the older woman, holding the long rein, caught in the treadmill of an afternoon long in the future. "She is at that enviable moment in life [I thought] when she believes she can go once around the ring, make one complete circuit, and at the end be exactly the same age as at the start." Everything in her movements, her expression, told you that for her the ring of time was perfectly formed, changeless, predictable, without beginning or end, like the ring in which she was traveling at this moment with the horse that wallowed under her. And then I slipped back into my trance, and time was circular again—time, pausing quietly with the rest of us, so as not to disturb the balance of a performer.

Her ride ended as casually as it had begun. The older woman stopped the horse, and the girl slid to the ground. As she walked toward us to leave, there was a quick, small burst of applause. She smiled broadly, in surprise and pleasure; then her face suddenly regained its gravity and she disappeared through the door.

It has been ambitious and plucky of me to attempt to describe what is indescribable, and I have failed, as I knew I would. But I have discharged my duty to my society; and besides, a writer, like an acrobat, must occasionally try a stunt that is too much for him. At any rate, it is worth reporting that long before the circus comes to town, its most notable performances have already been given. Under the bright lights of the finished show, a performer need only reflect the electric candle power that is directed upon him; but in the dark and dirty old training rings and in the makeshift cages, whatever light is generated, whatever excitement, whatever beauty, must come from original sources—from internal fires of professional hunger and delight, from the exuberance and gravity of youth. It is the difference between planetary light and the combustion of stars.

The South is the land of the sustained sibilant. Everywhere, for the appreciative visitor, the letter "s" insinuates itself in the scene: in the sound of sea and sand, in the singing shell, in the heat of sun and sky, in the sultriness of the gentle hours, in the siesta, in the stir of birds and insects. In contrast to the softness of its music, the South is also cruel and hard and prickly. A little striped lizard, flattened along the sharp green bayonet of a yucca, wears in its tiny face and watchful eye the pure look of death and violence. And all over the place, hidden at the bottom of their small sandy craters, the ant lions lie in wait for the ant that will stumble into their trap. (There are three kinds of lions in this region: the lions of the circus, the ant lions, and the Lions of the Tampa Lions Club, who roared their approval of segregation at a meeting the other day—all except one, a Lion named Monty Gurwit, who declined to roar and thereby got his picture in the paper.)

The day starts on a note of despair: the sorrowing dove, alone on its telephone wire, mourns the loss of night, weeps at the bright perils of the unfolding day. But soon the mockingbird wakes and begins an early rehearsal, setting the dove down by force of character, running through a few slick imitations, and trying a couple of original numbers into the bargain. The redbird takes it from there. Despair gives way to good humor. The Southern dawn is a pale affair, usually, quite different from our northern daybreak. It is a triumph of gradualism; night turns to day imperceptibly, softly, with no theatrics. It is subtle and undisturbing. As the first light seeps in through the blinds I lie in bed half awake, despairing with the dove, sounding the A for the brothers Alsop. All seems lost, all seems sorrowful. Then a mullet jumps in the bayou outside the bedroom window. It falls back into the water with a smart smack. I have asked several people why the mullet incessantly jump and I have received a variety of answers. Some say the mullet jump to shake off a parasite that annoys them. Some say they jump for the love of jumping—as the girl on the horse seemed to ride for the love of riding (although she, too, like all artists, may have been shaking off some parasite that fastens itself to the creative spirit and can be got rid of only by fifty turns around a ring while standing on a horse).

In Florida at this time of year, the sun does not take command of the day until a couple of hours after it has appeared in the east. It seems to carry no authority at first. The sun and the lizard keep the same schedule; they bide their time until the morning has advanced a good long way before they come fully forth and strike. The cold lizard waits astride his warming leaf for the perfect moment; the cold sun waits in his nest of clouds for the crucial time.

On many days, the dampness of the air pervades all life, all living. Matches refuse to strike. The towel, hung to dry, grows wetter by the hour. The newspaper, with its headlines about integration, wilts in your hand and falls limply into the coffee and the egg. Envelopes seal themselves. Postage stamps mate with one another as shamelessly as grasshoppers. But most of the time the days are models of beauty and wonder and comfort, with the kind sea stroking the back of the warm sand. At evening there are great flights of birds over the sea, where the light lingers; the gulls, the pelicans, the terns, the herons stay aloft for half an hour after land birds have gone to roost. They hold their ancient formations, wheel and fish over the Pass, enjoying the last of day like children playing outdoors after suppertime.

To a beachcomber from the North, which is my present status, the race problem has no pertinence, no immediacy. Here in Florida I am a guest in two houses—the house of the sun, the house of the State of Florida. As a guest, I mind my manners and do not criticize the customs of my hosts. It gives me a queer feeling, though, to be at the center of the greatest social crisis of my time and see hardly a sign of it. Yet the very absence of signs seems to increase one's awareness. Colored people do not come to the public beach to bathe, because they would not be made welcome there; and they don't fritter away their time visiting the circus, because they have other things to do. A few of them turn up at the ballpark, where they occupy a separate but equal section of the left-field bleachers and watch Negro players on the visiting Braves team using the same bases as the white players, instead of separate (but equal) bases. I have had only two small encounters with "color." A colored woman named Viola, who had been a friend of my wife's sister years ago, showed up one day with some laundry of ours that she had consented to do for us, and with the bundle she brought a bunch of nasturtiums, as a sort of natural accompaniment to the delivery of clean clothes. The flowers seemed a very acceptable thing and I was touched by them. We asked Viola about her daughter, and she said she was at Kentucky State College, studying voice.

The other encounter was when I was explaining to our cook, who is from Finland, the mysteries of bus travel in the American Southland. I showed her the bus stop, armed her with a timetable, and then, as a matter of duty, mentioned the customs of the Romans. "When you get on the bus," I said, "I think you'd better sit in one of the front seats—the seats in back are for colored people." A look of great weariness came into her face, as it does when we use too many dishes, and she replied, "Oh, I know—isn't it silly!"

Her remark, coming as it did all the way from Finland and landing on this sandbar with a plunk, impressed me. The Supreme Court said nothing about silliness, but I suspect it may play more of a role than one might suppose. People are, if anything, more touchy about being thought silly than they are about being thought unjust. I note that one of the arguments in the recent manifesto of Southern

Congressmen in support of the doctrine of "separate but equal" was that it had been founded on "common sense." The sense that is common to one generation is uncommon to the next. Probably the first slave ship, with Negroes lying in chains on its decks, seemed commonsensical to the owners who operated it and to the planters who patronized it. But such a vessel would not be in the realm of common sense today. The only sense that is common, in the long run, is the sense of change —and we all instinctively avoid it, and object to the passage of time, and would rather have none of it.

The Supreme Court decision is like the Southern sun, laggard in its early stages, biding its time. It has been the law in Florida for two years now, and the years have been like the hours of the morning before the sun has gathered its strength. I think the decision is as incontrovertible and warming as the sun, and, like the sun, will eventually take charge.

But there is certainly a great temptation in Florida to duck the passage of time. Lying in warm comfort by the sea, you receive gratefully the gift of the sun, the gift of the South. This is true seduction. The day is a circle—morning, afternoon, and night. After a few days I was clearly enjoying the same delusion as the girl on the horse—that I could ride clear around the ring of day, guarded by wind and sun and sea and sand, and be not a moment older.

P.S. (April 1962).    When I first laid eyes on Fiddler Bayou, it was wild land, populated chiefly by the little crabs that gave it its name, visited by wading birds and by an occasional fisherman. Today, houses ring the bayou, and part of the mangrove shore has been bulkheaded with a concrete wall. Green lawns stretch from patio to water's edge, and sprinklers make rainbows in the light. But despite man's encroachment, Nature manages to hold her own and assert her authority: high tides and high winds in the gulf sometimes send the sea crashing across the sand barrier, depositing its wrack on lawns and ringing everyone's front door bell. The birds and the crabs accommodate themselves quite readily to the changes that have taken place; every day brings herons to hunt around among the roots of the mangroves, and I have discovered that I can approach to within about eight feet of a Little Blue Heron simply by entering the water and swimming slowly toward him. Apparently he has decided that when I'm in the water, I am without guile—possibly even desirable, like a fish.

The Ringling circus has quit Sarasota and gone elsewhere for its hibernation. A few circus families still own homes in the town, and every spring the students at the high school put on a circus, to let off steam, work off physical requirements, and provide a promotional spectacle for Sarasota. At the drugstore you can buy a postcard showing the bed John Ringling slept in. Time has not stood still for anybody but the dead, and even the dead must be able to hear the acceleration of little sports cars and know that things have changed.

From the all-wise *New York Times*, which has the animal kingdom ever in mind, I have learned that one of the creatures most acutely aware of the passing of time is the fiddler crab himself. Tiny spots on his body enlarge during daytime hours, giving him the same color as the mudbank he explores and thus protecting him from his enemies. At night the spots shrink, his color fades, and he is almost invisible in the light of the moon. These changes are synchronized with the tides, so that each day they occur at a different hour. A scientist who experimented with the crabs to learn more about the phenomenon discovered that even when they are removed from their natural environment and held in confinement, the rhythm of their bodily change continues uninterrupted, and they mark the passage of time in their laboratory prison, faithful to the tides in their fashion.

# WHAT DO OUR HEARTS TREASURE?

*Bayou Louise, January 1966*

Up until a couple of years ago, the Christmases I have known have been in lands of the fir tree and pine. The same is true of my wife, who is a New Englander and whose Christmases have been observed in a cold setting, Bostonian in design. But times change, circumstances alter, health glides slowly downhill, and there is, of course, Christmas in lands of the palm tree and vine—which is what we were up against last month. Our Christmas, 1965, was spent in a rented house on the edge of a canal in Florida, locally called a bayou.

I knew there would have to be certain adjustments, emotional and physical, to this shift in ceremony, but I guess I was not quite prepared for them and had not really figured them out. It was obvious to both of us that we were not looking forward to being away from home at Christmas, but I busied myself with road maps and thermos arrangements and kept my mind off the Nativity. We arrived in Florida tired from the long motor journey but essentially cheerful and ready for anything.

The house we walked into had been engaged sight unseen, and this is always fun and full of jolts, like a ride at an amusement park. Our pleasure palace was built of cinder blocks and was painted shocking pink. The principal tree on the place was a tall power pole sprouting transformers; it stood a few feet from the canal and threw a pleasant shade across the drive. The house itself, we soon discovered, was wonderfully supplied with modern labor-saving appliances and almost completely bare of any other sort of furnishing. We found an automatic washing machine, a dryer, an automatic dishwasher, a reverse-cycle heating-and-air-conditioning unit that had just burned out its compressor and was lying in disarray behind a board fence outside, a disposal device that would grind up a grapefruit rind if you cut the rind into slices, a big refrigerator, an electric wall oven, an electric stove, an electric warming oven, and so on. All this was pretty good except that there was no ice bucket, no water pitcher, no rugs on the terrazzo floors, no pictures on the pastel walls, no bookshelves, no books, and no garbage pail. There were bathrooms everywhere you turned, but I saw no sign that anybody had ever done anything in the house except take baths and adjust the controls on the machinery.

When we were rested from our trip, we started buying things for the house, mostly from a large department store in town. This store fell into the habit of delivering most of our purchases not to us but to a house next door, whose owners were away. We got on the phone and stayed there for most of the daylight hours.

Several days before Christmas, I began to notice that my wife was suffering from crying spells, all of them of short duration. I would find her weeping quietly in what seemed like elegant, if uncomfortable, surroundings. "It's Vietnam that is making me feel this way," she said. But I did not believe it was Vietnam. I knew her well enough, in her December phase, to know that something far deeper than Southeast Asia was at work.

I was too busy to cry. There was a man that came each day to work on the collapsed heating system. He was from a firm called "Air Comfort" and was a fine, brave, taciturn man. I would find him in a kneeling position, as though he were a figure in a crèche, gazing at the tangle of tubes and wires left by the removal of the burned-out compressor. He, too, seemed melancholy, but did not weep. He kept his own counsel and did what he could, hour after hour, to remedy an almost impossible situation. I felt that if I hung around him long enough, I might catch the drift of the reverse-cycle system and pick up a crumb or two of knowledge that would stand me in good stead later on. On the west side of the building I found a pile of fatwood logs, and when the living room became chilly I would light a fire. The logs left no ash; it was as though you were burning clear kerosene. The weather held good, and we were not really cold. The sunsets were spectacular. But the sun always sank behind the Australian pines and the palms on the opposite shore across the Pass, and I knew that my wife and I were, unconsciously, watching it descend in its more familiar rim behind the birches, the black spruces, the firs, the hackmatacks across the road from our house in Maine. Like everything else in Florida, the birds seemed inappropriate. I happen to admire the

mourning dove, but by no stretch of the eardrum can its lament be
called Christmassy. I like to see the turkey buzzard wheeling in the sky,
but he is not a merry bird, like the chickadee; his vigil is for the dying.
There arrived in the mail a program of the Christmas ceremony in the
school at home, reporting that our youngest grandson had appeared in
a pageant called "Goodbye to Last Year's Toys," and that our grand-
daughter had recited something called "What Do Our Hearts Treasure?"

There was very little traffic in the canal. Once in a while a pint
whiskey bottle would float slowly by on the outgoing tide. A small power-
boat named Digitalis made an occasional sortie, and two boys in a
homemade bateau paddled through. Sometimes, toward the end of the
day, a little green heron showed up and fished from a mangrove
that overhung the water. The scene was idyllic. Christmas was in the
air, yet the air seemed too soft to sustain it. In the vast shopping
centers that ringed the city, Santa, in jumbo size, dominated the parking lots. In the commanding noonday sun, with the temperature in the
seventies, he seemed vastly overdressed in his red suit with the ermine
trimming—a saint who perspired under the arms. Through the arcades
in front of the shops sauntered an endless procession of senior citizens,
with their sad faces, their painful joints, their last-minute errands.

I went on an errand of my own. I visited a nursery and bought a
poinsettia plant, hoping to introduce a spot of the correct color into our
house. In the North, this errand would have enjoyed a certain stature,
but in Florida the thing seemed faintly ridiculous. Driving away from
the nursery with my prize, I passed a great forest of poinsettias bloom-
ing naturally in somebody's front yard. It seemed to take the point out
of my purchase. A lot of things are red in Florida—the powder-puff bush,
the red hibiscus, the red bougainvillaea, the cannas—all these blooms
make a monkey out of a husband carrying home a small red potted
plant.

We talked over the matter of the tree and decided that the
traditional Christmas tree would be silly under these circumstances.
We would get, we said, a tropical thing of some sort, that would look
good all winter in a corner of our stylish living room, next to the glass
wall through which we watched the tropical sunsets. The nursery came
up with something very fine indeed—a cluster of three little palmlike
trees called *Dracaena marginata* (the man called it *imaginata*, which I
liked better). The pot was handsome, and the trees looked like a miniature version of the classic oasis scene in the desert. When the plant was
delivered, a small chameleon arrived with it and soon made the living
room his own. He liked the curtain on the south wall, and would poke
his evil little head out and join us for cocktails. I named him Beppo.

Everyone admired our plant. The crying spells ceased, but it was plain that there was still something the matter; it wasn't Vietnam, it wasn't the reverse-cycle system, it was some kind of unreality that pervaded our lives.

On the twenty-second, a large package arrived from the North and I noted the familiar handwriting of our daughter-in-law. I carried the package into the living room, dumped it on the sofa, slit its throat with my jackknife, and left it for my wife to dissect. (She is methodical at Christmas and keeps a record of gifts and donors.) Soon I heard a sharp cry. "Come here! Look!" I found her standing on the hearth with her nose buried in a branch from a balsam fir, which she had hung over the fireplace. With it hung a harness strap of sleigh bells. The branch had unquestionably been whacked from a tree in the woods behind our son's house in Maine and had made the long trip south. It wore the look and carried the smell of authenticity. "There!" said my wife, as though she had just delivered a baby.

The package also disgorged a tiny red drum and two tiny drumsticks, made from bright red wrapping paper by a grandchild. And the package contained school photographs, which we eagerly studied. Our youngest grandson had done something odd with his mouth, in a manly attempt to defeat the photographer, and looked just like Jimmy Hoffa. "How marvelous!" said my wife.

We placed the toy drum at the base of *Dracaena marginata*. (What do our hearts treasure?) Not to be outdone, I constructed one small cornucopia out of the same bright red paper and hung it on a spiky frond of the tree. I fashioned a five-pointed silver star, strung it on a length of monofilament from my tackle box, and suspended it from the ceiling above the tree with a piece of magic tape. The star revolved slowly, catching the light at intervals—a holy mobile. The tree now seemed biblical and just right. We were in business at last. I gazed out across the pass to where the soft and feathery Australian pines were outlined against the bright sky. They had hardened up momentarily for this hour of splendor. They were spruce! They were birch! They were fir! Everywhere, everywhere, Christmas tonight!

V

❧❦❧

# MEMORIES

# AFTERNOON OF AN AMERICAN BOY

❧

When I was in my teens, I lived in Mount Vernon, in the same block with J. Parnell Thomas, who grew up to become chairman of the House Committee on Un-American Activities. I lived on the corner of Summit and East Sidney, at No. 101 Summit Avenue, and Parnell lived four or five doors north of us on the same side of the avenue, in the house the Diefendorfs used to live in.

Parnell was not a playmate of mine, as he was a few years older, but I used to greet him as he walked by our house on his way to and from the depot. He was a good-looking young man, rather quiet and shy. Seeing him, I would call "Hello, Parnell!" and he would smile and say "Hello, Elwyn!" and walk on. Once I remember dashing out of our yard on roller skates and executing a rink turn in front of Parnell, to show off, and he said, "Well! Quite an artist, aren't you?" I remember the words. I was delighted at praise from an older man and sped away along the flagstone sidewalk, dodging the cracks I knew so well.

The thing that made Parnell a special man in my eyes in those days was not his handsome appearance and friendly manner but his sister. Her name was Eileen. She was my age and she was a quiet, nice-looking girl. She never came over to my yard to play, and I never went over there, and, considering that we lived so near each other, we were remarkably uncommunicative; nevertheless, she was the girl I singled out, at one point, to be of special interest to me. Being of special interest to me involved practically nothing on a girl's part it simply meant that she was under constant surveillance. On my own part, it meant that I suffered an astonishing disintegration when I walked by her house, from embarrassment, fright, and the knowledge that I was in enchanted territory.

In the matter of girls, I was different from most boys of my age. I admired girls a lot, but they terrified me. I did not feel that I possessed the peculiar gifts or accomplishments that girls liked in their male companions—the ability to dance, to play football, to cut up a bit in public, to smoke, and to make small talk. I couldn't do any of these things successfully, and seldom tried. Instead, I stuck with the accomplishments I was sure of: I rode my bicycle sitting backward on the handle bars, I made up poems, I played selections from *Aïda* on the piano. In winter, I tended goal in the hockey games on the frozen pond in the dell. None of these tricks counted much with girls. In the four years I was in the Mount Vernon High School, I never went to a school dance and I never took a girl to a drugstore for a soda or to the Westchester Playhouse or to Proctor's. I wanted to do these things but did not have the nerve. What I finally did manage to do, however, and what is the subject of this memoir, was far brassier, far gaudier. As an exhibit of teen-age courage and ineptitude, it never fails to amaze me in retrospect. I am not even sure it wasn't un-American.

My bashfulness and backwardness annoyed my older sister very much, and at about the period of which I am writing she began making strong efforts to stir me up. She was convinced that I was in a rut, socially, and she found me a drag in her own social life, which was brisk. She kept trying to throw me with girls, but I always bounced. And whenever she saw a chance she would start the phonograph and grab me, and we would go charging around the parlor in the toils of the one-step, she gripping me as in a death struggle, and I hurling her finally away from me through greater strength. I was a skinny kid but my muscles were hard, and it would have taken an unusually powerful woman to have held me long in the attitude of the dance.

One day, through a set of circumstances I have forgotten, my sister managed to work me into an afternoon engagement she had with some others in New York. To me, at that time, New York was a wonderland largely unexplored. I had been to the Hippodrome a couple of times with my father, and to the Hudson-Fulton Celebration, and to a few matinées; but New York, except as a setting for extravaganzas, was unknown. My sister had heard tales of tea-dancing at the Plaza Hotel. She and a girl friend of hers and another fellow and myself went there to give it a try. The expedition struck me as a slick piece of arrangement on her part. I was the junior member of the group and had been roped in, I imagine, to give symmetry to the occasion. Or perhaps Mother had forbidden my sister to go at all unless another member of the family was along. Whether I was there for symmetry or for decency I can't really remember, but I was there.

The spectacle was a revelation to me. However repulsive the idea of dancing was, I was filled with amazement at the setup. Here were tables where a fellow could sit so close to the dance floor that he was practically on it. And you could order cinnamon toast and from the safety of your chair observe girls and men in close embrace, swinging along, the music playing while you ate the toast, and the dancers so near to you that they almost brushed the things off your table as they jogged by. I was impressed. Dancing or no dancing, this was certainly high life, and I knew I was witnessing a scene miles and miles ahead of anything that took place in Mount Vernon. I had never seen anything like it, and a ferment must have begun working in me that afternoon.

Incredible as it seems to me now, I formed the idea of asking Parnell's sister Eileen to accompany me to a tea dance at the Plaza. The plan shaped up in my mind as an expedition of unparalleled worldliness, calculated to stun even the most blasé girl. The fact that I didn't know how to dance must have been a powerful deterrent, but not powerful enough to stop me. As I look back on the affair, it's hard to credit my own memory, and I sometimes wonder if, in fact, the whole business isn't some dream that has gradually gained the status of actuality. A boy with any sense, wishing to become better acquainted with a girl who was "of special interest," would have cut out for himself a more modest assignment to start with—a soda date or a movie date—something within reasonable limits. Not me. I apparently became obsessed with the notion of taking Eileen to the Plaza and not to any darned old drugstore. I had learned the location of the Plaza, and just knowing how to get to it gave me a feeling of confidence. I had learned about cinnamon toast, so I felt able to cope with the waiter when he came along. And I banked heavily on the general splendor of the surroundings and the extreme sophistication of the function to carry the day, I guess.

I was three days getting up nerve to make the phone call. Meantime, I worked out everything in the greatest detail. I heeled myself with a safe amount of money. I looked up trains. I overhauled my clothes and assembled an outfit I believed would meet the test. Then, one night at six o'clock, when Mother and Father went downstairs to dinner, I lingered upstairs and entered the big closet off my bedroom where the wall phone was. There I stood for several minutes, trembling, my hand on the receiver, which hung upside down on the hook. (In our family, the receiver always hung upside down, with the big end up.)

I had rehearsed my first line and my second line. I planned to say, "Hello, can I please speak to Eileen?" Then, when she came to the phone, I planned to say, "Hello, Eileen, this is Elwyn White." From there on, I figured I could ad-lib it.

At last, I picked up the receiver and gave the number. As I had suspected, Eileen's mother answered.

"Can I please speak to Eileen?" I asked, in a low, troubled voice.

"Just a minute," said her mother. Then, on second thought, she asked, "Who is it, please?"

"It's Elwyn," I said.

She left the phone, and after quite a while Eileen's voice said, "Hello, Elwyn." This threw my second line out of whack, but I stuck to it doggedly.

"Hello, Eileen, this is Elwyn White," I said.

In no time at all I laid the proposition before her. She seemed dazed and asked me to wait a minute. I assume she went into a huddle with her mother. Finally, she said yes, she would like to go tea-dancing with me at the Plaza, and I said fine, I would call for her at quarter past three on Thursday afternoon, or whatever afternoon it was—I've forgotten.

I do not know now, and of course did not know then, just how great was the mental and physical torture Eileen went through that day, but the incident stacks up as a sort of unintentional un-American activity, for which I was solely responsible. It all went off as scheduled: the stately walk to the depot; the solemn train ride, during which we sat staring shyly into the seat in front of us; the difficult walk from Grand Central across Forty-second to Fifth, with pedestrians clipping us and cutting in between us; the bus ride to Fifty-ninth Street; then the Plaza itself, and the cinnamon toast, and the music, and the excitement. The thundering quality of the occasion must have delivered a mental shock to me, deadening my recollection, for I have only the dimmest memory of leading Eileen onto the dance floor to execute two or three unspeakable rounds, in which I vainly tried to adapt my violent sister-and-brother wrestling act into something graceful and appropriate. It must have been awful. And at six o'clock, emerging, I gave no thought to any further entertainment, such as dinner in town. I simply herded Eileen back all the long, dreary way to Mount Vernon and deposited her, a few minutes after seven, on an empty stomach, at her home. Even if I had attempted to dine her, I don't believe it would have been possible; the emotional strain of the afternoon had caused me to perspire uninterruptedly, and any restaurant would have been justified in rejecting me solely on the ground that I was too moist.

Over the intervening years, I've often felt guilty about my afternoon at the Plaza, and many years ago, during Parnell's investigation of writers, my feeling sometimes took the form of a guilt sequence in which

I imagined myself on the stand, in the committee room, being questioned. It went something like this:

PARNELL: Have you ever written for the screen, Mr. White?

ME: No, sir.

PARNELL: Have you ever been, or are you now, a member of the Screen Writers' Guild?

ME: No, sir.

PARNELL: Have you ever been, or are you now, a member of the Communist Party?

ME: No, sir.

Then, in this imaginary guilt sequence of mine, Parnell digs deep and comes up with the big question, calculated to throw me.

PARNELL: Do you recall an afternoon, along about the middle of the second decade of this century, when you took my sister to the Plaza Hotel for tea under the grossly misleading and false pretext that you knew how to dance?

And as my reply comes weakly, "Yes, sir," I hear the murmur run through the committee room and see reporters bending over their notebooks, scribbling hard. In my dream, I am again seated with Eileen at the edge of the dance floor, frightened, stunned, and happy—in my ears the intoxicating drumbeat of the dance, in my throat the dry, bittersweet taste of cinnamon.

I don't know about the guilt, really. I guess a good many girls might say that an excursion such as the one I conducted Eileen on belongs in the un-American category. But there must be millions of aging males, now slipping into their anecdotage, who recall their Willie Baxter period with affection, and who remember some similar journey into ineptitude, in that precious, brief moment in life before love's pages, through constant reference, had become dog-eared, and before its narrative, through sheer competence, had lost the first, wild sense of derring-do.

# FAREWELL, MY LOVELY!

❧❦❧

*(An aging male kisses an old flame good-bye,* circa *1936)*\*

I see by the new Sears Roebuck catalogue that it is still possible to buy an axle for a 1909 Model T Ford, but I am not deceived. The great days have faded, the end is in sight. Only one page in the current catalogue is devoted to parts and accessories for the Model T; yet everyone remembers springtimes when the Ford gadget section was larger than men's clothing, almost as large as household furnishings. The last Model T was built in 1927, and the car is fading from what scholars call the American scene—which is an understatement, because to a few million people who grew up with it, the old Ford practically *was* the American scene.

It was the miracle God had wrought. And it was patently the sort of thing that could only happen once. Mechanically uncanny, it was like nothing that had ever come to the world before. Flourishing industries rose and fell with it. As a vehicle, it was hard-working, commonplace, heroic; and it often seemed to transmit those qualities to the persons who rode in it. My own generation identifies it with Youth, with its gaudy, irretrievable excitements; before it fades into the mist, I would like to pay it the tribute of the sigh that is not a sob, and set down random entries in a shape somewhat less cumbersome than a Sears Roebuck catalogue.

---

\* This piece originally appeared in *The New Yorker* over the pseudonym Lee Strout White. It was suggested by a manuscript submitted by Richard L. Strout, of *The Christian Science Monitor*, and Mr. Strout, an amiable collaborator, has kindly allowed me to include it in this collection. The piece was published as a little book in 1936 by G. P. Putnam's Sons under the title "Farewell to Model T."

The Model T was distinguished from all other makes of cars by the fact that its transmission was of a type known as planetary—which was half metaphysics, half sheer friction. Engineers accepted the word "planetary" in its epicyclic sense, but I was always conscious that it also meant "wandering," "erratic." Because of the peculiar nature of this planetary element, there was always, in Model T, a certain dull rapport between engine and wheels, and even when the car was in a state known as neutral, it trembled with a deep imperative and tended to inch forward. There was never a moment when the bands were not faintly egging the machine on. In this respect it was like a horse, rolling the bit on its tongue, and country people brought to it the same technique they used with draft animals.

Its most remarkable quality was its rate of acceleration. In its palmy days the Model T could take off faster than anything on the road. The reason was simple. To get under way, you simply hooked the third finger of the right hand around a lever on the steering column, pulled down hard, and shoved your left foot forcibly against the low-speed pedal. These were simple, positive motions; the car responded by lunging forward with a roar. After a few seconds of this turmoil, you took your toe off the pedal, eased up a mite on the throttle, and the car, possessed of only two forward speeds, catapulted directly into high with a series of ugly jerks and was off on its glorious errand. The abruptness of this departure was never equaled in other cars of the period. The human leg was (and still is) incapable of letting in a clutch with anything like the forthright abandon that used to send Model T on its way. Letting in a clutch is a negative, hesitant motion, depending on delicate nervous control; pushing down the Ford pedal was a simple, country motion—an expansive act, which came as natural as kicking an old door to make it budge.

The driver of the old Model T was a man enthroned. The car, with top up, stood seven feet high. The driver sat on top of the gas tank, brooding it with his own body. When he wanted gasoline, he alighted, along with everything else in the front seat; the seat was pulled off, the metal cap unscrewed, and a wooden stick thrust down to sound the liquid in the well. There were always a couple of these sounding sticks kicking around in the ratty sub-cushion regions of a flivver. Refueling was more of a social function then, because the driver had to unbend, whether he wanted to or not. Directly in front of the driver was the windshield—high, uncompromisingly erect. Nobody talked about air resistance, and the four cylinders pushed the car through the atmosphere with a simple disregard of physical law.

There was this about a Model T: the purchaser never regarded his purchase as a complete, finished product. When you bought a Ford, you figured you had a start—a vibrant, spirited framework to which could be screwed an almost limitless assortment of decorative and functional hardware. Driving away from the agency, hugging the new wheel between your knees, you were already full of creative worry. A Ford was born naked as a baby, and a flourishing industry grew up out of correcting its rare deficiencies and combatting its fascinating diseases. Those were the great days of lily-painting. I have been looking at some old Sears Roebuck catalogues, and they bring everything back so clear.

First you bought a Ruby Safety Reflector for the rear, so that your posterior would glow in another's car's brilliance. Then you invested thirty-nine cents in some radiator Moto Wings, a popular ornament which gave the Pegasus touch to the machine and did something godlike to the owner. For nine cents you bought a fanbelt guide to keep the belt from slipping off the pulley.

You bought a radiator compound to stop leaks. This was as much a part of everybody's equipment as aspirin tablets are of a medicine cabinet. You bought special oil to prevent chattering, a clamp-on dash light, a patching outfit, a tool box which you bolted to the running board, a sun visor, a steering-column brace to keep the column rigid, and a set of emergency containers for gas, oil, and water—three thin, disc-like cans which reposed in a case on the running board during long, important journeys—red for gas, gray for water, green for oil. It was only a beginning. After the car was about a year old, steps were taken to check the alarming disintegration. (Model T was full of tumors, but they were benign.) A set of anti-rattlers (ninety-eight cents) was a popular panacea. You hooked them on to the gas and spark rods, to the brake pull rod, and to the steering-rod connections. Hood silencers, of black rubber, were applied to the fluttering hood. Shock-absorbers and snubbers gave "complete relaxation." Some people bought rubber pedal pads, to fit over the standard metal pedals. (I didn't like these, I remember.) Persons of a suspicious or pugnacious turn of mind bought a rear-view mirror; but most Model T owners weren't worried by what was coming from behind because they would soon enough see it out in front. They rode in a state of cheerful catalepsy. Quite a large mutinous clique among Ford owners went over to a foot accelerator (you could buy one and screw it to the floor board), but there was a certain madness in these people, because the Model T, just as she stood, had a choice of three foot pedals to push, and there were plenty of moments when both feet were occupied in the routine performance of duty and when the only way to speed up the engine was with the hand throttle.

Gadget bred gadget. Owners not only bought ready-made gadgets, they invented gadgets to meet special needs. I myself drove my car directly from the agency to the blacksmith's, and had the smith affix two enormous iron brackets to the port running board to support an army trunk.

People who owned closed models builded along different lines: they bought ball grip handles for opening doors, window antirattlers, and deluxe flower vases of the cut-glass antisplash type. People with delicate sensibilities garnished their car with a device called the Donna Lee Automobile Disseminator—a porous vase guaranteed, according to Sears, to fill the car with a "faint clean odor of lavender." The gap between open cars and closed cars was not as great then as it is now: for $11.95, Sears Roebuck converted your touring car into a sedan and you went forth renewed. One agreeable quality of the old Fords was that they had no bumpers, and their fenders softened and wilted with the years and permitted the driver to squeeze in and out of tight places.

Tires were 30 x 3½, cost about $12, and punctured readily. Everybody carried a Jiffy patching set, with a nutmeg grater to roughen the tube before the goo was spread on. Everybody was capable of putting on a patch, expected to have to, and did have to.

During my association with Model T's, self-starters were not a prevalent accessory. They were expensive and under suspicion. Your car came equipped with a serviceable crank, and the first thing you learned was how to Get Results. It was a special trick, and until you learned it (usually from another Ford owner, but sometimes by a period of appalling experimentation) you might as well have been winding up an awning. The trick was to leave the ignition switch off, proceed to the animal's head, pull the choke (which was a little wire protruding through the radiator) and give the crank two or three nonchalant upward lifts. Then, whistling as though thinking about something else, you would saunter back to the driver's cabin, turn the ignition on, return to the crank, and this time, catching it on the down stroke, give it a quick spin with plenty of that. If this procedure was followed, the engine almost always responded—first with a few scattered explosions, then with a tumultuous gunfire, which you checked by racing around to the driver's seat and retarding the throttle. Often, if the emergency brake hadn't been pulled all the way back, the car advanced on you the instant the first explosion occurred and you would hold it back by leaning your weight against it. I can still feel my old Ford nuzzling me at the curb, as though looking for an apple in my pocket.

In zero weather, ordinary cranking became an impossibility, except for giants. The oil thickened, and it became necessary to jack up the rear wheels, which, for some planetary reason, eased the throw.

The lore and legend that governed the Ford were boundless. Owners had their own theories about everything; they discussed mutual problems in that wise, infinitely resourceful way old women discuss rheumatism. Exact knowledge was pretty scarce, and often proved less effective than superstition. Dropping a camphor ball into the gas tank was a popular expedient; it seemed to have a tonic effect on both man and machine. There wasn't much to base exact knowledge on. The Ford driver flew blind. He didn't know the temperature of his engine, the speed of his car, the amount of his fuel, or the pressure of his oil (the old Ford lubricated itself by what was amiably described as the "splash system"). A speedometer cost money and was an extra, like a windshield wiper. The dashboard of the early models was bare save for an ignition key; later models, grown effete, boasted an ammeter which pulsated alarmingly with the throbbing of the car. Under the dash was a box of coils, with vibrators which you adjusted, or thought you adjusted. Whatever the driver learned of his motor, he learned not through instruments but through sudden developments. I remember that the timer was one of the vital organs about which there was ample doctrine. When everything else had been checked, you "had a look" at the timer. It was an extravagantly odd little device, simple in construction, mysterious in function. It contained a roller, held by a spring, and there were four contact points on the inside of the case against which, many people believed, the roller rolled. I have had a timer apart on a sick Ford many times. But I never really knew what I was up to— I was just showing off before God. There were almost as many schools of thought as there were timers. Some people, when things went wrong, just clenched their teeth and gave the timer a smart crack with a wrench. Other people opened it up and blew on it. There was a school that held that the timer needed large amounts of oil; they fixed it by frequent baptism. And there was a school that was positive it was meant to run dry as a bone; these people were continually taking it off and wiping it. I remember once spitting into a timer; not in anger, but in a spirit of research. You see, the Model T driver moved in the realm of metaphysics. He believed his car could be hexed.

One reason the Ford anatomy was never reduced to an exact science was that, having "fixed" it, the owner couldn't honestly claim that the treatment had brought about the cure. There were too many authenticated cases of Fords fixing themselves—restored naturally to health after a short rest. Farmers soon discovered this, and it fitted nicely with their draft-horse philosophy: "Let 'er cool off and she'll snap into it again."

A Ford owner had Number One Bearing constantly in mind. This bearing, being at the front end of the motor, was the one that always burned out, because the oil didn't reach it when the car was climbing hills. (That's what I was always told, anyway.) The oil used to recede and leave Number One dry as a clam flat; you had to watch that bearing like a hawk. It was like a weak heart—you could hear it start knocking, and that was when you stopped to let her cool off. Try as you would to keep the oil supply right, in the end Number One always went out. "Number One Bearing burned out on me and I had to have her replaced," you would say, wisely; and your companions always had a lot to tell about how to protect and pamper Number One to keep her alive.

Sprinkled not too liberally among the millions of amateur witch doctors who drove Fords and applied their own abominable cures were the heaven-sent mechanics who could really make the car talk. These professionals turned up in undreamed-of spots. One time, on the banks of the Columbia River in Washington, I heard the rear end go out of my Model T when I was trying to whip it up a steep incline onto the deck of a ferry. Something snapped; the car slid backward into the mud. It seemed to me like the end of the trail. But the captain of the ferry, observing the withered remnant, spoke up.

"What's got her?" he asked.

"I guess it's the rear end," I replied, listlessly. The captain leaned over the rail and stared. Then I saw that there was a hunger in his eyes that set him off from other men.

"Tell you what," he said, carelessly, trying to cover up his eagerness, "Let's pull the son of a bitch up onto the boat, and I'll help you fix her while we're going back and forth on the river."

We did just this. All that day I plied between the towns of Pasco and Kennewick, while the skipper (who had once worked in a Ford garage) directed the amazing work of resetting the bones of my car.

Springtime in the heyday of the Model T was a delirious season. Owning a car was still a major excitement, roads were still wonderful and bad. The Fords were obviously conceived in madness: any car which was capable of going from forward into reverse without any perceptible mechanical hiatus was bound to be a mighty challenging thing to the human imagination. Boys used to veer them off the highway into a level pasture and run wild with them, as though they were cutting up with a girl. Most everybody used the reverse pedal quite as much as the regular foot brake—it distributed the wear over the bands and wore them all down evenly. That was the big trick, to wear all the bands down evenly, so that the final chattering would be total and the whole unit scream for renewal.

The days were golden, the nights were dim and strange. I still recall with trembling those loud, nocturnal crises when you drew up to a signpost and raced the engine so the lights would be bright enough to read destinations by. I have never been really planetary since. I suppose it's time to say good-bye. Farewell, my lovely!

# THE YEARS OF WONDER

❧

Russia's foolish suggestion that a dam be thrown across Bering Strait brings back happy memories of that body of water and of certain youthful schemes and follies of my own. I passed through the Strait and on into the Arctic many years ago, searching for a longer route to where I didn't want to be. I was also in search of walrus. A dam, I am sure, would have been an annoyance.

I was rather young to be so far north, but there is a period near the beginning of every man's life when he has little to cling to except his unmanageable dream, little to support him except good health, and nowhere to go but all over the place. This period in my life lasted about eight years, and I spent the summer of one of those years in and around Alaska. It was the summer of 1923. In those days, I kept a diary, entering in it whatever was uppermost in my mind. I called it my journal; the word "journal," I felt, lent a literary and manly flavor to the thing. Diaries were what girls kept. A couple of years ago, when Alaska achieved statehood, I began digging into my journal for the year 1923, hoping to discover in its faded pages something instructive about the new state. This account, then, is a delayed account—some thirty-seven years late. I doubt that the reader will be able to put together a picture of Alaska from reading it, but he may catch a glimpse of the young diarist. And of the 1920s, that notorious decade that was almost a delirium.

My trip to Alaska, like practically everything else that happened to me in those busy years, was pure accident. I was living in Seattle; I was unemployed, my job on a newspaper having blown up in mid-June;

and although I had no reason for going to Alaska, I had no reason for staying away, either. The entries in my journal covering the four-week period between the loss of my job and the start of my trip to the north reveal a young man living a life of exalted footlessness. I was a literary man in the highest sense of the term, a poet who met every train. No splendor appeared in the sky without my celebrating it, nothing mean or unjust took place but felt the harmless edge of my wildly swinging sword. I walked in the paths of righteousness, studying girls. In particular, I studied a waitress in a restaurant called the Chantecler. I subscribed to two New York dailies, the *World* and the *Evening Post*. I swam alone at night in the canal that connects Lake Union and Lake Washington. I seldom went to bed before two or three o'clock in the morning, on the theory that if anything of interest were to happen to a young man it would almost certainly happen late at night. Daytimes, I hung around my room in Mrs. Donohue's boarding house, reading the "Bowling Green" and the "Conning Tower," wondering what to do next, and writing.

My entry for June 15, 1923, begins, "A man must have something to cling to. Without that he is as a pea vine sprawling in search of a trellis." Obviously, I was all asprawl, clinging to Beauty, which is a very restless trellis. My prose style at this time was a stomach-twisting blend of the Bible, Carl Sandburg, H. L. Mencken, Jeffrey Farnol, Christopher Morley, Samuel Pepys, and Franklin Pierce Adams imitating Samuel Pepys. I was quite apt to throw in a "bless the mark" at any spot, and to begin a sentence with "Lord" comma.

On June 19, I recorded my discharge from the *Times* and noted that the city editor said it was "no reflection on my ability." I didn't believe then, and do not believe now, that it was no reflection on my ability. As a newspaper reporter, I was almost useless, and it came as no surprise when one more trellis collapsed on me. When I left the *Times* office with my final pay check in my pocket, I "sauntered" down Pine Street. I can still recall experiencing an inner relief—the feeling of again being adrift on life's sea, an element I felt more at home in than in a city room. On June 25, I clipped a sonnet sequence by Morley from the "Bowling Green" and pasted it in the journal. The second sonnet began, "So put your trust in poets." As though I needed to be told that!

On July 2, I entered in my journal a copy of a poem I had written and mailed anonymously to the Reverend Mark A. Matthews, pastor of the First Presbyterian Church, who had preached a sermon I found offensive. A résumé of the sermon had appeared in the Monday morning paper. Dr. Matthews had attacked nonchurchgoers, of whom I was one.

On the following Sunday, I departed from my usual stance and became a churchgoer, attending the morning service at the First Presbyterian to make a routine check on my man. "The smugness of his doctrine," I wrote in my journal, "made the air stifling." Probably what really made the air stifling for me was that in his sermon the minister made no mention of having received my stinging communication.

For one week I worked on Hearst's *Post-Intelligencer*, commonly called the *P.I.*, substituting for a reporter on vacation. My entry for July 18 (1:30 A.M.) begins, "A man scarce realizes what a terrible thing scorn is until he begins to despise himself." I doubt that I found myself despicable; I simply found life perplexing. I did not know where to go. On Friday, July 20 (3 A.M.), appears the abrupt entry, "I sail Monday on S.S. Buford for Skagway." No explanation or amplification follows, only an account of an evening spent with a girl who lived on Lake Union. (She fed me bread and apple jelly.)

I did, however, clip from the *P.I.* and paste into my journal the item that started me on my way to Alaska. The story was headed

S. F. CHAMBER
TO SEE ALASKA

and began:

> The resources and trade conditions of Alaska will be studied by a delegation from the San Francisco Chamber of Commerce, which will leave San Francisco today on the steamer *Buford* for an 8,300 mile trip to Alaska and Siberia, via Seattle. The group will also include citizens of other cities, among them ten Boston capitalists, and the trip will be in charge of B. S. Hubbard, vice president of the Schwabacher-Frey Stationery Company.

A number of things must have attracted me to this item in the news. First, the ship was to call at Seattle. I was a dockside regular at this period, and any ship at all was of interest to me. Second, Alaska was in the opposite direction from home, where I considered it unsuitable to be at my age. Third, a Chamber of Commerce was involved, and this opened up familiar vistas. As a reporter, I had spent many a lunch hour covering the noonday gatherings of fraternal and civic groups; Seattle was a hotbed of Elks, Eagles, Moose, Lions, Kiwanians, Rotarians, and members of the Young Men's Business Association. I had broken the hard roll countless times with Chamber of Commerce people, had laughed courteously at their jokes and listened patiently to their tales of industrial growth. I was under the influence of Mencken and Lewis, and felt proud disdain for business and for businessmen. It was important to me at that time to move among people toward whom I felt aloof and superior, even though I secretly envied their ability to earn a living.

Perhaps the clincher in the news story of the *Buford* was the list of the ports of call, names that were music to the ear of youth: Ketchikan, Taku Glacier, Juneau, Skagway, Sitka, Cordova, Seward, Kodiak, Cold Bay, Lighthouse Rocks, Dutch Harbor, Bogoslof Island, the Pribilof Islands, Cape Chaplin, Anadir. "From Nome, they [the voyagers] will pass the ice pack, proceeding to East Cape, Siberia, and then return to Nome. On the home trip they will stop at St. Michael, Akutan and Seattle, the entire trip requiring forty days."

Forty days! To me, forty days was a mere siesta in time's long afternoon, and I could cling, for lack of anything else, to the ship. The Pribilof Islands with ten Boston capitalists—sheer enchantment! All I needed was a job on the ship, and this I determined to get. The *Buford* arrived in due course and tied up to Pier 7. Every day while she was there, I sneaked aboard and hung about the corridors, waylaying ship's officers and offering my services in any capacity. When, after three days, I found no taker, I made inquiries and learned that for $40 I could sail as a first-class passenger as far as Skagway, which is at the head of the Inside Passage. This enabled me to shift my strategy; I *had* $40 and I decided to launch myself in the direction of the Arctic by the sheer power of money. Once firmly entrenched in the ship, I could from that vantage point pursue my job-hunting. The second steward gave me a bit of encouragement. "Anything can happen in a ship," he said. And he turned out to be right.

To start for Alaska this way, alone and with no assurance of work and a strong likelihood of being stranded in Skagway, was a dippy thing to do, but I believed in giving Luck frequent workouts. It was part of my philosophy at that time to keep Luck toned up by putting her to the test; otherwise she might get rusty. Besides, the 1920s, somehow or other, provided the winy air that supported dippiness. The twenties even supported the word "dippy."

You might suppose that the next few entries in my journal, covering the days when I must have been winding up my affairs and getting ready to sail on a long voyage of discovery, would offer a few crumbs of solid information. Not at all. From Friday morning, when I announced that I would soon be off, until the departure of the *Buford*, several days later, my journal contains no helpful remarks, no hint of preparation, no facts about clothes, money, friends, family, anything. A few aphorisms; a long, serious poem to the girl on Lake Union ("Those countless, dim, immeasurable years," it begins); a Morley clipping from the "Bowling Green" about writing ("A child writes well, and a highly trained and long-suffering performer may sometimes write with intelligence. It is the middle stages that are appalling. . . ."); a short effort in vers libre written on Sunday morning and describing my boardinghouse slatting around in the doldrums of a summer Sabbath—that is all I find in these tantalizing pages. Mr. Morley was right; the middle stages are appalling. As a diarist, I was a master of suspense, leaving to the reader's imagination everything pertinent to the action of my play. I operated, generally, on too high a level for routine reporting, and had not at that time discovered the eloquence of facts. I can see why the *Times* fired me. A youth who persisted in rising above facts must have been a headache to a city editor.

Memory helps out on a couple of points. I recall that winding up my affairs was chiefly a matter of getting a Ford coupé repossessed by the finance company. My other affairs were portable and would go along —a Corona typewriter, a copy of *Lyric Forms from France*, and my wardrobe, which fitted cozily into one droopy suitcase. I owned an unabridged Webster's, but I am quite sure I did not take it—probably placed it in safekeeping with a friend. The luckiest thing that happened to me was that my wardrobe included a very old and shabby flannel shirt and a dirty pair of dungarees. Without these I would have been in some difficulty later on.

The *Buford* did not get away until almost ten on Tuesday evening, thirty-four hours behind schedule. As the lines were cast off, I stood at the starboard rail and watched the lights of the city—the Bon Marché sign, the tower of the Smith Building—and was shaken by the sudden loud blast of the whistle giving finality to my adventure. Then, it would appear, I sat right down and wrote what was for me a fairly lucid account of the departure. I listed some of the items that had come aboard: beeves, hams, nuts, machinery for Cold Bay, oranges, short ribs, and a barber's chair. I noted that when this last item was carried up the plank, the passengers lining the rail broke into applause. (Already they were starved for entertainment.)

At sundown the following evening, July 25, we passed a tall gray ship that rode at anchor in a small cove near a fishing village. On board was President Harding, homeward bound from Alaska. A band on his ship played, and the President came to the rail and waved a handkerchief borrowed from his wife. The incident caused a stir among the passengers and crew of our ship; seeing the President of the United States in such an unlikely spot, on our way to the mysterious North, was reassuring. About a week later came the radiogram telling of his death.

The voyage of the *Buford* carrying the men of commerce to the

Arctic wasteland was an excursion both innocent and peculiar. It inaugurated a new steamship line, the Alaskan-Siberian Navigation Company, and I think the company had been hard up for passengers and had persuaded the Chamber to conduct a trade tour and bring wives. The *Buford* herself, however, was in no way peculiar; she was a fine little ship. She had been a troop carrier in the war, and afterward had been reconverted to carry passengers and freight. She was deep, was not overburdened with superstructure, and had a wide, clear main deck. Painted in tall block letters on her topsides and extending half her length were the words SAN FRANCISCO CHAMBER OF COMMERCE. This enormous label gave her a little the look of a lightship—all name and no boat—and in many a desolate northern port, where the only commerce was with Eskimos who swarmed aboard to peddle ivory paper cutters, the label acquired a bizarre and wistful meaning.

One of the things I know now, and did not know at the time, is that the *Buford* was being bought from the government on the installment plan. The owners never managed to complete their payments, and by 1925 she was being referred to in the San Francisco *Chronicle* as "the hard-luck ship *Buford*." Everything she touched turned to dross. The owners not only never completed their payments, they never fully completed the reconversion of the ship, either. I remember a room in the 'tween-decks that obviously dated from troop-carrying days. It was a spacious room furnished with a truly magnificent battery of urinals and toilets standing at attention and perfectly exposed—a palace of open convenience, seldom visited, except by me, who happened, at one juncture, to live close by. A lonely, impressive room. I have an idea that when the owners took possession of their ship, they must have taken one look at this panorama of plumbing and decided to let it stand. To have laid a wrench to it would have cost a fortune.

Our commander was Captain Louis L. Lane, a handsome, sociable man who delighted the ladies by his strong profile and reassured us all by his fine handling of the ship. He had been in the Arctic before, loved it, and was known and welcomed everywhere. I think he quite enjoyed the adventurous role he was cast in: shepherd of a crowd of landlubbers and dudes in wild, remote places where he had local knowledge and could display his special talents. No gunkhole was too small for Captain Lane to squeeze the *Buford* into. Before we were done with the voyage, though, I got the impression that our captain operated under unusual difficulties. The strong tides and treacherous currents of the Inside Passage, the cold, enveloping fogs of the Bering Sea, the shifting floes of the ice pack in the lonely, silent, too bright Arctic—these were strain enough on a man, but they were slight compared to the cold white bank of boredom that gradually enveloped the passengers, several of whom, I believe, would gladly have paid any reasonable sum to have the ship turn about and head back for the Golden Gate. Captain Lane in mid-passage was the host at a party that was not going too well.

All pleasure cruises have moments of tedium, but usually the passengers can relax on sunny decks, swim in warm pools, go ashore every day or two where the ladies can plunder the shops and the men can stretch their legs and bend their elbows. The *Buford*, skirting the long coastline of Alaska in the early twenties, did not offer much relief of this sort. For some the *Buford* became a high-class floating jail—the food good, the scenery magnificent, but no escape. A hundred and seventy-odd passengers did a six-week stretch, and their spirits sagged as the scenery became increasingly familiar. In the fog, the scenic effect was dampening to many a spirit; for long periods the forecastlehead was barely visible from the door of the main cabin. The horn sounded daylong and nightlong.

Whoever planned this odd voyage for the expansion of trade had, of course, foreseen the need of entertainment and had done his best. Provision had been made for music, dancing, gaming, and drinking. Music was in charge of the Six Brown Brothers, a saxophone combo that had once performed in a show with Fred Stone. I have a fine, sharp photograph of the Brothers taken at the Akutan whaling station; they are standing in front of a dead whale, their saxophones at the ready. Adventure was in charge of H. A. Snow, a big-game hunter, who brought along his elephant gun, his movie camera, and his son Sydney. The ship was well stocked with private supplies of liquor. One of the owners of the ship, J. C. Ogden, came along for the ride, and this gave the thing the air of a real outing. But although there was an occasional diversion, the days were largely without incident and without cheer. Even such advertised treats as the stop at the Pribilofs to see the seal rookeries proved anticlimactic to many of the students of trade conditions; the place smelled bad and the seals looked like the ones you had seen in zoos and circuses. Some of the passengers, having gone to the great trouble and expense of reaching the Pribilof Islands, chose, when they got there, to remain on board and play bridge. As for me, I never had a dull moment, I lived on three successive levels socially, a gradual descent that to me seemed a climb: first the promenade deck, then the main deck, then below. I was busy, but not too busy to journalize, and I was young enough to absorb with gratitude and wonder the vast, splendid scene of Alaska in the time before the airplane brought it to our door and when it was still inaccessible and legendary.

When, in Seattle, I presented myself to the purser as a paying passenger, he assigned me to a small room with another man. This fellow turned out to be an oddball like me—not a member of the Chamber. He was a Laplander, a short, stocky man with a long mustache. His clothes were rough; he had no white shirts and almost no English. "I go Nomee," was all he could tell me at first. His name was Isak Nakkalo, and he was a reindeer butcher on his way to a job. Isak and I dwelt in peace and in silence day after day, until life changed abruptly for me and I began my descent. All up the Inside Passage, while the *Buford* skirted headlands and dodged rocks and reefs, Isak took no part in the social life aboard ship, but I did. I struck up a few acquaintances, danced to the sweet jazz of the Brown Brothers, nursed my clean shirts to get the maximum mileage out of them, and displayed affability (if not knowledge) in the matter of trade relations. I also lived a secret life. At every opportunity, I bearded stewards, engineers, and deck officers, and asked for work. My encounters with these people must have mystified them; at sea, a first-class passenger looking for work is irregular. I was probably worse than irregular; I was annoying.

Ketchikan was our first Alaskan port of call and the scene of the passengers' first disillusionment. In the minds of most of us aboard was an image of Alaska formed by Robert W. Service and Jack London—a land of deep snow, igloos, Eskimos, polar bears, rough men, fancy women, saloons, fighting sled dogs, intense cold, and gold everywhere. Ketchikan as we rounded the bend, delivered a shattering blow to this fine image; the village was a warm, mosquitoey place, smelling of fish. Not an igloo was in sight, and on the dock to greet us was a small, moth-eaten band of Shriners in their caps. But, image or no image, this was our frontier, and long before the ship was close enough for voices to carry, the passengers began shouting questions to the group ashore. One of our shipboard Shriners ached to know whether there was going to be a ceremonial that night. The distant welcoming group cupped their ears. "I say is there going to be a ceremonial tonight?" he bellowed. The words were lost in air. Mr. Hubbard, our tour master, began bellowing, too. He wanted to know whether a representative of the Ketchikan Commercial Club was on hand.

I sat on a bollard in the warm sun, watching these antics indulgently, I, a graduate of the University of Mencken and Lewis, studying the spectacle of Babbittry northbound—men visiting a strange land yet craving not strangeness but a renewal of what was familiar. I can still recall the agitation of Mr. Hubbard on this occasion—a pioneer in a sack suit glimpsing his frontier at last and taut with emotion. As the ship was being warped alongside, Mr. Hubbard saw the boatswain swing himself over the rail, grasp a hawser, and slide down onto the dock. Eager to make contact with the Commercial Club man, Mr. Hubbard stepped over the rail and took hold of the hawser. But the dock was a long way down, and there was still an ugly gully of water between ship and dock. Twice Mr. Hubbard flexed his legs in a test take-off, both times lost his nerve. His face wore a grim look, and he soon had an audience, just as a suicide on a ledge gets one. For a few tense moments, the launching of Mr. Hubbard into Alaska held everyone spellbound, but it never came off. Prudence conquered zeal, and our first brush with the frontier was a defeat for the spirit of San Francisco.

Later, when I went ashore, via the plank, I "lounged down the street" (I was always "lounging" or "sauntering" in my journal) and bought a copy of *Faint Perfume*, by Zona Gale. Because the town smelled of fish, I considered this purchase clownish. Of such flimsy delights were my days made in those delectable years.

That evening, the Shriners had their ceremonial, the Commercial Club had its meeting, the ladies from the ship bought great numbers of Indian baskets, and one of the oilers from the *Buford*'s engine-room crew managed to get ashore and establish trade relations with a half-breed girl. "Big, like that," he told me afterward. (I was already cultivating the society of firemen and sailors, hoping to be admitted.) When everyone had satisfied his own peculiar needs and refreshed himself in the way he knew best, the *Buford* let go her lines and continued north through the tortuous straits of the Alexander Archipelago. I was an extremely callow and insecure young man, but as I examine my record of Ketchikan and translate it from the Chinese in which it is written, I can see that I was not alone in my insecurity; all of us were seeking reassurance of one sort or another—some with mystic rites and robes, some with the metaphysics of commerce, some with expensive Indian baskets and inexpensive Indian girls. I was enraptured with my surroundings—contemptuous of all, envious of all, proud, courageous, and scared to death.

On the morning of Sunday, July 29, we sighted Taku Glacier, a scheduled point of interest. When we brought it abeam, Captain Lane stopped the ship and everyone rushed on deck. "The bridegroom," I noted in my journal, "dashed to get his polo coat and his yellow gloves. The bride put on her polo coat to match. Everybody put on something special. Walter Brunt, potentate of Islam Temple, put on his monkey cap in case he should get into a photograph with the glacier in the background."

The whale boat was lowered and Sydney Snow was rowed off to get pictures of the *Buford* against the glacier. But Captain Lane was not easily satisfied; he wanted his charges to see that a glacier is really a river of ice, discharging into the sea. Taku, in the manner of glaciers, was sulking in its tent and taking its own sweet time about discharging into the sea; it needed prodding. Accordingly, Mr. Snow was called on to stir things up. He hurried to the bridge with his elephant gun and opened fire on Taku, while Sydney, in the whaleboat, cranked away at his camera. Nothing happened. For about an hour, there was desultory fire from the bridge while the passengers hung expectantly at the rail. Then they wearied of the spectacle of a reluctant glacier, and most of them drifted away toward the dining saloon. A few minutes before noon, whether from rifle fire or from sheer readiness, a piece of ice did fall into the sea. It made a fine splash. Passengers who had deserted the deck rushed back but were, of course, too late.

As I stood at the rail studying Taku Glacier, I was joined by the *Buford's* storekeeper, a solemn, thoughtful man. For a few moments he stared quietly at the great wall of ice. "How do you like it?" I asked, between volleys. He took my question seriously and his answer was slow in coming. "I don't care for it," he replied, at last, and walked aft to resume his duties. As our voyage progressed and we ventured farther and farther into nowhere, with sea and sky and fog and ice and the white wings of gulls for our backdrop, the storekeeper's measured words became more and more expressive of the inner feelings of many of the tourists; they did not care for it.

At Juneau, I watched one of the Brown Brothers fishing in the rain, and wrote an unrhymed poem: "Grapefruit and oranges in the green water off Juneau dock—grapefruit and oranges, part of the ship's scum." Sandburg had me by the throat in those days. Alaskan towns, I reported in my journal, "are just murmurings at the foot of mountains."

One of the faintest of these murmurings was Skagway, where my ticket ran out. The *Buford* tied up at the dock there on the last day of July. My search for a job on board had been vain. I put my Corona in its case, packed my bag, and went on deck to sit awhile in sorrow and in fear, delaying until the last possible moment my walk down the plank and into the forlorn street of Skagway—a prospector twenty-five years late and not even primarily interested in gold.

While I was sitting there on deck (my journal says I was "browsing" there), trying to sort out my troubles and wondering how I had managed to get myself into this incredible mess, I received a summons to the bridge. A Miss Linderman, according to my account, presented herself to me and delivered the message. "The captain wants to see you right away" was all she said. Oddly enough, I did not associate this summons with my job-hunting; I had no idea what was up, and felt like a schoolboy called to the principal's office. The message seemed ominous, but less ominous than the imminent trip down the gangplank into murmurous Skagway. I hustled to the bridge.

Captain Lane stared at me for a moment. Then he said, "We can put you on as night saloonsman for the remainder of the voyage—workaway passage. Is that satisfactory?"

"Yes, sir," I replied. I didn't know what a night saloonsman was, or a workaway passage, but I was in no mood for quibbling, and if Captain Lane had offered to tow me astern at the end of a long rope I would have grabbed the chance. I thanked my captain, reported to the second steward, and that night turned up in the dining saloon wearing a white jacket and carrying a napkin slung over my left forearm, in the manner of right-handed waiters the world over. The crisis of Skagway was behind me, and pretty soon Skagway was, too, as the *Buford* steamed west toward the Aleutians at her steady pace of eleven knots.

I cannot recall Miss Linderman—she is a name on a page, that is all—but among the handful of women who have distinguished themselves in some great way in my life she occupies a high position. I never found out exactly what happened; I never even tried to find out. This much is clear: the news that a job-hunter was loose on board finally reached the captain, just as the news would have reached him that a harmless snake was loose in the hold, and he reluctantly disposed of the matter in the easiest way, as he settled many another small but pesky problem in the business of running that crazy tour.

(Since beginning this account, I've been looking into the files of the San Francisco *Chronicle* for 1923 for news of the *Buford* and its company. One of the owners of the line, it appears, was a Mr. John Linderman, and the passenger list shows the presence on board of several Linderman girls—his daughters, I suppose. So I guess I was bailed out of Skagway by the daughter of an owner. Inasmuch as Mr. Linderman and his partner Mr. Ogden were buying the ship on the installment plan, and had slim prospects of making the thing pay, I think the management was foolhardy to take on another mouth to feed. But I still value Miss Linderman highly.)

Working in a ship is a far better life than sailing in one as a passenger. Alaska, the sea, and the ship herself became real to me as soon as I was employed; before that, all three had suffered from a sort of insubstantiality. Passengers never really come to know a ship; too much is hidden from their sight, too little is demanded of them. They may love their ship, but without their participating in her operation the identification is not established. As saloonsman, I was a participant—at first a slightly sick participant. I worked from eight in the evening till six in the morning. I set tables, prepared late supper for thirty, served it (sometimes carrying a full tray in a beam sea), cleaned the tables, washed the dishes, stropped the glasses, swept down the companionway leading to the social hall, and shined brass. This was hard work, dull work, and, until my stomach adjusted to the ripe smell of the pantry, touchy work. But when, at around three o'clock, I stepped out onto the forward deck for a smoke, with the sky showing bright in the north and the mate pacing the bridge and the throaty snores of the passengers issuing from the staterooms, the ship would throb and tremble under me and she was *my* ship, all mine and right on course, alive and purposeful and exciting. No longer was the *Buford* merely taking me from one benighted port to another; now she was transporting me from all my yesterdays to all my tomorrows. It was I who seemed to make her go, almost as though I were a quartermaster with my hand on the wheel.

My metamorphosis from passenger to saloonsman took the passengers by surprise and created a certain awkwardness at the late supper. A few of the first-class people knew me by name and most of them knew me by sight; naturally they felt uneasy when they found me at their service. There was the matter of tipping. Should a girl with whom I had danced between Seattle and Skagway leave a coin for me when I handed her a cold cut between Skagway and Cordova? A delicate question. One elderly female, flustered at seeing me in saloonsman's garb, cried, "Goodness! How long have *you* been a waitress?" I regarded my change in status as extremely comical, played it deadpan, and made quite a to-do about it in my journal, greatly exaggerating its comic value. Embarrassed at first, I soon felt an elevation of spirit and wore my white jacket like a plume. In my mouth was the taste of a fresh superiority over my fellow man; not only was I leading a secret literary life among the mercantile crowd but I was now a busy, employed man, gainfully occupied among wastrels and idlers. Always hungry myself and indulging in snacks at every opportunity, I nevertheless adopted a patronizing air toward those who appeared for the pre-bedtime meal, regarding their appetite at that hour as gross and contemptible. The hardest part of the job for me was remembering orders; I would stand attentively listening to a group of four telling me what they wanted, and by the time I reached the pantry the whole recital would be gone from my head. As a member of the Steward Department, I was permitted by the rules to go on deck to catch some air but was not permitted to sit down while on deck. I ceased mingling with the passengers and joined the much juicier fraternity of pantrymen and cooks, denizens of the glory hole in the stern of the ship next to the steering engine—a noisy, aromatic place, traditional seat of intrigue and corruption. I joined the glory-hole crowd, but I was not shifted to the glory hole itself; instead, I was assigned a bunk in a small, airless inside room, first class, with a young man named J. Wilbur Wolf. Wilbur was the other night saloonsman, and, like me, was burdened with a college education and an immaculate past. The second steward, a cagey man, chose not to inject Wilbur and me into the glory hole, where we properly belonged. The second may have feared that our morals would be corrupted, but I think he simply did not wish to disturb the gamy society of the hole by introducing two young dudes of almost unparalleled innocence. It would have made him uneasy.

At Cordova, we received by radio the news of Harding's death, and I copied into my journal the notice on the ship's bulletin board:

SAN FRANCISCO

President Warren G. Harding died here tonight at 7:30 o'clock. He was stricken without any warning. Mrs. Harding was with him at the last. See the second steward about your laundry.

"Here," I wrote in pensive vein, "is a very fine illustration of how the world jogs on, come what may." Apparently the realization that people would continue to have their dirty clothes washed after the death of Warren Gamaliel Harding struck me forcibly.

At all events, the *Buford* jogged on, come what might. As she glided up the wide aisle of Resurrection Bay toward Seward, the Brown Brothers gathered in the social hall and rehearsed suitable numbers for an impromptu memorial service. Hearing the sad sounds of their muted horns drifting out and mingling with the crying of gulls, I was afflicted with melancholy at the loss of my President—I felt bereft. Mr. Harding is not greatly mourned these days, but we of the *Buford* blew him a heartfelt tribute from Seward that night, on six jolly saxophones hastily converted to solemnity.

In those northern waters in 1923, Captain Lane guided the *Buford* much in the manner of early aviators: he flew by the seat of his pants. Approaching Kodiak, we ran into thick weather. All afternoon the ship crept blindly through a cold, drizzly fog. We felt obliged to make Kodiak because we had a passenger to discharge, and for the newborn Alaskan-Siberian Navigation Company the discharge of even one passenger was an event of considerable moment, tending to add luster and credibility to the trip. The passenger in this case was an Airedale terrier, but that didn't diminish the matter. With visibility close to zero, the skipper became unsure of his position, and his uncertainty was magically transmitted to the passengers. I heard a couple of ladies nervously ask an officer whether we shouldn't just drop anchor and wait for the weather to clear. (This would probably have been one of the longest sea waits on record.) After a while, a fishing boat appeared under our bow, its crew gave us our position by shouting and pointing, and away we went on an altered course. Captain Lane went ashore that night after a hard day at the chart table. He did not get back to the ship till late. I was called to his cabin at three in the morning to clear away glasses and bottles. I find the following entry, written an hour earlier:

> Monday morning    4 bells.    Kodiak
> The brass is shined. The dishes are put away. Wilbur sits across the aisle, dozing at another table. In the pantry the coffee urn simmers and from the ceiling the steam drops in little globules. The Skipper is not aboard yet, as far as we can tell. At any rate he hasn't appeared for his coffee: we have a place neatly set for him with cold meats, bread, and relishes.

This entry bears the telltale mark of a writer at work. The sixth sentence first read, "At any rate he hasn't appeared for his coffee yet," and I edited it, crossing out the word "yet," which was a sensible move, rhetorically, and shows that I was working away at a hard trade at a late hour. Wilbur, he who dozed, was also a diarist, although I didn't know it at the time. Two night saloonsmen, both of them diarists—a strange, unearthly ship in a strange, cold sea! A portion of Wilbur's diary is now in my possession. His widow recently sent it to me—a tiny notebook crammed with loathing for the menial life. "No more of this 'working your way' stuff—if I can't go first class I stay at home." Wilbur's urge to restore himself to a decent place in society was as compelling as my own urge to make my way farther down in the ship, sink to the depths and try the rapture of human dereliction and drudgery.

My next entry is a poem called "Lament." It begins:

> Millions of songs are knocking round, back and forth, inside my head:
>     songs of praise and of wonder. But I can not give birth even to one
>     song.

An odd statement. I was giving birth almost continuously, like a hamster. None of the songs had any merit, but there was no lack of parturition.

The passengers' disappointment with the Territory of Alaska was often quite apparent. Dutch Harbor, our next stop, did nothing to lift their spirits. A few deserted houses, a family of Indians, a sow and her three young ones—hardly a place made to order for San Francisco ladies bent on sightseeing. I went ashore and followed a muddy path over a small hill and sat down in the grass where I could look across at Unalaska. This village, seen from that distance, was a picture-book place —a single row of white frame buildings, one of them a little Greek Orthodox church with two green onion spires. Behind the town, rising out of the sea in soft and billowing folds, were green treeless hills draped in swirls of drifting fog. They seemed incredibly lofty and massive, those hills—a backdrop for a dream sequence. I wanted desperately to visit Unalaska, but was not free to go, since I had duties on board.

While I sat there, staring, two ladies from the *Buford* came along and stopped in front of me.

"Is there anything over there worth seeing?" one of them asked, thinking I had been there. "From here, it looks to me as if it was pretty dead. If there's something special about that church, I want to go on, but otherwise, if there isn't anything special, I don't care about going. Do you, Kate?"

Kate shook her head. The two of them seemed ineffably sad and uprooted.

I told them I hadn't been to Unalaska but guessed there was nothing special. And on that report they turned listlessly back toward the ship.

Later on, I contrived to get over to the village; a boy in a small boat ferried me across. By some standards, the place could have been called dead, but, walking the length of Unalaska at the foot of the green, tumbled hills, alone and wonder-struck, I felt more alive than I had ever felt before in my life. I was about as far west as a man could conveniently get on this continent, I was a long, long way from home, songs of praise knocked in my head, and I felt a gush of exhilaration. Added to my cup of pleasure was the knowledge that when I returned to the ship I could go to bed instead of having to work all night; my job had changed abruptly. For the remainder of the voyage, I was to be messboy to the firemen.

At dawn that day, the second steward, my boss, had appeared in the pantry, where I was deep in dishes. "You can knock off," he said. "Tomorrow I'm putting you on as firemen's messboy—take care of eight men, firemen's mess, and you won't need the white coat. We'll sign you on the articles at fifty a month."

Although the second did not mention it, I had heard rumors of a fight below in the ship—someone had got knifed—and I was reasonably certain that my new job was connected with this affair. I figured I was the replacement for the knifee. This turned out to be correct. At any rate, I obeyed orders; I went to my room, fished my old flannel shirt and dirty trousers from my bag, and turned in, wondering why I was to receive fifty dollars for feeding eight people when I had been receiving nothing but my passage for feeding about thirty. I knew there was a catch in it somewhere, but I dropped off to sleep. At six the following morning, I reported for work. This was the true beginning of the voyage for me; I was below at last, where the ship's heartbeat was audible and her body odor undispersed.

Why did I long to be below? I don't know. I just remember that I did and that this descent seemed a difficult but necessary step up life's ladder. The whole Alaskan experience was a subconscious attempt to escape from the world, to put off whatever was in store for me; the farther down inside a ship I went, the better the hiding place. Moreover, I wanted to test myself—throw myself into any flame that was handy, to see if I could stand the heat.

The firemen's messroom proved to be a dandy crucible. No young man could have asked for a more direct exposure to heat, fumes, toil, and trouble. The room was small and rank-smelling, with a porthole a few feet above the waterline. When I close my eyes these days and think of Alaska, the picture always comes to me in a round frame, for I viewed much of our future forty-ninth state through the porthole of the firemen's mess, and the picture has a special smell—a blend of cabbage, garbage, steam, filth, fuel oil, engine oil, exhausted air, exhausted men. It is a smell you get nowhere but in a ship.

At one end of the room was a warming table through which live steam passed, a little of it always escaping in whispers and causing the room to overheat. In the center stood the mess table, flanked by two benches. On the side away from the porthole were a sink, a garbage can, and our shrine—the coffee urn. This urn was hooked up to the ship's steam lines. It had an intake valve, an exhaust valve, and a glass gauge in which the coffee slowly rose and fell with the motion of the ship. I soon learned to tell the *Buford*'s angle of heel by glancing at my gauge. Filth set the tone of the room, and the smell was steady and reliable. Filth had accumulated in subtle ways: bits of tired soap stashed away in tin cans, morsels of rotten meat tucked between the pipes overhead, slices of raisin bread that had been deflowered and left to die, cheese that had been placed in safekeeping behind the urn—everywhere trinkets and keepsakes. The former messboy, like so many millions of people on land and on sea, had saved against a rainy day. It was easy to see why the firemen had taken matters into their own hands, finally, and brought his regime to a bloody close. But I think untidiness was only part of the story.

As I stood there on an empty stomach at six o'clock on that first morning and received my instructions from the second steward, I felt dizzy, sick, and scared. The instructions were sketchy, and the second acted as though he wanted to get away while I was still conscious and willing. He told me I was to carry the firemen's grub down from the main galley, serve it, clean up afterward, make the bunks in the forecastle, empty the garbage into a chute in the ship's side, keep the coffee always fresh and hot, keep the toilets clean, and do what the men said. "You take care of them—you do what they tell you," he said. "I'm still your boss, and if you get into any bad trouble, let me know. But they're the ones you have to satisfy." Then he introduced me curtly to my opposite number, a Puerto Rican youth named Luis, who was the sailors' messboy, and who would show me the ropes. The second then departed. I don't recall that he ever showed up again in the small world I now inhabited.

Luis was a twitchy youth swathed in a long, dirty sweater dangling to his knees. He had two eyes, but only one of them was on duty; the other peered straight ahead into another—and, I think, better—world.

"What job you come from?" he asked.

"Night saloon," I answered.

"Ahhh! Then you know how to steal. That is good." He seemed vastly relieved. My men, he explained, would expect delicacies obtainable only by the light-fingered.

Being shown the ropes by Luis turned out to be a dizzying experience—like being taught to fly a plane by a bright child. "Come ong, boy!" he said, and started out on the run, singing "Rock of Ages" in Spanish. Luis was evanescent, volatile, and loaded with interesting fancies and misconceptions, many of which did not pertain to the mess. He thought seals could fly, and he thought Harding had just been married, not buried. Steam valves mystified and excited him, and he couldn't keep his hands off them. As he scampered here and there, with me tagging along, he warned me about the low state to which I had fallen. The black gang, he said, were the lowest bunch in the ship, and I would be their servant, which made me low man. He described the firemen as having conceits and passions that were incredibly irregular and troublesome. And he warned me about the language in the messroom and forecastle. "Gee, boy," he said sorrowfully, "they use awfool language. Sonna mon beetsch, it is terrible the way they talk, those bastards."

I wasn't worried about any naughty words I might hear, but I had other worries. I knew I was a lamb set down among wolves, and I was greatly concerned lest the firemen, my masters, remember my face as belonging to first class and find out about my past, which was too dainty for a messroom. I was marred by gentility and stained with education. Worst of all, I had come aboard first class, and, thanks to the caprice of the second steward, I still occupied part of a first-class cabin. I knew well enough that these incriminating facts would have to be concealed if I were to survive. I felt like a man who was committed some monstrous crime in the past, one he will have to live down by good conduct. Stealing seemed my golden chance to redeem myself from my early infamy. I determined to be very brave and steal carefully and well. I decided to do my work, give good service, and keep my trap shut. My assets were that I was wearing a two-day beard and clothes that bore the clear imprint of toil.

The first breakfast was crucial and was served in a dense cloud of live steam. Luis had flipped the valves of my coffee urn in passing, the urn had erupted, and the room had become a Turkish bath. I could barely see the men's faces through the murk, blackened and stained as they were with engine-room oil and dirt. But they couldn't see mine, either, which was a break. They complained angrily about the steam bath, and when they found a new boy serving them, their curiosity was aroused, and I was required to answer questions and fill them in on my past. This I did in broad strokes, using place names and dismal events, always derogatory to management. Everywhere I had worked I had got fired, I said. The men were pleased with this familiar indignity, and they loved place names. (I was well fixed for names, as I had spent the previous summer crossing the continent, working at odd jobs.) In Cody, I said, I had sandpapered an open-air dance floor all day for a lousy three bucks. In Minneapolis, I had peddled roach powder, door to door. In Big Timber, I had worked as a hay hand. And everywhere I had got sacked. This was my simple card of admission. Sight unseen, the men hated all my past employers. I was now their boy. As I dodged about, dishing up oatmeal and trying to subdue the urn, my courage began to return. After the first loud outburst, the men settled into a dull guzzle and the question period came to an end. One or two of the faces looked positively amiable. Two of my fellows, I later found out, had been in jail, which I regarded as adventurous and laudable, and one of them was suffering from a venereal disease, which I found disquieting and worrisome. The memory of the famous Army film *Fit to Fight* was still fresh, and I assumed that I would soon contract the disease merely from using the same cutlery.

My name, I discovered, was Mess. "Get me an orange tonight, Mess!" one of the wipers said as he left the room after my debut. I knew from the sound of his voice that this was a direct order. I perceived, too, that the wiper was less interested in the sweetness of an orange than in the sweetness of having a personal servant to bedevil. Below decks, fresh fruit was not part of the diet; to get an orange, you had to either grow one or steal one. In the days that followed, I learned to pinch goodies at the source, or from staterooms with their doors left open. This was part of the routine at sea. I became a floating Robin Hood, providing my men with delicacies by robbing the rich. It was part of the stratagem of survival, theirs and mine, and I laid my snares for a dill pickle as artfully as a trapper for a mink. The men themselves were not unreasonable. While I was carrying out my first assignment, I was in a cold sweat, fearing that the sight of one orange in the messroom might lead to a demand for oranges right across the board. This proved not to be the case. My firemen did not crowd their luck. And except in rough weather, when their deranged stomachs caused them to delve into the vast lore of seasick remedies and dreams of miracle cures effected by combining the most rare and unlikely substances, they asked of me only tasks I could humanly perform. Thanks to my former job in the saloon, I had valuable contacts in vital supply centers. In Wilbur Wolf I had an actual confederate, who saved odds and ends from the night buffet and turned them over to me as slyly as though we were pushing dope. Never knowing when a fireman would strike, I kept goodies always on hand in a hiding place by my bunk, as a man in rattler country keeps a snake-bite kit at the ready.

After breakfast the first morning, as the firemen drifted off to their duties and the *Buford* steamed north into the Bering Sea, I scrubbed the room, threw out the foul trophies, washed the cloth bag in the coffee urn, and stole an orange. The first day passed without mishap. I went on deck just long enough to see the *Buford* dive into a wall of cold white fog. A lookout had been placed on the forecastlehead, and Tony, the giant Negro watchman, was heaving the lead. Although I was busy getting squared away in my new job, my journal for that date contains a long, fancy description of the heaving of the lead. I was tired, but not too tired for a burst of showy prose.

The task of carrying the big stewpots of food down the almost vertical ladder from the galley proved to be the most formidable part of a messboy's job—far more ticklish than stealing. These caldrons were as big as a bushel basket. They had two opposing handles riveted to the rim. Even when empty they were heavy, and when full of stew they were very, very heavy, as well as piping hot, and they required, of course, the use of both hands, leaving no hand for oneself. In a smooth sea, the trip down the ladder with one of these pots was, for a novice, sobering. In a rough sea, with the ship pitching and rolling, the descent appeared at first glance impossible. The ladder would lose its slant in mid-journey; slowly it would approach the perpendicular, then it would achieve the perpendicular. In a really heavy sea, it would go right past the perpendicular. Luis showed me how to get down. The trick was to wait at the top, stewpot gripped tightly, until the ladder presented a favorable angle for descent. Then you started down cautiously, gaining a round or two. As the ladder began straightening under you, you quickly poked one foot back between the rounds and hooked your toe around the side of the ladder, as an acrobat supports himself when hanging by his feet from a trapeze. As soon as the ladder's cycle was complete and it started back toward a favorable angle, you disengaged your foot and gained another couple of rounds, and so on down until the trip was completed. Those moments of being suspended between decks with a heavy pot full of hot stew and with the combined weight of body and stew supported by one leg and a terrible strain on the other leg seemed interminable. But I was young, and my ankles were as strong as my opinions. Fortunately, I mastered the ladder trick before the *Buford* ran into a whole gale in the North Pacific on her way home. By that time, I was an accomplished artist.

In the *Buford*, the sailors and the firemen were two distinct societies; they lived apart, ate apart, and thought apart. A ship is no melting pot; it hardens its class distinctions until the social bones are ankylosed. Fireman scorns sailor, sailor derides fireman, on general principles. This is, I guess, traditional, and helps keep everyone toned up. In dress and appearance, the *Buford*'s sailors were a cut above the firemen; they shaved oftener and kept their clothes clean, thus by personal daintiness further arousing the scorn of the firemen. Each group took entire credit for making the ship go and vehemently denied that the work of the other group had any nautical significance whatever. This argument—who makes the ship go?—was pursued endlessly, until logic reeled. I heard it discussed by the hour in my mess as I stood dunking dishes. My men were, in fact, nourished more on argument than on stew meat; the most trivial subject awakened their forensic powers and stirred their passions.

At St. Paul, in the Pribilof Islands, I went ashore during a lull in the mess, trotted out to the rookery, and watched the seals. Each big bull was surrounded by his harem. Many of the cows had had their pups, and the place was like a gay, foul-smelling nursery during a children's party, with fights breaking out among the elders. I could have watched the fun for days but had to hurry back to my urn. Luis was dispirited when I reported that seals could not fly. He was filling a ketchup jar—a moment of high drama complicated by this saddening piece of news.

At St. Lawrence Island, we anchored off the village of Gambell and set a missionary and his wife ashore, a Mr. and Mrs. Nickerson. It was the end of the voyage for them. Twenty Eskimos came aboard, loaded with ivory goods and sealskin objects. They spoke no English except for a few key phrases like "seventy-five cents," which they uttered clearly and firmly. They could also say "napkin ring" and "paper knife" very nicely. The ladies of San Francisco, starving for loot and long absent from the bazaars, clutched wildly for the prizes and bid loudly against each other. I watched from a vantage point while a pair of sealskin slippers was bid up from a dollar to six-fifty. The Eskimo hesitated. At this moment, one of my firemen stuck his head up from a companionway, caught the fellow's eye, and beckoned to him. The Eskimo left the ladies and walked over to my man, who thereupon produced from his shirt two dirty cakes of soap and a roll of toilet paper. These items were accepted instantly and the slippers changed hands— a severe setback for the trail blazers of the San Francisco Chamber of Commerce. The ladies were furious. A few of the more alert and energetic ones rushed off to their staterooms and returned with soap and tissue, but trade between San Francisco, Alaska, and Siberia had taken an ugly turn, and the *Buford*'s high purpose seemed momentarily clouded. At noon, Luis and I served lunch to the Eskimos in the sailors' mess, Luis fairly transported by contact with savages in a strange land. Later, the six Brown Brothers unlimbered their horns, and the Eskimos danced, with surprising frenzy. None of them had ever heard a sax, and the sound made them drunk.

At St. Michael, we loaded fish. My poem for August 15 ran:

All day long barrels of fish went across the sky with a rattle,
Swung up from the lighter across the sky and down into the hold of the
vessel.
The quartermaster had square shoulders and he drove the winches—all day
long.
And at evening, when the sky got orange, and gray clouds mustered for a
sunset, the fair-haired girl came and stood at the rail to watch the square-
shouldered quartermaster.
She's his girl, I said. They'll get married, and the boys will grow up to be
square-shouldered like the father.
A sea gull lifted itself from the water and glided peacefully into the orange
west.

The quality of my verse plunged steadily down as the *Buford* plunged steadily north. One trouble the poet had was sheer fatigue; he was a mighty tired poet at the end of a day.

On Friday, August 17, the *Buford* anchored off Nome; we had reached the gateway to the top of the world. The sea was rough, and for a while we were unable to unload cargo. All sorts of rumors were astir—that we were low on water, that we were low on oil, that we would not go to the ice pack, that we would be a week late getting back to the States. The tug *Genevieve* came alongside, and with some others I went down a ladder and got a ride ashore. *Genevieve* made hard work of it, and two ladies were stricken with nausea and were in bad shape when they set foot on the beach. On Saturday night, at about nine o'clock, I stood outside the office of the Nome *Nugget,* across from the Nome Tailoring Company, and watched the first copies of that weekly paper come off the press. The *Nugget* office was full of men and dogs. I bought a copy for twenty-five cents and read the streamer head: GREAT FUTURE ASSURED NOME; NOME–SAN FRANCISCO JOIN HANDS NORTH OF 53. It was an eerie moment in mercantile history, this joining of San Francisco and Nome. The ship was dressed in flags, and the local population of the dreary little town was delighted to see visitors come ashore, even if they vomited on arrival. I do not know how fruitful the occasion turned out to be in the world of trade; the only fruit I saw with my own eyes was in the window of Mrs. Wanger's shop, where a classy new line of fall hats and dresses that had been hustled ashore from the *Buford* was on display. I strolled about the ghostly town in the bright night and took in the sights—the North Pole Bakery, the Nome Sheet Metal Works, the Dream Theatre, Andrew Box's Elite Baths & Hotel (Steam-Heated Rooms), and Mrs. Wanger's red-hot finery.

The *Nugget* was celebrating the event with a special four-page supplement dedicated to amity and trade. On the editorial page appeared an apology:

TO OUR PATRONS REGARDS THE DELAY OF THE PAPER

We wish to take this opportunity to say to the readers of the Nugget that due to the fact that we have added another four pages to today's edition we feel that an explanation is in order for our delay in having the paper out on time. In order to add this amount to the paper we worked all night Friday night not going to bed at all.

The "we" of this notice was George S. Maynard, owner and publisher of the *Nugget* and Mayor of Nome, a real night owl.

I've often wondered how San Francisco's business giants felt when they glimpsed those tumbledown, almost deserted hamlets of the North. Nome must have been a particularly heavy shock. Nome's rickety houses were strung out in a long line fronting the main street. Everybody in Nome lived out of tin cans, and the disposal system was simple and direct; the empties got heaved out of rear windows, and landed on the beach. The beach was an enormous dump, with the accumulated pile of cans comparing favorably with the buildings themselves as an architectural mass. I'll say this for Nome, though: at a certain hour of the day, when the sun hit the place just right, the dump produced an extraordinary phenomenon. The top layer of cans would suddenly catch the sun's rays, and when this happened the crescent beach, viewed from the deck of a ship in the roadstead, would appear to burst into flames, and the down-at-heel gold town for a few breathtaking moments would wear a circlet of fire.

My strongest memory of Nome is of the close shave I had while there. I went to my garbage chute one morning and dumped a big load of slops overside, not knowing that a lighter had tied up to the ship during the night. The garbage took one of the lightermen fairly in the head. He was a big man, and he came aboard bellowing that he would kill whoever had done it. I rushed up to first class and hid, and he never found me. The episode gave me quite a turn, though. I can still see him, with all that stuff in his hair and blood in his eye, coming up the ladder to get me.

From Nome, the *Buford* steamed to Teller, where about a dozen white men remained from a gold-rush population of ten thousand, and then passed through Bering Strait and headed for the ice pack through quiet seas. We were the first passenger ship to invade this part of the world. Here in the Arctic, I began to feel the inadequacy of my wardrobe; I hadn't even brought along a pair of wool socks. Nights were cold and bright; the ship proceeded without running lights. One of our missions was to touch at Wrangell Island and take off two men stranded there. There had been a lot of talk about this, but the whole business fell through; at 70 degrees North Latitude our path was blocked by ice, and we never reached Wrangell. Instead, we hunted walrus.

When the ice was sighted, Captain Lane went aloft in the shrouds and peered ahead through binoculars while the passengers watched admiringly from the deck. Soon our captain came down and ordered the ship stopped. Then, to my great surprise, he left us. With ice closing in all around us, he simply beat it—went off for a hunt in a double kayak with three Eskimos we had taken aboard at Nome. It gave everybody an uneasy feeling—the ship nuzzled by ice, and no captain on board. The hunting party was gone a long while. The passengers, alert and interested at first, grew weary of watching and waiting, and when the hunters finally returned, empty-handed, everyone felt let down. Next day, the hunters had better luck; seven walruses were shot. They were swung aboard by the boom tackle and dumped on the forward deck, where they immediately began to ripen. These huge corpses stayed with us for days; the heads and skins fetched up at last in the Oakland

Museum, whose curator, if the wind was right, must have known long in advance that they were coming. My whole account of the trip in the Arctic Ocean follows:

> Wed. Aug. 22. The walrus hunt. Consensus of opinion among ladies was that the icebergs were beautiful but the walruses were disgusting. Mr. Snow, sitting on walrus and thinking of funny sayings. Luis, the sailor's mess—"Surely this world it is a beautiful thing." The bob-haired girl went on deck just long enough to find out what walrus looked like, and then went back to the chief engineer's room to play cards.

(There was always a card game in the chief's room—that is one of the few things I remember about Alaska. I also remember seeing a polar bear in its natural habitat. Luis was right; surely this world it is a beautiful thing.)

At about three o'clock in the afternoon of the twenty-third, Luis darted into my messroom, flipped all valves, and made an announcement: "Come ong, boy! Come quick, quick! Assia!" He drew the name out lingeringly—"Ass-ee-a." He was all dolled up in a clean shirt, ready to go ashore and send postcards. Together we rushed on deck, and there it was—Asia, a bleak headland called Cape Serdze, with patches of snow spotting the ground. Whales were all around us as we closed with the land; they blew and slapped their flukes. All over the deck lay the stinking walruses, the massive carcasses slashed and gouged by the knives of our hungry Eskimos, who gnawed at the raw trophies as you might work away at a cheese if you were in need of a snack. Blood leaked from the mutilated animals. It spread in rivulets across the deck and responded to the slight roll of the ship. The passengers, for their part, responded to the name Siberia; it was our Arctic *pièce de résistance*, justifying the trip and putting the authentic touch on the name Alaskan–Siberian Navigation Company. Mr. Snow went forward to the forecastlehead and cracked jokes about the Bolsheviki.

"No one knew what to expect," I wrote. "There was a good deal of speculation at first about whether the ship would be fired on. In a general way, the passengers felt that there was something hostile about Russia." Hostile or not, the San Francisco Chamber of Commerce was experiencing its most adventurous hour, and possibly its most footless, and I don't doubt that if we had been fired on, Mr. Snow would have returned the fire with what ammunition remained after our assaults on Taku and on the walruses. Mr. Hubbard, wandering gingerly among pools of blood, saw that Siberia was represented by a couple of dozen furry Eskimos and one squaw man; they came aboard from a skin boat as soon as the *Buford* dropped her hook. On shore we could see dogs curled up asleep among patches of tired snow. At this point, I shall quote from that other diarist of the *Buford*, J. Wilbur Wolf. Wilbur managed to get ashore. "Here," he wrote, "I witnessed the first real Eskimo huts. How shy the natives are, and how unsanitary."

Wilbur traded a few pieces of silver for a Siberian gun holster, Mr. Snow traded an old cap for a polar-bear skin, and we were off for East Cape, which proved to be a repetition of Serdze—headlands, a gray beach, a gray shack flying a small red flag, skin dwellings, vagrant fogs, snow in patches along the shore, and low hills hinting at the vast continent that lay beyond the fog and beyond the power of the imagination. (It may have been memories of the utter drabness of Siberia that caused the *Buford*'s co-owner Mr. Ogden to seek greener pastures for his boat; her next excursion was to Samoa and the Marquesas—a financial bust like the Siberian affair, but at least a languorous one.) Emotionally, the *Buford* and her passengers had had it; we were ready for home. Captain Lane guided his ship across the Strait, called again at Nome, just long enough to take on ten passengers, and then started the homeward journey, with parting salutes from the Coast Guard cutter *Bear*, the tug *Genevieve*, the Hudson's Bay Company's ship, and a whistle ashore. We steamed to False Pass, took aboard some workers from the cannery, and struck boldly out across the North Pacific in a direct line for Seattle. We had not been at sea long when the gale hit.

The new passengers at Nome had put a strain on the *Buford*'s accommodations, and Wilbur and I had been the first to feel the squeeze. We had been booted out of first class. There seemed to be no place to put us until some genius in the Steward Department remembered the ship's prison. This was a tiny steel cell, six feet by six feet, containing two hard, narrow bunks, one above the other—a cute little poky, well off the beaten track. It was located in the 'tween-decks, and Wilbur and I, after the surprise had worn off, were well pleased with it. For my part, I was glad to move into the brig because it relieved me of my fear of being discovered in first class by a fireman. Wilbur liked our new home because it was an outside room. "Somehow or other," he wrote in his diary, "a person can always adapt himself to new environment."

The gayest feature of our new environment was a large, noisy soil pipe running vertically through the room from a very popular toilet on the deck above. We arranged our clothes, wrapped in a sheet, behind this pipe. The door of our cell was heavy steel, and there was a steel sill about a foot high that you stepped over to get in or out. "We have fitted the cell out like a palace," wrote Wilbur in the first fine flush of nest-building. "Advantages: more secrecy [this was for hiding stolen food]; more light, outside room; better air, and more independence. The disadvantages will loom up later, I suppose."

They weren't long looming up. Our pint-sized palace felt the impact of the gale as soon as the *Buford* took her first big roll. The deadlight was leaky; it kept air out but let sea water in, in the mysterious manner of deadlights. Trapped by the high sill, the water in the room built up to a mean depth of about ten inches. Wilbur's stomach collapsed with the first roll of the ship, and he went to bed in the lower bunk, where he lay for three days *in extremis*, his groans blending with the mighty complaints of the soil pipe, his bunk awash like some bleak outer ledge, subject to the incessant rising and falling of our interior tides.

Most of the *Buford*'s passengers, from long days and nights of wining and dining, fell horribly ill. More than half the crew were sick. My messroom was almost deserted, but as a matter of routine I had to set food on the table, regardless of the men's ability to retain it. I was also very busy mixing the extraordinary cocktails by which my men hoped to get relief from their agonies—pineapple ice cream laced with piccalilli, prune juice and tomato juice in equal parts with a sprinkle of mace, soft-boiled egg and marinated carrot, ginger snaps with ketchup.

On the second day of the storm, I had no sooner got the table set for lunch than the *Buford* rolled everything off onto the deck. The ship, which had been so quiet in the Arctic, set up a frightful banging. Down in the hold, the cargo shifted, and the sailors—those that could still stand—worked all one night getting it back in place. Barrels of fish, loose in the cold room, thrashed around and broke the refrigeration pipes, letting brine out all over the deck. On the main deck forward, some Husky dogs that were being brought back to the States by the more enterprising of our souvenir hunters took an awful beating from the storm. Two, I think, were washed overboard. Others got loose and wandered into the paint room, and soon were beyond recognition. Two of my firemen showed up in my messroom and engaged in a long, closely reasoned argument about whether one of them was sick and had vomited. During the storm, Luis lost his job—I never learned why.

For most of the passengers, the voyage ended on a note of nausea and gloom. For me, it ended on a note of triumph. The three gale-tossed days gave me a feeling of elation and well-being; it seemed exciting to be up and about, busily tending the sick and doing my duty. I felt victorious and hearty. My stomach held together and I was able to watch my first great storm at sea unimpaired. Even when a heavy mess bench fell on my foot and broke one toe, the accident and the pain failed to quiet my enthusiasm for the life of a messboy in a full gale. I was drunk with power, the Florence Nightingale of the mess and the brig, and this sensation of drunkenness was heightened by a trick I invented as an antisickness device; instead of bracing myself against the lurches of the ship, I let myself go and yielded to her every pitch and roll, on the theory that bodily resistance is—in part, at least—the true cause of nausea. There may have been nothing to this eccentric notion of mine, but for three days in the wild North Pacific I reeled crazily through the corridors, responding to the sea physically, as though the sea were a dancing partner whose lead I followed.

In a matter of hours, my long, evasive excursion to the far north would be over. I was headed now toward the south and the east, toward unemployment and the insoluble problem of what to do with myself. My spice route to nowhere was behind me; I would soon be host again to the specter that I commonly entertained—the shape of a desk in an office, the dreaded tick of the nine-to-five day, the joyless afternoons of a Sunday suburb, the endless and ineffectual escapes that unemployed young men practice (a trip to the zoo, a walk in the night, the opium pipe of a dark cinema). The shape was amorphous—I seldom attempted to fill in the outlines; it hung above me like a bird of death. But in the final hours of the *Buford* the gale granted me a reprieve. In the fury of the storm, thought was impossible; the future was expunged by wind and water; I lived at last in the present, and the present was magnificent —rich and beautiful and awesome. It gave me all the things I wanted from life, and it was as though I drank each towering wave as it came aboard, as though I would ever after be athirst. At last I had adjusted, temporarily, to a difficult world and had conquered it; others were sick, I bloomed with health. In the noise of battle, all the sad silences of my brooding and foreboding were lost. I had always feared and loved the sea, and this gale was my bride and we had a three-day honeymoon, a violent, tumultuous time of undreamed-of ecstasy and satisfaction. Youth is almost always in deep trouble—of the mind, the heart, the flesh. And as a youth I think I managed to heap myself with more than my share. It took an upheaval of the elements and a job at the lowest level to give me the relief I craved.

The honeymoon was soon over; the wind abated, the *Buford* recovered her poise. On September 4, we docked at Seattle. I collected my pay and went ashore. My next entry is dated September 6, from a room in the Frye Hotel—a poem called "Chantecler."

> How many orders of beef have you passed over the counter,
> Girl with white arms, since I've been gone?
> How many times have you said,
> "Gravy?"
>
> Your arms are still white,
> And you're still the thing in all the room
> That transcends foodstuffs.

By standing there
You make the restaurant part of September,
And September, girl, is part of the world—
A sad-voiced, beautiful part.

How many orders of beef have you passed over the counter,
Girl with white arms, since I've been gone?

Like so many other questions that stirred in me in those years of
wonder and of wandering, this one was to go forever unanswered.

# ONCE MORE TO THE LAKE

*August 1941*

One summer, along about 1904, my father rented a camp on a lake in Maine and took us all there for the month of August. We all got ring-worm from some kittens and had to rub Pond's Extract on our arms and legs night and morning, and my father rolled over in a canoe with all his clothes on; but outside of that the vacation was a success and from then on none of us ever thought there was any place in the world like that lake in Maine. We returned summer after summer—always on August 1 for one month. I have since become a salt-water man, but sometimes in summer there are days when the restlessness of the tides and the fearful cold of the sea water and the incessant wind that blows across the afternoon and into the evening make me wish for the placidity of a lake in the woods. A few weeks ago this feeling got so strong I bought myself a couple of bass hooks and a spinner and returned to the lake where we used to go, for a week's fishing and to revisit old haunts.

I took along my son, who had never had any fresh water up his nose and who had seen lily pads only from train windows. On the jour-ney over to the lake I began to wonder what it would be like. I won-dered how time would have marred this unique, this holy spot—the coves and streams, the hills that the sun set behind, the camps and the paths behind the camps. I was sure that the tarred road would have found it out, and I wondered in what other ways it would be deso-lated. It is strange how much you can remember about places like that once you allow your mind to return into the grooves that lead back. You remember one thing, and that suddenly reminds you of another thing. I guess I remembered clearest of all the early mornings, when the lake was cool and motionless, remembered how the bedroom smelled of the lumber it was made of and of the wet woods whose scent entered through the screen. The partitions in the camp were thin and did not extend clear to the top of the rooms, and as I was always the first up I would dress softly so as not to wake the others, and sneak out into the sweet outdoors and start out in the canoe, keeping close along the shore in the long shadows of the pines. I remembered being very careful never to rub my paddle against the gunwale for fear of disturbing the stillness of the cathedral.

The lake had never been what you would call a wild lake. There were cottages sprinkled around the shores, and it was in farming country although the shores of the lake were quite heavily wooded. Some of the cottages were owned by nearby farmers, and you would live at the shore and eat your meals at the farmhouse. That's what our family did. But although it wasn't wild, it was a fairly large and undisturbed lake and there were places in it that, to a child at least, seemed infinitely remote and primeval.

I was right about the tar: it led to within half a mile of the shore. But when I got back there, with my boy, and we settled into a camp near a farmhouse and into the kind of summertime I had known, I could tell that it was going to be pretty much the same as it had been before—I knew it, lying in bed the first morning, smelling the bedroom and hearing the boy sneak quietly out and go off along the shore in a boat. I began to sustain the illusion that he was I, and therefore, by simple transposition, that I was my father. This sensation persisted, kept cropping up all the time we were there. It was not an entirely new feeling, but in this setting it grew much stronger. I seemed to be living a dual existence. I would be in the middle of some simple act, I would be picking up a bait box or laying down a table fork, or I would be saying something, and suddenly it would be not I but my father who was saying the words or making the gesture. It gave me a creepy sensation.

We went fishing the first morning. I felt the same damp moss covering the worms in the bait can, and saw the dragonfly alight on the tip of my rod as it hovered a few inches from the surface of the water. It was the arrival of this fly that convinced me beyond any doubt that everything was as it always had been, that the years were a mirage and that there had been no years. The small waves were the same, chucking the rowboat under the chin as we fished at anchor, and the boat was the same boat, the same color green and the ribs broken in the same places, and under the floorboards the same fresh-water leavings and débris—the dead helgramite, the wisps of moss, the rusty discarded fishhook, the dried blood from yesterday's catch. We stared silently at the tips of our rods, at the dragonflies that came and went. I lowered the tip of mine into the water, tentatively, pensively dislodging the fly, which darted two feet away, poised, darted two feet back, and came to rest again a little farther up the rod. There had been no years between the ducking of this dragonfly and the other one—the one that was part of memory. I looked at the boy, who was silently watching his fly, and it was my hands that held his rod, my eyes watching. I felt dizzy and didn't know which rod I was at the end of.

We caught two bass, hauling them in briskly as though they were mackerel, pulling them over the side of the boat in a businesslike manner without any landing net, and stunning them with a blow on the back of the head. When we got back for a swim before lunch, the lake was exactly where we had left it, the same number of inches from the dock, and there was only the merest suggestion of a breeze. This seemed an utterly enchanted sea, this lake you could leave to its own devices for a few hours and come back to, and find that it had not stirred, this constant and trustworthy body of water. In the shallows, the dark, water-soaked sticks and twigs, smooth and old, were undulating in clusters on the bottom against the clean ribbed sand, and the track of the mussel was plain. A school of minnows swam by, each minnow with its small individual shadow, doubling the attendance, so clear and sharp in the sunlight. Some of the other campers were in swimming, along the shore, one of them with a cake of soap, and the water felt thin and clear and unsubstantial. Over the years there had been this person with the cake of soap, this cultist, and here he was. There had been no years.

Up to the farmhouse to dinner through the teeming, dusty field, the road under our sneakers was only a two-track road. The middle track was missing, the one with the marks of the hooves and the splotches of dried, flaky manure. There had always been three tracks to choose from in choosing which track to walk in; now the choice was narrowed down to two. For a moment I missed terribly the middle alternative. But the way led past the tennis court, and something about the way it lay there in the sun reassured me; the tape had loosened along the backline, the alleys were green with plantains and other weeds, and the net (installed in June and removed in September) sagged in the dry noon, and the whole place steamed with midday heat and hunger and emptiness. There was a choice of pie for dessert, and one was blueberry and one was apple, and the waitresses were the same country girls, there having been no passage of time, only the illusion of it as in a dropped curtain—the waitresses were still fifteen; their hair had been washed, that was the only difference—they had been to the movies and seen the pretty girls with the clean hair.

Summertime, oh, summertime, pattern of life indelible, the fade-proof lake, the woods unshatterable, the pasture with the sweetfern and the juniper forever and ever, summer without end; this was the background, and the life along the shore was the design, the cottagers with their innocent and tranquil design, their tiny docks with the flagpole and the American flag floating against the white clouds in the blue sky, the little paths over the roots of the trees leading from camp to camp and the paths leading back to the outhouses and the can of lime for sprinkling, and at the souvenir counters at the store the miniature birch-bark canoes and the postcards that showed things looking a little better than they looked. This was the American family at play, escaping the city heat, wondering whether the newcomers in the camp at the head of the cove were "common" or "nice," wondering whether it was true that the people who drove up for Sunday dinner at the farmhouse were turned away because there wasn't enough chicken.

It seemed to me, as I kept remembering all this, that those times and those summers had been infinitely precious and worth saving. There had been jollity and peace and goodness. The arriving (at the beginning of August) had been so big a business in itself, at the railway station the farm wagon drawn up, the first smell of the pine-laden air, the first glimpse of the smiling farmer, and the great importance of the trunks and your father's enormous authority in such matters, and the feel of the wagon under you for the long ten-mile haul, and at the top of the last long hill catching the first view of the lake after eleven months of not seeing this cherished body of water. The shouts and cries of the other campers when they saw you, and the trunks to be unpacked, to give up their rich burden. (Arriving was less exciting nowadays, when you sneaked up in your car and parked it under a tree near the camp and took out the bags and in five minutes it was all over, no fuss, no loud wonderful fuss about trunks.)

Peace and goodness and jollity. The only thing that was wrong now, really, was the sound of the place, an unfamiliar nervous sound of the outboard motors. This was the note that jarred, the one thing that would sometimes break the illusion and set the years moving. In those other summertimes all motors were inboard; and when they were at a little distance, the noise they made was a sedative, an ingredient of summer sleep. They were one-cylinder and two-cylinder engines, and some were make-and-break and some were jump-spark, but they all made a sleepy sound across the lake. The one-lungers throbbed and fluttered, and the twin-cylinder ones purred and purred, and that was a quiet sound, too. But now the campers all had outboards. In the daytime, in the hot mornings, these motors made a petulant, irritable sound; at night, in the still evening when the afterglow lit the water, they whined about one's ears like mosquitoes. My boy loved our rented outboard, and his great desire was to achieve single-handed mastery over it, and authority, and he soon learned the trick of choking it a little (but not too much), and the adjustment of the needle valve. Watching him I would remember the things you could do with the old one-cylinder engine with the heavy flywheel, how you could have it eating out of your hand if you got really close to it spiritually. Motorboats in those days didn't have clutches, and you would make a landing by shutting off the motor at the proper time and coasting in with a dead rudder. But there was a way of reversing them, if you learned the trick, by cutting the switch and putting it on again exactly on the final dying revolution of the flywheel, so that it would kick back against compression and begin reversing. Approaching a dock in a strong following breeze, it was difficult to slow up sufficiently by the ordinary coasting method, and if a boy felt he had complete mastery over his motor, he was tempted to keep it running beyond its time and then reverse it a few feet from the dock. It took a cool nerve, because if you threw the switch a twentieth of a second too soon you would catch the flywheel when it still had speed enough to go up past center, and the boat would leap ahead, charging bull-fashion at the dock.

We had a good week at the camp. The bass were biting well and the sun shone endlessly, day after day. We would be tired at night and lie down in the accumulated heat of the little bedrooms after the long hot day and the breeze would stir almost imperceptibly outside and the smell of the swamp drift in through the rusty screens. Sleep would come easily and in the morning the red squirrel would be on the roof, tapping out his gay routine. I kept remembering everything, lying in bed in the mornings—the small steamboat that had a long rounded stern like the lip of a Ubangi, and how quietly she ran on the moonlight sails, when the older boys played their mandolins and the girls sang and we ate doughnuts dipped in sugar, and how sweet the music was on the water in the shining night, and what it had felt like to think about girls then. After breakfast we would go up to the store and the things were in the same place—the minnows in a bottle, the plugs and spinners disarranged and pawed over by the youngsters from the boys' camp, the Fig Newtons and the Beeman's gum. Outside, the road was tarred and cars stood in front of the store. Inside, all was just as it had always been, except there was more Coca-Cola and not so much

Moxie and root beer and birch beer and sarsaparilla. We would walk out with the bottle of pop apiece and sometimes the pop would back-fire up our noses and hurt. We explored the streams, quietly, where the turtles slid off the sunny logs and dug their way into the soft bottom; and we lay on the town wharf and fed worms to the tame bass. Everywhere we went I had trouble making out which was I, the one walking at my side, the one walking in my pants.

One afternoon while we were there at that lake a thunderstorm came up. It was like the revival of an old melodrama that I had seen long ago with childish awe. The second-act climax of the drama of the electrical disturbance over a lake in America had not changed in any important respect. This was the big scene, still the big scene. The whole thing was so familiar, the first feeling of oppression and heat and a general air around camp of not wanting to go very far away. In mid-afternoon (it was all the same) a curious darkening of the sky, and a lull in everything that had made life tick; and then the way the boats suddenly swung the other way at their moorings with the coming of a breeze out of the new quarter, and the premonitory rumble. Then the kettle drum, then the snare, then the bass drum and cymbals, then crackling light against the dark, and the gods grinning and licking their chops in the hills. Afterward the calm, the rain steadily rustling in the calm lake, the return of light and hope and spirits, and the campers running out in joy and relief to go swimming in the rain, their bright cries perpetuating the deathless joke about how they were getting simply drenched, and the children screaming with delight at the new sensation of bathing in the rain, and the joke about getting drenched linking the generations in a strong indestructible chain. And the comedian who waded in carrying an umbrella.

When the others went swimming, my son said he was going in, too. He pulled his dripping trunks from the line where they had hung all through the shower and wrung them out. Languidly, and with no thought of going in, I watched him, his hard little body, skinny and bare, saw him wince slightly as he pulled up around his vitals the small, soggy, icy garment. As he buckled the swollen belt, suddenly my groin felt the chill of death.

# VI

DIVERSIONS AND
OBSESSIONS

# THE SEA AND
# THE WIND THAT BLOWS

❧

Waking or sleeping, I dream of boats—usually of rather small boats under a slight press of sail. When I think how great a part of my life has been spent dreaming the hours away and how much of this total dream life has concerned small craft, I wonder about the state of my health, for I am told that it is not a good sign to be always voyaging into unreality, driven by imaginary breezes.

I have noticed that most men, when they enter a barber shop and must wait their turn, drop into a chair and pick up a magazine. I simply sit down and pick up the thread of my sea wandering, which began more than fifty years ago and is not quite ended. There is hardly a waiting room in the East that has not served as my cockpit, whether I was waiting to board a train or to see a dentist. And I am usually still trimming sheets when the train starts or the drill begins to whine.

If a man must be obsessed by something, I suppose a boat is as good as anything, perhaps a bit better than most. A small sailing craft is not only beautiful, it is seductive and full of strange promise and the hint of trouble. If it happens to be an auxiliary cruising boat, it is without question the most compact and ingenious arrangement for living ever devised by the restless mind of man—a home that is stable without being stationary, shaped less like a box than like a fish or a bird or a girl, and in which the homeowner can remove his daily affairs as far from shore as he has the nerve to take them, close-hauled or running free—parlor, bedroom, and bath, suspended and alive.

Men who ache all over for tidiness and compactness in their lives often find relief for their pain in the cabin of a thirty-foot sailboat at anchor in a sheltered cove. Here the sprawling panoply of The Home is compressed in orderly miniature and liquid delirium, suspended between the bottom of the sea and the top of the sky, ready to move on in the morning by the miracle of canvas and the witchcraft of rope. It is small wonder that men hold boats in the secret place of their mind, almost from the cradle to the grave.

Along with my dream of boats has gone the ownership of boats, a long succession of them upon the surface of the sea, many of them makeshift and crank. Since childhood I have managed to have some sort of sailing craft and to raise a sail in fear. Now, in my seventies, I still own a boat, still raise my sail in fear in answer to the summons of the unforgiving sea. Why does the sea attract me in the way it does? Whence comes this compulsion to hoist a sail, actually or in dream? My first encounter with the sea was a case of hate at first sight. I was taken, at the age of four, to a bathing beach in New Rochelle. Everything about the experience frightened and repelled me: the taste of salt in my mouth, the foul chill of the wooden bathhouse, the littered sand, the stench of the tide flats. I came away hating and fearing the sea. Later, I found that what I had feared and hated, I now feared and loved.

I returned to the sea of necessity, because it would support a boat; and although I knew little of boats, I could not get them out of my thoughts. I became a pelagic boy. The sea became my unspoken challenge: the wind, the tide, the fog, the ledge, the bell, the gull that cried help, the never-ending threat and bluff of weather. Once having permitted the wind to enter the belly of my sail, I was not able to quit the helm; it was as though I had seized hold of a high-tension wire and could not let go.

I liked to sail alone. The sea was the same as a girl to me—I did not want anyone else along. Lacking instruction, I invented ways of getting things done, and usually ended by doing them in a rather queer fashion, and so did not learn to sail properly, and still cannot sail well, although I have been at it all my life. I was twenty before I discovered that charts existed; all my navigating up to that time was done with the wariness and the ignorance of the early explorers. I was thirty before I learned to hang a coiled halyard on its cleat as it should be done. Until then I simply coiled it down on deck and dumped the coil. I was always in trouble and always returned, seeking more trouble. Sailing became a compulsion: there lay the boat, swinging to her mooring, there blew the wind; I had no choice but to go. My earliest boats were so small that when the wind failed, or when I failed, I could switch to manual control—I could paddle or row home. But then I graduated to boats that only the wind was strong enough to move. When I first dropped off my mooring in such a boat, I was an hour getting up the nerve to cast off the pennant. Even now, with a thousand little voyages notched in my belt, I still feel a memorial chill on casting off, as the gulls jeer and the empty mainsail claps.

Of late years, I have noticed that my sailing has increasingly become a compulsive activity rather than a simple source of pleasure. There lies the boat, there blows the morning breeze—it is a point of honor, now, to go. I am like an alcoholic who cannot put his bottle out of his life. With me, I cannot not sail. Yet I know well enough that I have lost touch with the wind and, in fact, do not like the wind anymore. It jiggles me up, the wind does, and what I really love are windless days, when all is peace. There is a great question in my mind whether a man who is against wind should longer try to sail a boat. But this is an intellectual response—the old yearning is still in me, belonging to the past, to youth, and so I am torn between past and present, a common disease of later life.

When does a man quit the sea? How dizzy, how bumbling must he be? Does he quit while he's ahead, or wait till he makes some major mistake, like falling overboard or being flattened by an accidental jibe? This past winter I spent hours arguing the question with myself. Finally, deciding that I had come to the end of the road, I wrote a note to the boatyard, putting my boat up for sale. I said I was "coming off the water." But as I typed the sentence, I doubted that I meant a word of it.

If no buyer turns up, I know what will happen: I will instruct the yard to put her in again—"just till somebody comes along." And then there will be the old uneasiness, the old uncertainty, as the mild southeast breeze ruffles the cove, a gentle, steady, morning breeze, bringing the taint of the distant wet world, the smell that takes a man back to the very beginning of time, linking him to all that has gone before. There will lie the sloop, there will blow the wind, once more I will get under way. And as I reach across to the red nun off the Torry Islands, dodging the trap buoys and toggles, the shags gathered on the ledge will note my passage. "There goes the old boy again," they will say. "One more rounding of his little Horn, one more conquest of his Roaring Forties." And with the tiller in my hand, I'll feel again the wind imparting life to a boat, will smell again the old menace, the one that imparts life to me: the cruel beauty of the salt world, the barnacle's tiny knives, the sharp spine of the urchin, the stinger of the sun jelly, the claw of the crab.

# THE RAILROAD

Allen Cove, January 28, 1960

What's the railroad to me?
I never go to see
Where it ends.
It fills a few hollows,
And makes banks for the swallows,
It sets the sand a-blowing,
And the blackberries a-growing.

Henry Thoreau, who wrote those lines, was a student of railroading. He was a devotee, though seldom a passenger. He lived, of course, in the morningtime of America's railroads. He was less concerned with where the railroad ended than with what the railroad meant, and his remarks on the Fitchburg seem fadeproof in the strong light of this century, their liturgical quality still intact.

And what's the railroad to me? I have to admit that it means a great deal to me. It fills more than a few hollows. It is the link with my past, for one thing, and with the city, for another—two connections I would not like to see broken. The railroads of Maine are eager to break these connections, having found them to be unprofitable, and are already at work on the problem. They hope to discontinue all passenger service within the state, and although they failed in their first try, in 1959, they may do better in the year ahead.

Bangor is the second-oldest railroad town in New England; a steam train pulled out of Bangor, bound upriver for Old Town, on November 6, 1836. The running time for the twelve-mile trip was two and a half hours, the conductor's name was Sawyer, passengers were aboard, and the fare was thirty-seven and a half cents. That was the first steam train to roll in Maine, the second to roll in New England. Soon Bangor may set another mark in rail history; it may watch the departure of the last train, and as this sad hulk moves off down the track (if it ever does), Maine will become the first state in the Union, except for Hawaii, to have no rail passenger service between its major cities.

What's the railroad to me? It is a lingering pain in the heart, an old friend who has tired of me and my antics. Unlike Thoreau, whose rail adventures were largely intellectual, I do go to see where the railroad ends. On some occasions—as on next Monday, for instance —I have no choice but to go; I will pay the tariff cheerfully and stare at the bare blackberry vines with affection. But the sleeper I had planned to take, the sleeper out of Bangor, has been pulled off, and I will have to find another one, a hundred and forty miles to the westward. (The distance to the depot gets longer and longer.) I live in the twilight of railroading, the going down of its sun. For the past few months I've been well aware that I am the Unwanted Passenger, one of the last survivors of a vanishing and ugly breed. Indeed, if I am to believe the statements I see in the papers, I am all that stands between the Maine railroads and a bright future of hauling fast freight at a profit. It makes me feel like a spoilsport.

But I have other sensations, too. I bought this house almost thirty years ago, confident that whatever else happened to me, the railroad would always pick me up and carry me here and there, to and fro. This morning our village lies under several thicknesses of snow. Snow has fallen almost without interruption for a week, beginning with a north-east storm, tapering off to dull weather in which the low clouds spat snow day and night, and today another storm from the northeast. The highway is a ready cake mix of snow, ice, sand, salt, and trouble. Within the fortnight there has been the greatest rash of air disasters in my memory. And on top of everything the railroad, which is my old love, is sick of me and the likes of me, and I feel that my connections have been broken, as sharply as by the man in coveralls who crawls between the cars and knocks apart the steam line with his hammer. My thoughts, as they sometimes do on sad occasions, revert to Concord and another railroad in another century.

"On this morning of the Great Snow, perchance," wrote Thoreau, "which is still raging and chilling men's blood, I hear the muffled tone of their engine bell from out the fog bank of their chilled breath, which announces that the cars *are coming*, without long delay, notwithstanding the veto of a New England north-east snowstorm. . . ." How different my village from his village, my century from his century! The only bell that is audible to me in this snowstorm is the one that rings inside my head, which announces that the cars *are going*—soon, perhaps, to be gone for good. For although the passengers' dilemma here in Maine is still unresolved, there is a strong suspicion that we are living on borrowed time; the railroads would like to chop my head off instanter and be done, but the Public Utilities Commission, after looking at all sides of the matter, has given me a stay of execution, on good behavior. It stipulates that I must travel more often and that I must not go first class.

Maine has two railroads—the Bangor & Aroostook and the Maine Central. One serves the north country, hauling potatoes and newsprint from field and forest; the other serves the midsection, hauling mail and packages of bonbons between Portland and Bangor, with an occasional sortie to Vanceboro. Both roads carry passengers when any show up. A third road, the Boston & Maine, dips into the state as far as Portland. A fourth, the Canadian Pacific, comes in briefly across the border.

Several months ago, the two principal railroads petitioned the commission to be allowed to quit carrying passengers and thus free their talents for the exciting and rewarding task of moving freight and mail. Public hearings were held; for the most part they were poorly attended. While the commissioners listened, the railroad men told grim tales of ruin and utter desolation. At one hearing in Portland, a lawyer for the Maine Central summed up the disjointed times when he said, "We are right now engaged in the diagnosis of a very sick patient." At another hearing, a man speaking for a cat-food factory in Lubec— makers of Puss 'n Boots cat food—rose to say that unless the Maine Central could wriggle free from the stifling grip of its passengers, Puss 'n Boots might have to move on to a happier and more progressive territory. The future of America's cats seemed suddenly at stake.

All in all, the year 1959 was a schizophrenic time for Maine's railroads. On Monday you would open your morning paper and find a display ad seeking your patronage and describing the rapturous experience of riding the rails. On Tuesday you would open the same paper and get a tongue-lashing from an impatient spokesman for the line, pointing out that the railroad would be bringing prosperity right this minute if only you, the passenger, would stand to one side and allow the freights to roll. "I am refreshed and expanded when the freight train rattles past me," wrote Thoreau. So, without any question, is E. Spencer Miller, president of the Maine Central. And so, for that matter, are all of us refreshed, though for a different reason, when, after a long wait in a motionless car on a silent siding, we hear a freight train at last rattle past us, hauling its cartons of food to faraway cats and releasing us hungry passengers for the continuance of our journey.

To the lay passenger, or to the traveling layman, the bookkeeping of railroads is as mysterious as the backing up of a train in the night. Even to a public-utilities commission the account books of railroads are something less than perfectly transparent. The Maine railroads' books were, of course, opened to the commission, and some of the figures got into the papers. Every railroad, I gather, keeps two sets of books, one on its freight operation, the other on its passenger operation; and every once in a while the books themselves manage to draw close together and a sort of seepage takes place from one set to the other, so that to the unpracticed eye, it is hard to tell how deeply a profitable sack of potatoes is being eaten into by those rats, the passengers. But there is no question that we passengers, of late years, have *been* gnawing away at the potatoes. Some of us do it in desperation, because we are starving to death between station stops. No food is carried on the train that brings me up the Kennebec, and a passenger must live by his wits off the land. At Waterville, on the eastbound run of the State of Maine, there is a midmorning pause, and while mail sacks are being tossed about in the genial and relaxed way that has characterized the handling of mail since the beginning of time, the engineer and the passengers (all six of us) gather at the snack counter in the depot, where we huddle over coffee and doughnuts, some of us passengers breaking a thirteen-hour fast that began 456.6 miles to the westward in the cornucopia civilization of Grand Central. These late breakfasts in Waterville come to an end as ritualistically as does the President's press conference in Washington when one of the reporters rises and says "Thank you, Mr. President." In Waterville, it is the engine driver himself who breaks up the party. He simply steps down from his stool, adjusts his cap, and walks away, which is the signal for us passengers to climb back into our places behind him in the train.

I suppose the very quality in railroads that has endeared them to me all my life, their traditionalism, has helped bring them (and me) to our present plight. England is about the most traditional institution I know of, but American railroads run a close second. "What has always been shall always be" is their motto. For almost a hundred years the Iron Horse was America's mount; the continent was his range, and the sound his hoofs made in the land was the sound of stability, majesty, punctuality, and success. "Far through unfrequented woods on the confines of towns, where once only the hunter penetrated by day, in the darkest night dart these bright saloons without the knowledge of their inhabitants; this moment stopping at some brilliant station-house in town or city, where a social crowd is gathered, the next in the Dismal Swamp, scaring the owl and fox. The startings and arrivals of the cars are now the epochs in the village day. They go and come with such regularity and precision, and their whistle can be heard so far, that the farmers set their clocks by them, and thus one well-conducted institution regulates a whole country." It was all true. And gradually the railroads fell in love with the sound of their own whistle, with the brightness of the saloons and the brilliance of the station houses, and even after the whistle dwindled to little more than a faint pooping in the hills and the saloons were withdrawn from service and the lights in the station houses went out, the railroads stubbornly stuck to their accustomed ways and the ways of the horse. Some of the station houses were so solidly built they still stand, monuments to darkness and decay. The depot in Bangor, built in 1907, is a notable example of a railroad's addiction to the glorious past. Give it bars at the windows and it could as well be a federal penitentiary. Give it a moat with a drawbridge and it could be the castle where the baron lives. (On wet days it actually acquires a sort of moat, through which we surviving passengers wade and plunge with our luggage to gain the platform.) Reduce it to miniature size and it could be a model-railroad station built out of beautiful tiny blocks by yesterday's child. It is, in short, everything except what it ought to be—a serviceable shelter for arriving and departing passengers—and any railroad that hopes to attract customers and survive as a profitable carrier would certainly have to raze it as a first step toward the new day. Come to think of it, the depot at Bangor, although fit for a baron, was at one time the property of a hustling railroad called the European & North American, whose dream was to bring Europe closer by rushing people by rail to St. John, where an ocean liner would speed them on their way. The property in Bangor on which the present station stands fell into the hands of the Maine Central in 1882, when that railroad leased the European & North American. The lease was to run for nine hundred and ninety-nine years, and although the European was dissolved a while back, there seems a good likelihood that the depot will still be standing in the year 2881, its men's room still well patronized and its freight office ablaze with lights.

I made my first rail journey into Maine in the summer of 1905, and have been riding to and fro on the cars ever since. On that first trip, when I was led by the hand into the green sanctuary of a Pullman drawing room and saw spread out for my pleasure its undreamed-of facilities and its opulence and the porter holding the pillow in his mouth while he drew the clean white pillowcase up around it and the ladder to the upper and the three-speed electric fan awaiting my caprice at the control switch and the little hammock slung so cunningly to receive my clothes and the adjoining splendor of the toilet room with its silvery appointments and gushing privacy, I was fairly bowled over with childish admiration and glee, and I fell in love with railroading then and there and have not been the same boy since that night.

We were a family of eight, and I was the youngest member. My father was a thrifty man, and come the first of August every summer, he felt that he was in a position to take his large family on a month's vacation. His design, conceived in 1905 and carried out joyously for many summers, was a simple one: for a small sum he rented a rough camp on one of the Belgrade lakes, then turned over the rest of his savings to the railroad and the Pullman Company in return for eight first-class round-trip tickets and plenty of space on the sleeper—a magnificent sum, a magnificent gesture. When it came to travel, there was not a second-class bone in my father's body, and although he spent thousands of hours of his life sitting bolt upright in dusty day coaches, commuting between Mount Vernon and Grand Central, once a year he put all dusty things aside and lay down, with his entire family, in Pullman perfection, his wife fully dressed against the possibility of derailment, to awake next morning in the winy air of a spruce-clad land and to debouch, surrounded by his eager children and full of the solemnity of trunk checks, onto the platform of the Belgrade depot, just across the tracks from Messalonskee's wild, alluring swamp. As the express train pulled away from us in Belgrade on that August morning of 1905, I got my first glimpse of this benign bog, which did not seem dismal to me at all. It was an inseparable part of the first intoxication of railroading, and, of all natural habitats, a swamp has ever since been to me the most beautiful and most seductive.

Today, as my thoughts wander affectionately back over fifty-five years of railroading, the thing that strikes me as most revealing about that first rail trip in 1905 is the running time of the train. We left New York at eight o'clock in the evening and arrived at Belgrade next morning at half past nine—a thirteen-and-a-half-hour run, a distance of four hundred and fifteen miles, a speed of thirty-one miles an hour. And what is the speed of our modern Iron Horse in this decade as he gallops through the night? I timed him from New York to Bangor not long ago, divided the mileage by the number of hours, and came up with the answer: thirty-four miles an hour. Thus, in fifty-five years, while the motorcar was lifting its road speed to the dazzling rate of seventy miles an hour on the thruways, and the airplane was becoming a jet in the sky, the railroad steadfastly maintained its accustomed gait, between thirty and thirty-five miles an hour. This is an impressive record. It's not every institution that can hold to an ideal through fifty-five years of our fastest-moving century. It's not every traveler who is content to go thirty-four, either. I am not sure that even I, who love the rails, am content. A few of us visionaries would like to see the railroad step up the pace from thirty-four to forty, so we could leave New York after dinner at night and get home in time for lunch next day. (I've just learned that the Maine Central has a new schedule, effective early next month. Soon I can leave New York after dinner and be home the following *afternoon* in time for dinner. There's to be a four-hour lay-over in Portland, an eighteen-hour trip all told. Thus the speed of my Horse has just dropped from thirty-four miles an hour to twenty-eight. He's a very sick Horse.)

The slowness of rail travel is not because the Horse is incapable of great speed but because the railroad is a gossip; all along the line it stops to chat at back porches, to exchange the latest or borrow a cup of sugar. A train on its leisurely course often reminds me of a small boy who has been sent on an errand; the train gets there eventually, and so does the boy, but after what adventures, what amusing distractions and excursions, what fruitful dawdling! A railroad has a thousand and one things on its mind, all of them worthy, many of them enchanting, but none of them conducive to swift passage for a seated customer. I think if a railroad is to profit from a passenger run, it will have to take the word "run" seriously and conquer its insatiable curiosity about what is happening along the route. Some railroads manage to do this, and I notice that when they do, their cars are usually well filled, and their pockets, too.

There are other reasons the Horse is so slow-paced. The State of Maine leaves Portland in the evening and trots along briskly till it gets to Lowell Junction, around midnight. Here it leaves the main line of the Boston & Maine and goes adventuring on a stretch of single track toward Worcester, fifty miles away. This piece of track is well known to sleepy passengers snug in their beds. It was built by a Girl Scout troop while on maneuvers. The girls felled the trees for the ties, collected gravel from abandoned guppy tanks for the fill, and for rails they got hold of some twisted I-beams from condemned buildings. Even the engine driver has a healthy respect for this remarkable section of roadbed; he slows the train to a walk, obeying his instinct for self-preservation as well as the strict safety rules of the railroad. For about an hour, the creeping train is contorted in the most violent way, and the patient passenger slats back and forth in his berth, drugged with sleep, fear, and pain.

Tomorrow night, the last sleeping car leaves Bangor for New York. I shall not be aboard but shall be thinking of it and wishing it well as it rolls through Etna and skirts the swamp. When, the other day, the news broke that the through sleeping car was to be dropped, the papers carried a statement from Harold J. Foster, our traffic manager: "The service was, we hoped, one which would build railroad patronage between Maine points and New York City on an overnight basis. The sleeper has been poorly patronized, although we advertised its convenience in a consistent program in newspapers and on radio." Mr. Foster's words are true; the sleeper was poorly patronized, except on the occasions when bad weather grounded the planes, and except by a few eccentrics like me, who enjoy railroading and patronized it well. The *convenience* of the service was advertised, but not, of course, its inconveniences, which the traveling public was familiar with anyway —its high tariff, its low speed, its luggage problems, and (in my case) its depot fifty miles from home.

Not all sick railroads die; some have been known to make a startling recovery. The Long Island recovered when New York State forgave it its taxes. (I don't know whether its sins were forgiven, too, but at least its taxes were.) The Chicago & Northwestern recovered when someone thoughtfully equipped it with comfortable cars and modern conveniences, and when it was permitted to drop a few unprofitable trains. In Philadelphia, a nonprofit corporation formed for the purpose of improving passenger service is even now blowing new life into the rails that carry people to the city. This amounts to a municipal sub- sidy, and may easily benefit the community far in excess of its cost. About a year ago, the Rock Island Lines tried an experiment; it reduced first-class fares instead of raising them. The test lasted several months, and during that time there was a twenty-five percent increase in pas- sengers carried.

Several other roads reduced fares and found that business picked up. I believe that a number of things are happening that will bring passenger trains back into favor and into the profit column, which is where everyone wants them to be. America's growth is phenomenal, its habits are changeable and unpredictable, its people are always on the move. Railroads, which commonly look backward, should look ahead. Already some cities are experiencing death by motorcar; Los Angeles is the most noticeable one, where the fast-breeding automobile has had a population explosion comparable to the lemming's and will soon have to rush into the sea to make room for oncoming generations of fertile automobiles and to save the people from stagnation and asphyxiation. Railroad men should take heart when they gaze at the automobile in its area of greatest concentration and its hour of greatest triumph.

As for planes, planes have broken the speed of sound and are reaching for the speed of light to see if they can't smash that, too, and soon we will fly to the coast and get there before we start and so will be cheated of the journey—a dreamlike transportation system that gradually gets to be nightmarish, with people whipped so rapidly from point to point that they are in danger of becoming a race of waltzing mice. (I see that 1960, according to the Chinese calendar, is the Year of the Mouse, but I think it may turn out to be the Year of the Waltzing Mouse, so feverish have our lives become.) If our future journeys are to be little different from flashes of light, with no interim landscape and no interim thought, I think we will have lost the whole good of journeying and will have succumbed to a mere preoccupation with getting there. I believe journeys have value in themselves, and are not just a device for saving time—which never gets saved in the end anyway. Railroad men should take courage when they look at a jet plane, or even at a poky old airliner circling at two hundred miles an hour over an airport waiting for the fog to lift or for its nose wheel to lock into position. The railroad has qualities none can take away, virtues that have never been surpassed. A well-driven train moving smoothly and strongly over a well-laid roadbed offers a traveler advantages and conveniences not to be had in any other form of transportation. Unlike the motorcar, the train does not have to be steered. Unlike the plane, the train can slow down in thick weather. Unlike the bus, the train does not have to pull over to the left every few minutes to pass what is up ahead.

Maine's railroad men are perhaps more downhearted than most, because this state is relatively unpopulous and is for that reason a tough nut for a passenger line to crack. Even Maine's largest cities are not yet large enough to show much urban sprawl, and a motorist does not ordinarily encounter serious traffic delays in the outskirts. In good weather, it is usually more convenient for a resident of Bangor to drive to Portland than go by rail. In my own case, I can drive from my house to Portland in four hours, assuming that I can drive at all, but to get to Portland by train I must first spend an hour and a half getting to the depot in Bangor, then four hours on the train—a total of five hours and a half.

One of the jokers of railroading in Maine is the mail contract. In this neck of the woods, passengers and mail are usually found riding the rails together, and the schedule of a train is geared to the delivery of letters, not of people. The Bangor & Aroostook has just been working on a schedule designed to satisfy both the Public Utilities Commission, which insists that passenger be carried during 1960, and the Post Office Department, which insists that any letter posted in one part of Maine before five o'clock in the afternoon be able to reach any other part of Maine in time for the morning delivery next day. Today the new schedule was announced; a passenger northbound for Caribou will take his departure at twenty minutes past one in the morning from a rendezvous called Northern Maine Junction, just outside of Bangor, presumably clutching an alarm clock in one hand and snowshoes in the other. I suppose this is the best train the Bangor & Aroostook could work out under existing conditions, but I doubt whether it will attract customers to the rails in great numbers, although I'd like to make the trip once myself just for the richness of the experience.

The railroads want and need mail contracts, but the job of carrying the mail turns a railroad into the creature of the federal government. Uncle Sam can put the finger on any train in America and order it to carry the mail. He pays for this, of course, but he also runs his own show. A train's scheduled departure can be delayed indefinitely by the mail. Furthermore, the postal department determines *how* the mail is to be handled; the railroad has no say in the matter. A train stop becomes an interlude for mail sorting—sorting of sacks, that is. The reason my engine driver can take a coffee break at Waterville is that each mail sack is thrown out separately, and the pitcher keeps filling in the catcher. Twenty-five sacks of mail, if they were palletized, could be removed from a mail car in twenty-five seconds, but that's not the way the government wants it. Instead of twenty-five seconds, the operation takes twenty-five minutes. It seems to me that if the government has the power to immobilize some trains for the benefit of the mail, it has an obligation to speed up other trains for the benefit of the passengers.

If Maine's railroads are to stay alive and haul passengers, they will need help from villages, cities, the state, and the federal government, and I think they should get it. A state without rail service is a state that is coming apart at the seams, and when a train stops at a village depot anywhere in America and a passenger steps off, I think that village is in an enviable condition, even if the lone passenger turns out to be a bank robber who does nothing better than stir the air up for a little while. But I think railroads will have to help themselves, too. They should raise their sights, not their fares. And they should stop sulking in their tent, and, instead, try to beat the motorcar at its own game, which, if I do not misread the signs, should get easier as the years go on. There may even be a way to divorce the rail passenger from that fat wife of his, the mail sack—a marriage that has been un-happy all along. I believe that if railroads would improve their services by ten percent, they would increase their business by twenty. They must tidy things up. "This closed car smells of salt fish," wrote Thoreau, sniffing the air as the train rushed by, and his words were echoed by several Maine citizens at the recent hearings when they got on the subject of the untidiness of day coaches.

Railroads are immensely complex, and they seem to love com-plexity, just as they love ritual and love the past. Not all sick roads die, as I have pointed out, but a road can sometimes put on a pretty good show of dying, and then its ritual seems to be part of the scheme of dying. During 1959, because of some sickness of my own, and of my wife's, and of other members of our two families, she and I patron-ized the railroad more often than usual, observing its agony while using what remained of its facilities. There was one memorable night last fall, when, sitting forlorn in the deserted waiting room of the Portland depot, waiting to take the sleeper for New York, we seemed actually to be the principal actors in the deathbed scene of railroading in Amer-ica; no Hollywood director could have improved on the thing. For reasons too dull to go into, we were taking our departure from Portland instead of Bangor. The old station hung tomblike above and around our still forms, drear and drafty. (No social crowd was gathered here.) The only other persons in the place were the ticket agent, at ease behind his counter, and a redcap in slow conversation with two friends. Now and then the front door would open and a stray would enter, some fellow to whom all railroad stations are home. Shortly before train time, a porter appeared, dragging a large wooden table and two chairs, and set the stage for the rites of ticket-taking. The table looked to be the same age as the depot and to have been chewed incessantly by porcupines. Two conductors in faded blue now walked stiffly onto the set and seated themselves at the table. My wife and I, catching the cue, rose and approached the oracle, and I laid our tickets down in front of one of the men. He grasped them, studied them closely, as though he had never seen anything quite like them in all his life, then turned to his companion and shouted, for all to hear in the room where no one was, "B in the Twenty-three!" To which the other replied, in a tremendous voice, "B in the Twenty-three!" (and seemed to add, *for the last two passengers on earth*"). Then he tore off the stub and handed it to me.

The words of the ceremony, spoken so loudly, although familiar to us seemed unnaturally solemn and impressive, and we felt more as though we were taking marriage vows than taking a train. After the ceremony was over, we followed the redcap with our luggage, walking slowly out, the last two passengers, into the cold train shed, and picked our way across the tracks toward our waiting sleeper. Halfway there, we passed an ancient trainman, his arms full of kerosene lanterns, on his way to harness the Horse with the honored trappings of the past. There was something ineffably sad about the departure of this train; death seemed in the air.

When I came to live in Maine, the depot was twenty-three miles away, in Ellsworth. Then the depot got to be fifty miles away, in Bangor. After tomorrow night, it will be a hundred and forty miles away (for a sleeping car), in Portland. A year from now, there may be no depot in the whole state—none with a light burning, that is. I cannot conceive of my world without a rail connection, and perhaps I shall have to pull up stakes and move to some busier part of the swamp, where the rails have not been abandoned. Whether I move away or stay put, if the trains of Maine come to a standstill I will miss them greatly. I will miss cracking the shade at dawn—and the first shafts of light in the tinted woods, and the old excitement. I'll miss the Canada geese in the Kennebec in the seasons of migration, and the breakfast in bed, drinking from the punctured can of grapefruit juice as we proceed gravely up the river, and the solid old houses of Gardiner, and Augusta's little trackslide glade with the wooden staircase and the vines of the embankment and the cedar waxwing tippling on berries as I tipple on juice. I'll miss the peaceful stretches of the river above Augusta, with the stranded sticks of pulpwood along the banks; the fall overcast, the winter brightness; the tiny blockhouse of Fort Halifax, at Winslow, mighty bastion of defense; and at Waterville the shiny black flanks of Old No. 470, the Iron Horse that has been enshrined right next to what used to be the Colby campus—the steam locomotive that pulled the cars on the last prediesel run from Portland to Bangor.

Early last spring, as my train waited on a siding for another train to go through, I looked out of the window and saw our conductor walking in the ditch, a pocketknife in his hand. He passed out of sight and was gone ten minutes, then reappeared. In his arms was a fine bunch of pussy willows, a gift for his wife, I don't doubt. It was a pleasing sight, a common episode, but I recall feeling at the time that the scene was being overplayed, and that it belonged to another century. The railroads will have to get on with the action if they are to boost that running speed from twenty-eight to forty and lure customers.

Perhaps the trains will disappear from Maine forever, and the conductor will then have the rest of his life to cut pussies along the right of way, with the sand a-blowing and the blackberries a-growing. I hope it doesn't happen in my lifetime, for I think one well-conducted institution may still regulate a whole country.

P.S. (May 1962).     Death came quickly to the railroads of Maine. The passenger trains not only disappeared "in my lifetime," they disappeared in what seemed like a trice. The trains are gone, the station houses are gone. I was watching television one day and saw the tower of Portland's Union Station fall over, struck down by a large steel ball swinging from the boom of a crane. I could feel the blow in the pit of my stomach.

The freights are running as usual, and at higher speeds, but the expected spurt in business and profits has not occurred. At the annual meeting of the Maine Central a few weeks ago, the president of the line told the stockholders that "sunshine and shadow" lay ahead for them. The cat-food factory in Lubec has decided to close down, and this event casts a long shadow over the stockholders by jeopardizing the branch line that runs from Ayer's Junction to Eastport; it may have to be abandoned unless some business can be taken away from the truckers. I don't know why the cat-food plant is quitting; perhaps Puss has lost her appetite, or possibly the people who operate the cannery would prefer to live where there is passenger rail service.

A lady in North Belgrade wrote me not long ago and said, "Though the great change has been made, it is still the freight train that we depend on to warn us about the weather. If we can hear the freight come through Oakland at nine in the evening, we know that the wind is the wrong way and there will be rain." I still believe the wind is the wrong way and there will be rain; a land without rail service is a land in decline, or in suspension.

In the West, railroading still enjoys good health, and a few of the Eastern trains are rolling at a profit, notably the trains that connect Florida with the cities of the North. But in the East generally, the sickness spreads. The New Haven, in a bankrupt condition, filed for reorganization last summer; the Boston & Maine is in hard shape; the merged Erie-Lackawanna is poorly despite the merger; and the B. & O. doesn't feel good at all.

Railroading in America enjoyed its monopoly status much too long for its own good, and the characteristic American genius for new shapes, new ideas, new ways to exploit demand, although it infects every other business, has been lacking in railroading. Inflexibility is still the trouble with the Iron Horse. I am reasonably sure that there are thousands of car owners who would like to go to Florida or California by train if without any fuss they could drive their car, fully loaded, on board the train, as onto a ferryboat, and drive it off when they reached their destination. This kind of piggyback ride would eliminate the long, arduous drive through what one of my correspondents calls a "homogenized" landscape, it would save spending nights in motels and eating meals along the way, and it would save general wear and tear on man and machine. If it works in Europe, perhaps it could be made to work here, where distances are much greater. The *Bluenose*, a car-carrying ship plying between Nova Scotia and Bar Harbor, is a sellout every summer; people are willing to pay to avoid the long drive around.

In those last days of the rails in Maine, I remember most clearly the remark of a Bangor citizen, which I read in the paper. This fellow walked downtown on the day after the razing of the depot; he stared in surprise at the new vista. "Hey!" he said. "You can see Brewer from Exchange Street!" (Brewer is Bangor's twin, a few hundred yards distant across the river.)

In the old days, when the railroads were in their prime, you couldn't see Brewer from Exchange Street, but you could close your eyes and see the continent of America stretched out in front of you, with the rails running on endlessly into the purple sunset, as in an overwritten novel. I loved it when I couldn't see Brewer from Exchange Street, the rest of the view was so good.

# VII

❧

# BOOKS, MEN,
# AND WRITING

# THE ST. NICHOLAS LEAGUE

*December, 1934*

There is no doubt about it, the fierce desire to write and paint that burns in our land today, the incredible amount of writing and painting that still goes on in the face of heavy odds, are directly traceable to the *St. Nicholas Magazine*. In the back pages of that wholesome periodical, in the early days of the century, there flourished a group of minors known as the St. Nicholas League. The members wrote poems and prose, took snapshots with box cameras, drew pictures at random, and solved puzzles. They submitted the results of their fervor to the League, and the lucky ones pocketed the Gold or the Silver Badge of extreme merit.

A surprising number of these tiny geniuses are still at it today, banging away with pen or brush for dear life. A hardy and sentimental old League alumnus like myself comes across their names in odd places—in the fall book list, in the classified phone directory, or among a bunch of Pulitzer Prize-winners—and thinks back to that "union of cheerful, fun-loving industrious young people, bound together by worthy aims and accomplishments and stimulated by a wide range of competitions that offer to every member a chance of recognition and success." We were an industrious and fiendishly competitive band of tots; and if some of us, in the intervening years of careless living, have lost or mislaid our silver badge, we still remember the day it came in the mail: the intensity of victory, the sweetness of young fame, a pubescent moment immortalized by one of our League members in October of 1904, a lad named Robert E. Jones, who wrote to the editor, from Milton, N.H.:

Dear St. Nicholas: My badge came last night and I am more than delighted with it. I shall always keep it, and shall always look back with pleasure to the time "when my first picture was printed." I mean to work hard this summer all by myself, and shall send in more drawings, even better, I hope, than the one which was printed. Thanking you again for the beautiful badge, I remain, Most gratefully yours, Robert E. Jones.

Incidentally, the hope expressed in Robert's letter was fulfilled. He did work hard. Late that same year he was crowned with the badge of pure gold and became an Honor Member. They say he is even now doing the same high grade of work in the field of stage design.

Occasionally a writer or an artist, in a fit of biographical confession, jokingly admits to his public that he once won a badge from the St. Nicholas League. His jocosity is to hide his emotion. Nothing has ever taken the place of the League in his life. The Pulitzer Prize was a pleasant reward to Edna St. Vincent Millay, I have no doubt; but it was faint fun compared to her conquest in 1907 when, as E. *Vincent* Millay, 15, of Camden, Me., she opened her August number of *St. Nicholas* and found, "accepted for publication," her poem beginning "Shine on me, oh, you gold, gold sun." This poem was called "Vacation Song." Here are the first and last stanzas:

Shine on me, oh, you gold, gold sun,
Smile on me, oh, you blue, blue skies,
Sing birds! and rouse the lazy breeze
That, in the shadow, sleeping lies,
Calling, "Awaken! Slothful one
And chase the yellow butterflies."

Oh, mower! All the world's at play,—
Leave on the grass your sickle bright;
Come, and we'll dance a merry step
With the birds and leaves and the gold sunlight,
We'll dance till the shadows leave the hills
And bring to the fields the quiet night.

Even in 1907 Edna was already an honor member of the League. She had won honorable mention in June 1904, for a prose piece called "A Family Tradition." She had scored again in November 1905, February and September 1906, and really hit her stride in the spring of 1907. Three years later, her bureau drawer heaped with all the trophies the League could bestow on an illustrious member, Miss Millay, now a ripe girl of eighteen, sat down and penned her valedictory, published in the October issue:

Dear St. Nicholas: I am writing to thank you for my cash prize and to say good-bye, for "Friends" was my last contribution. I am going to buy with my five dollars a beautiful copy of "Browning," whom I admire so much that my prize will give me more pleasure in that form than in any other.

Although I shall never write for the League again, I shall not allow myself to become a stranger to it. You have been a great help and a great encouragement to me, and I am sorry to grow up and leave you. Your loving graduate, Edna Vincent Millay.

Thus Edna walked statelily out of the League, a copy of Browning in her hand, leaving a youngster named Scott Fitzgerald holding the fort in the same issue with a prize-winning photograph called "Vacation Scene." The poem "Friends," for which she received five dollars, is reprinted hereunder. The editor seemed to have had some vague notion that he was dealing with an authentic talent, for the verses appeared at the head of the League section and were prefaced with this editorial comment: "This contribution is a little gem in smoothness and perfection of its rhythm, in its deft use of contrast, and in its naturalness of expression from first to last."

### Friends

### I. He

I've sat here all the afternoon, watching her busy fingers send
That needle in and out. How soon, I wonder, will she reach the end?
Embroidery! I can't see how a girl of Molly's common sense
Can spend her time like that. Why, now—just look at that! I may be dense,
But, somehow, I don't see the fun in punching lots of holes down through
A piece of cloth; and, one by one, sewing them up. But Molly'll do
    A dozen of them, right around
    That shapeless bit of stuff she's found.
    A dozen of them! Just like that!
    And think it's sense she's working at.
But then, she's just a girl (although she's quite the best one of the lot)
And I'll just have to let her sew, whether it's foolishness or not.

### II. She

He's sat here all the afternoon, talking about an awful game;
One boy will not be out till June, and then he may be always lame.
Foot-ball! I'm sure I can't see why a boy like Bob—so good and kind—
Wishes to see poor fellows lie hurt on the ground. I may be blind,
But somehow, I don't see the fun. Some one calls, "14-16-9";
You kick the ball, and then you run and try to reach a white chalk-line.
    And Bob would sit right there all day
    And talk like that, and never say

A single word of sense; or so
  It seems to me. I may not know.
But Bob's a faithful friend to me. So let him talk that game detested,
And I will smile and seem to be most wonderfully interested.

I suppose there exist a few adults who never even heard of the St. Nicholas League—people whose childhood was spent on the other side of the railroad tracks reading the *Youth's Companion*; whose fathers didn't give them a subscription to *St. Nick* and who consequently never knew what it was to stand, as we League members stood, "for intelligent patriotism, and for protection of the oppressed, whether human beings, dumb animals or birds." I well remember how vital to one's progress in the League was kindness-to-animals. Without kindness-to-animals, you didn't get far in the St. Nicholas League, unless, like Edna Millay, you were really talented. (A lot of us boys had no perceptible talent, but were just sissies who stayed indoors and read magazines while normal kids were out playing I Spy.) It was a buddy of mine two houses up the block, an observant child named E. Barrett Brady, wise in the ways of the world, who put me on to kindness-to-animals in its relation to winning a silver or a gold badge. Barrett said it was worth while to put plenty of it in. As I look through the back numbers and examine my own published works, I detect running through them an amazing note of friendliness toward dumb creatures, an almost virulent sympathy for dogs, cats, horses, bears, toads, and robins. I was kind to animals in all sorts of weather almost every month for three or four years. The results were satisfactory. I won both the silver and the gold badge, and was honorably mentioned several times. This precocious anticipation of an editor's needs is a sad and revealing chapter in my life; I was after results, apparently, and was not writing, or drawing, for Art's own sake. Still, the League motto was "Live to learn and learn to live."

Membership in the League was anyone's for the asking. The first thing that happened when you joined was that they sent you a copper button, engraved with the League's name and the League emblem (the stars and stripes) in colors (red, white, and blue). This button was, as advertised, "beautiful in design and workmanship." Sweet as it was, it was just a starter, just a taste of what life was to be like. That was the beauty of the League—it came through handsomely every so often with some tangible reward. Each month six silver badges and six gold badges were distributed among the twelve successful adolescents of the month, for the best two drawings, the best two poems, the best two stories or essays, the best two amateur photographs, the best two puzzles, and the best two sets of answers to the puzzles in the previous issue. These puzzles, let me say, were sons of guns. It was a never-failing source of wonder that anybody ever managed to get all the answers. Someone always did, though. A child named Ringgold W. Lardner was on the honor roll for puzzles in April 1900; and Stephen Benét, John C. Farrar, Alan Dunn, Wilella Waldorf, and Louis Kronenberger all made the puzzle award in their time. Each month subjects were suggested for drawings and poems (or you could choose your own subject). In the drawing group there was always the chance to try a "Heading for January" or a "Heading for September" or whatever the forthcoming month happened to be. There were no dues of any sort, which perhaps accounts for the League's piling up some two hundred thousand members in its thirty-five years of existence.

We Leaguers were busy youngsters. Many of us had two or three strings to our bows and were not content till we had shone in every department, including wild-life photogaphy. Little Robert Benchley was an exception. He was elevated to the roll of honor in September 1903, for a drawing called "The Dollies' Lesson," the same month that Newman Levy won distinction in drawing and Conrad P. Aiken was mentioned for a poem called "A Lullaby." But although Benchley got in near the start of the League (it was organized in 1899), he showed no perseverance. "The Dollies' Lesson" was his only appearance. He dropped out early and was never heard from again, reminding one forcibly of one of the tenets of the League, that "book study alone is not followed by the best results. Direct friendship with the woods and fields and healthful play are necessary to the proper development of both mind and body." Benchley, knowing little of the woods and fields, and nothing about kindness to animals, was an ephemeral member.

Most of us were stayers. Aiken appeared in print four times in 1903 and once in 1904. E. Babette Deutsch rang the bell no fewer than nineteen times during her childhood; John C. Farrar twenty-two; E. Vincent Millay twenty; Susan Warren Wilbur twenty-one. Joseph Auslander made ten successful appearances in two years, and was twice publicly reprimanded by having his name published on the "Careless Roll"—once for no address, once for sending in a contribution without the proper endorsement. (All League contributors had to get a parent or guardian to write on the back "This is Joseph's own work" and sign it. If you forgot to, your name was published among the Careless.) Morris Ryskind was careless twice in the spring of 1913, but later redeemed himself with a poem, "Dawn," and a prose piece, "A Family Tradition," both of which would have been published had space permitted.

It would have been unsafe to predict the professional future of the Leaguers from the type of work they turned in. Viola Beerbohm Tree drew pictures for the League and turned out to be an actress. Laura

Benét wrote several prose pieces and turned into a poet. Elinor Wylie (Elinor M. Hoyt) distinguished herself twice, both times for drawing; and that young comer Ringgold W. Lardner gained double honors—in verse and in puzzles. (Note: his poem was not considered good enough to publish, and was merely mentioned.) Cornelia Otis Skinner wrote a poem. J. Deems Taylor and Janet Flanner, in a mad May of 1901, rose to fame together, each with a drawing called "Household Joys," a suggested subject. Master Taylor scored again later, copping a silver badge in December 1901, for his photograph "Moonrise in December," a snapshot of an extremely peaceful snow scene. Alan Seeger succeeded with a photograph "From My Best Negative." Sigmund G. Spaeth, with his eye on timely topics, wrote a poem about the first springtime of the twentieth century. John C. Mosher took signal honors with his camera in 1906, and, had space permitted, would have enlivened the January 1906 issue with his pleasing photograph "The View from My Home." Norman Geddes was mentioned in 1909 for a drawing, "My Best Friend's Favorite Occupation." And so it went. They were happy days.

Contributions came even from across the sea. A little English girl named Vita V. Sackville-West, bursting with an ancient pride, wrote in 1902 from Knole, Sevenoaks, Kent, England:

> Dear St. Nicholas League: This story about my home is quite true, and it may amuse you. The archbishops of England possessed Knole first. It then passed into the hands of Queen Elizabeth, who gave it to my ancestor, Thomas Sackville. After Thomas's death, Knole went to Richard Sackville, who was Thomas's brother. It then became the seat of the dukes of Dorset, and then it belonged to the earls of that county, and from then the Sackvilles have had it. There are 365 rooms in Knole, 52 staircases, and 7 courts. A priest's cell was found this year. The altar in the chapel was given by Mary of Scotland just before she was executed. Knole began to be built in 1100 or 1200 up to 1400. Most of the kings and queens of England have made Knole a present. We have here the second organ that was made in England. There are 21 show rooms in the house. Vita V. Sackville-West.

And another little English girl, Stella Benson, was taking cash prizes for her verses, and writing thank-you letters to the editor telling him she didn't really deserve any money.

We Leaguers even grew up and married one another. I married a League girl (silver badge for prose); and I see by the files that William R. Benét did, too. His girl was Elinor M. Hoyt, who received honorable mention for "A Heading for March" in 1901, three months before William received honorable mention for a poem "When School Is Done." My girl's sister was a gold-badge holder: she won it in wild-life photography by sneaking up with her camera on an affable duck in a public park in Worcester, Mass. And speaking of photography, one of the most unflinching of the League's camera enthusiasts, judging from published results, was a tot named Lois B. Long. Apparently she was banging away with her Brownie from morning till night, and as a result we have, credited to her, a picture of a girl standing in a wheat field, a picture called "Face to Face," another called "At the Corner," and another called "Where I Spent My Vacation."

We were a hardy and a versatile lot, all right. There were William Faulkner, Alice Hughes, Norman Klein, John Macy, Corey Ford, Frances Frost, Ward Greene, John S. Martin, Margaret E. Sangster, Niven Busch, Jr., Robert Garland, Peggy Bacon, Faith Baldwin, Margaret Kennedy, Clarence C. Little, Reginald Marsh, Bennett Cerf, Kay Boyle, Alice Harvey, Frieda Inescort, Weare Holbrook, Horatio Winslow, Lee Simonson, Marjorie Allen Seiffert, Richard Whorf, Anne Parrish, Leane Zugsmith, Clement Wood, Edmund Wilson, Lyle Saxon, Marion Strobel, Mary F. Watkins, all the Benéts, Jeanne de Lamarter, Henry Dreyfuss, Susan Ertz, Elizabeth Hawes, and how many others I'll never know.

For ten years (from 1899 to 1909) the League was edited by Albert Bigelow Paine. I bought a copy of *St. Nicholas* the other day to see what changes time had wrought. The magazine is now grown tall and limp, like *Collier's*—strange to the touch. The format is changed, but the League goes on, in its fashion. The proprietors have, it seems, eased the bitter problem of silver, gold, and cash awards by tying up, in the approved American manner, with manufacturers of the indispensable tools of the arts, fountain pens and drawing materials. I noted, uneasily, that a current minor named Ruth Blaesing, 13, was receiving for her "Ode to the Earth" not the silver badge of courage but the Waterman Pen Company's award of a fountain pen. And that Rose Doyle, 13, was receiving, for her drawing, the "First Higgins' Ink Award."

But the cheering thing was that the contributions in the current issue showed the same tenderness for life, the same reverent preoccupation with Nature, the same earnest morality that we early Leaguers showed in the days of our glory. No graduate can read over the old copies without a lump in the throat; for beneath the callow phrase and the young solemnity, the roots of beauty sometimes throve. Listen to the Miss Millay of November 1908, and you can hear already the singer singing:

> How lovely is the night, how calm and still!
> Cool shadows lie upon each field and hill,
> From which a fairy wind comes tripping light,

Perching on bush and tree in airy flight.
Across the brook and up the field it blows,
And to my ear there comes, where'er it goes,
A rustling sound as if each blade of grass
Held back a silken skirt to let it pass.

This is the bedtime of the weary day;
Clouds wrap him warmly in a blanket gray;
From out the dusk where creek and meadow lie,
The frogs chirp out a sleepy lullaby;
A single star, new-kindled in the west,
A flickering candle, lights the day to rest.

O lovely night, sink deep into my heart;
Lend me thy tranquillity a part;
Of calmness give to me a kindly loan,
Until I have more calmness of my own.
And, weary day, O let thy candle-light,
And let thy lullaby be mine tonight.

And hark to the William R. Benét, of Watervliet Arsenal, West Troy, N.Y., examining the harvest at the age of fifteen:

Yon lie the fields all golden with grain
    (Oh, come, ye Harvesters, reap!)
The dead leaves are falling with autumn's brown stain
    (Oh, come, ye Harvesters, reap!)
For soon sinks the sun to his bed in the west,
And cawing the crows fly each one to his nest;
The grain will soon wither, so harvest your best.
    (Oh, come, ye Harvesters, reap!)

Hear young Briton Niven Busch, Jr., before he had discovered the cinema, finding peace in August 1919, in a calm sonnet beginning:

Beneath the radiance of the quiet stars
The earth lies beautiful as in a dream.

And search the heart of youth with fourteen-year-old Stella Benson:

Borne upwards on its gold and silver wings
    Rises the Heart of Youth,
With its fond hopes and sweet imaginings
It wanders through this sordid world, nor brings
To mind the hard, undecorated truth;
And future cares and sorrows left behind
Are spurned, because the Heart of Youth is blind.

The League is still our white plume. We graduates know what it was like to wear it. These later, slight victories, such as they are, fail to make the heart pound; the twilight of an Honor Member is a dim and unsubstantial time. Give me again October 1914 and my drawing (which would have been published had space permitted) called "The Love of a Mother Rabbit."

# A SLIGHT SOUND AT EVENING

*Allen Cove, Summer, 1954*

In his journal for July 10-12, 1841, Thoreau wrote: "A slight sound at evening lifts me up by the ears, and makes life seem inexpressibly serene and grand. It may be in Uranus, or it may be in the shutter." The book into which he later managed to pack both Uranus and the shutter was published in 1854, and now, a hundred years having gone by, *Walden,* its serenity and grandeur unimpaired, still lifts us up by the ears, still translates for us that language we are in danger of forgetting, "which all things and events speak without metaphor, which alone is copious and standard."

*Walden* is an oddity in American letters. It may very well be the oddest of our distinguished oddities. For many it is a great deal too odd, and for many it is a particular bore. I have not found it to be a well-liked book among my acquaintances, although usually spoken of with respect, and one literary critic for whom I have the highest regard can find no reason for anyone's giving *Walden* a second thought. To admire the book is, in fact, something of an embarrassment, for the mass of men have an indistinct notion that its author was a sort of Nature Boy.

I think it is of some advantage to encounter the book at a period in one's life when the normal anxieties and enthusiasms and rebellions of youth closely resemble those of Thoreau in that spring of 1845 when he borrowed an ax, went out to the woods, and began to whack down some trees for timber. Received at such a juncture, the book is like an invitation to life's dance, assuring the troubled recipient that no matter what befalls him in the way of success or failure he will always be welcome at the party—that the music is played for him, too, if he will but listen and move his feet. In effect, that is what the book is—an invitation, unengraved; and it stirs one as a young girl is stirred by her first big party bid. Many think it a sermon; many set it down as an attempt to rearrange society; some think it an exercise in nature-loving; some find it a rather irritating collection of inspirational puffballs by an eccentric show-off. I think it none of these. It still seems to me the best youth's companion yet written by an American, for it carries a solemn warning against the loss of one's valuables, it advances a good argument for traveling light and trying new adventures, it rings with the power of positive adoration, it contains religious feeling without religious images, and it steadfastly refuses to record bad news. Even its pantheistic note is so pure as to be noncorrupting—pure as the flute-note blown across the pond on those faraway summer nights. If our colleges and universities were alert, they would present a cheap pocket edition of the book to every senior upon graduating, along with his sheepskin, or instead of it. Even if some senior were to take it literally and start felling trees, there could be worse mishaps: the ax is older than the Dictaphone and it is just as well for a young man to see what kind of chips he leaves before listening to the sound of his own voice. And even if some were to get no farther than the table of contents, they would learn how to name eighteen chapters by the use of only thirty-nine words and would see how sweet are the uses of brevity.

If Thoreau had merely left us an account of a man's life in the woods or if he had simply retreated to the woods and there recorded his complaints about society, or even if he had contrived to include both records in one essay, *Walden* would probably not have lived a hundred years. As things turned out, Thoreau, very likely without knowing quite what he was up to, took man's relation to Nature and man's dilemma in society and man's capacity for elevating his spirit and he beat all these matters together, in a wild free interval of self-justification and delight, and produced an original omelette from which people can draw nourishment in a hungry day. *Walden* is one of the first of the vitamin-enriched American dishes. If it were a little less good than it is, or even a little less queer, it would be an abominable book. Even as it is, it will continue to baffle and annoy the literal mind and all those who are unable to stomach its caprices and imbibe its theme. Certainly the plodding economist will continue to have rough going if he hopes to emerge from the book with a clear system of economic thought. Thoreau's assault on the Concord society of the mid-nineteenth century has the quality of a modern Western: he rides into the subject at top speed, shooting in all directions. Many of his shots ricochet and nick him on the rebound, and throughout the melee there is a horrendous cloud of inconsistencies and contradictions, and when the shooting dies down and the air clears, one is impressed chiefly by the courage of the rider and by how splendid it was that somebody should have ridden in there and raised all that ruckus.

When he went to the pond, Thoreau struck an attitude and did so deliberately, but his posturing was not to draw the attention of others to him but rather to draw his own attention more closely to himself. "I learned this at least by my experiment: that if one advances confidently in the direction of his dreams, and endeavors to live the life which he has imagined, he will meet with a success unexpected in common hours." The sentence has the power to resuscitate the youth drowning in his sea of doubt. I recall my exhilaration upon reading it, many years ago, in a time of hesitation and despair. It restored me to health. And now in 1954 when I salute Henry Thoreau on the hundredth birthday of his book, I am merely paying off an old score—or an installment on it.

In his journal for May 3-4, 1838—Boston to Portland—he wrote: "Midnight—head over the boat's side—between sleeping and waking— with glimpses of one or more lights in the vicinity of Cape Ann. Bright moonlight—the effect heightened by seasickness." The entry illuminates the man, as the moon the sea on that night in May. In Thoreau the natural scene was heightened, not depressed, by a disturbance of the stomach, and nausea met its match at last. There was a steadiness in at least one passenger if there was none in the boat. Such steadiness (which in some would be called intoxication) is at the heart of *Walden* —confidence, faith, the discipline of looking always at what is to be seen, undeviating gratitude for the life-everlasting that he found growing in his front yard. "There is nowhere recorded a simple and irrepressible satisfaction with the gift of life, any memorable praise of God." He worked to correct that deficiency. *Walden* is his acknowledgment of the gift of life. It is the testament of a man in a high state of indignation because (it seemed to him) so few ears heard the uninterrupted poem of creation, the morning wind that forever blows. If the man sometimes wrote as though all his readers were male, unmarried, and well-connected, it is because he gave his testimony during the callow years. For that matter, he never really grew up. To reject the book because of the immaturity of the author and the bugs in the logic is to throw away a bottle of good wine because it contains bits of the cork.

Thoreau said he required of every writer, first and last, a simple and sincere account of his own life. Having delivered himself of this chesty dictum, he proceeded to ignore it. In his books and even in his enormous journal, he withheld or disguised most of the facts from which an understanding of his life could be drawn. *Walden*, subtitled "Life in the Woods," is not a simple and sincere account of a man's life, either in or out of the woods; it is an account of a man's journey into the mind, a toot on the trumpet to alert the neighbors. Thoreau was well aware that no one can alert his neighbors who is not wide-awake himself, and he went to the woods (among other reasons) to make sure that he would stay awake during his broadcast. What actually took place during the years 1845-47 is largely unrecorded, and the reader is excluded from the private life of the author, who supplies almost no gossip about himself, a great deal about his neighbors and about the universe.

As for me, I cannot in this short ramble give a simple and sincere account of my own life, but I think Thoreau might find it instructive to know that this memorial essay is being written in a house that, through no intent on my part, is the same size and shape as his own domicile on the pond—about ten by fifteen, tight, plainly finished, and at a little distance from my Concord. The house in which I sit this morning was built to accommodate a boat, not a man, but by long experience I have learned that in most respects it shelters me better than the larger dwelling where my bed is, and which, by design, is a manhouse not a boathouse. Here in the boathouse I am a wilder and, it would appear, a healthier man, by a safe margin. I have a chair, a bench, a table, and I can walk into the water if I tire of the land. My house fronts a cove. Two fishermen have just arrived to spot fish from the air—an osprey and a man in a small yellow plane who works for the fish company. The man, I have noticed, is less well equipped than the hawk, who can dive directly on his fish and carry it away, without telephoning. A mouse and a squirrel share the house with me. The building is, in fact, a multiple dwelling, a semidetached affair. It is because I am semi-detached while here that I find it possible to transact this private busi ness with the fewest obstacles.

There is also a woodchuck here, living forty feet away under the wharf. When the wind is right, he can smell my house; and when the wind is contrary, I can smell his. We both use the wharf for sunning, taking turns, each adjusting his schedule to the other's convenience. Thoreau once ate a woodchuck. I think he felt he owed it to his readers, and that it was little enough, considering the indignities they were suffering at his hands and the dressing-down they were taking. (Parts of *Walden* are pure scold.) Or perhaps he ate the woodchuck because he believed every man should acquire strict business habits, and the woodchuck was destroying his market beans. I do not know. Thoreau had a strong experimental streak in him. It is probably no harder to eat a woodchuck than to construct a sentence that lasts a hundred years. At any rate, Thoreau is the only writer I know who prepared himself for his great ordeal by eating a woodchuck; also the only one who got a hangover from drinking too much water. (He was drunk the whole time, though he seldom touched wine or coffee or tea.)

Here in this compact house where I would spend one day as deliberately as Nature if I were not being pressed by the editor of a magazine, and with a woodchuck (as yet uneaten) for neighbor, I can feel the companionship of the occupant of the pond-side cabin in Walden woods, a mile from the village, near the Fitchburg right of way. Even my immediate business is no barrier between us: Thoreau occasionally batted out a magazine piece, but was always suspicious of any sort of purposeful work that cut into his time. A man, he said, should take care not to be thrown off the track by every nutshell and mosquito's wing that falls on the rails.

There has been much guessing as to why he went to the pond. To set it down to escapism is, of course, to misconstrue what happened. Henry went forth to battle when he took to the woods, and *Walden* is the report of a man torn by two powerful and opposing drives—the desire to enjoy the world (and not be derailed by a mosquito wing) and the urge to set the world straight. One cannot join these two successfully, but sometimes, in rare cases, something good or even great results from the attempt of the tormented spirit to reconcile them. Henry went forth to battle, and if he set the stage himself, if he fought on his own terms and with his own weapons, it was because it was his nature to do things differently from most men, and to act in a cocky fashion. If the pond and the woods seemed a more plausible site for a house than an in-town location, it was because a cowbell made for him a sweeter sound than a churchbell. *Walden*, the book, makes the sound of a cowbell, more than a churchbell, and proves the point, although both sounds are in it, and both remarkably clear and sweet. He simply preferred his churchbell at a little distance.

I think one reason he went to the woods was a perfectly simple and commonplace one—and apparently he thought so, too. "At a certain season of our life," he wrote, "we are accustomed to consider every spot as the possible site of a house." There spoke the young man, a few years out of college, who had not yet broken away from home. He hadn't married, and he had found no job that measured up to his rigid standards of employment, and like any young man, or young animal, he felt uneasy and on the defensive until he had fixed himself a den. Most young men, of course, casting about for a site, are content merely to draw apart from their kinfolks. Thoreau, convinced that the greater part of what his neighbors called good was bad, withdrew from a great deal more than family: he pulled out of everything for a while, to serve everybody right for being so stuffy, and to try his own prejudices on the dog.

The house-hunting sentence above, which starts the chapter called "Where I Lived, and What I Lived For," is followed by another passage that is worth quoting here because it so beautifully illustrates the off-beat prose that Thoreau was master of, a prose at once strictly disciplined and wildly abandoned. "I have surveyed the country on every side within a dozen miles of where I live," continued this delirious young man. "In imagination I have bought all the farms in succession, for all were to be bought, and I knew their price. I walked over each farmer's premises, tasted his wild apples, discoursed on husbandry with him, took his farm at his price, at any price, mortgaging it to him in my mind; even put a higher price on it—took everything but a deed of it— took his word for his deed, for I dearly love to talk—cultivated it, and him too to some extent, I trust, and withdrew when I had enjoyed it long enough, leaving him to carry it on." A copy-desk man would get a double hernia trying to clean up that sentence for the management, but the sentence needs no fixing, for it perfectly captures the meaning of the writer and the quality of the ramble.

"Wherever I sat, there I might live, and the landscape radiated from me accordingly." Thoreau, the home-seeker, sitting on his hummock with the entire State of Massachusetts radiating from him, is to me the most humorous of the New England figures, and *Walden* the most humorous of the books, though its humor is almost continuously subsurface and there is nothing deliberately funny anywhere, except a few weak jokes and bad puns that rise to the surface like the perch in the pond that rose to the sound of the maestro's flute. Thoreau tended to write in sentences, a feat not every writer is capable of, and *Walden* is, rhetorically speaking, a collection of certified sentences, some of them, it would now appear, as indestructible as they are errant. The book is distilled from the vast journals, and this accounts for its intensity: he picked out bright particles that pleased his eye, whirled them in the kaleidoscope of his content, and produced the pattern that has endured—the color, the form, the light.

On this its hundredth birthday, Thoreau's *Walden* is pertinent and timely. In our uneasy season, when all men unconsciously seek a retreat from a world that has got almost completely out of hand, his house in the Concord woods is a haven. In our culture of gadgetry and the

multiplicity of convenience, his cry "Simplicity, simplicity, simplicity!"
has the insistence of a fire alarm. In the brooding atmosphere of war
and the gathering radioactive storm, the innocence and serenity of his
summer afternoons are enough to burst the remembering heart, and one
gazes back upon that pleasing interlude—its confidence, its purity, its
deliberateness—with awe and wonder, as one would look upon the face
of a child asleep.

"This small lake was of most value as a neighbor in the intervals
of a gentle rain-storm in August, when, both air and water being perfectly still, but the sky overcast, midafternoon had all the serenity of
evening, and the wood-thrush sang around, and was heard from shore
to shore." Now, in the perpetual overcast in which our days are spent,
we hear with extra perception and deep gratitude that song, tying
century to century.

I sometimes amuse myself by bringing Henry Thoreau back to life
and showing him the sights. I escort him into a phone booth and
let him dial Weather. "This is a delicious evening," the girl's voice says,
"when the whole body is one sense, and imbibes delight through every
pore." I show him the spot in the Pacific where an island used to be,
before some magician made it vanish. "We know not where we are," I
murmur. "The light which puts out our eyes is darkness to us. Only that
day dawns to which we are awake." I thumb through the latest copy of
*Vogue* with him. "Of two patterns which differ only by a few threads
more or less of a particular color," I read, "the one will be sold readily,
the other lie on the shelf, though it frequently happens that, after the
lapse of a season, the latter becomes the most fashionable." Together we
go outboarding on the Assabet, looking for what we've lost—a hound,
a bay horse, a turtledove. I show him a distracted farmer who is trying
to repair a hay baler before the thunder shower breaks. "This farmer,"
I remark, "is endeavoring to solve the problem of a livelihood by a
formula more complicated than the problem itself. To get his shoestrings
he speculates in herds of cattle."

I take the celebrated author to Twenty-One for lunch, so the
waiters may study his shoes. The proprietor welcomes us. "The gross
feeder," remarks the proprietor, sweeping the room with his arm, "is a
man in the larva stage." After lunch we visit a classroom in one of those
schools conducted by big corporations to teach their superannuated
executives how to retire from business without serious injury to their
health. (The shock to men's systems these days when relieved of the
exacting routine of amassing wealth is very great and must be
cushioned.) "It is not necessary," says the teacher to his pupils, "that

a man should earn his living by the sweat of his brow, unless he sweats easier than I do. We are determined to be starved before we are hungry."

I turn on the radio and let Thoreau hear Winchell beat the red hand around the clock. "Time is but the stream I go a-fishing in," shouts Mr. Winchell, rattling his telegraph key. "Hardly a man takes a half hour's nap after dinner, but when he wakes he holds up his head and asks, 'What's the news?' If we read of one man robbed, or murdered, or killed by accident, or one house burned, or one vessel wrecked, or one steamboat blown up, or one cow run over on the Western Railroad, or one mad dog killed, or one lot of grasshoppers in the winter—we need never read of another. One is enough."

I doubt that Thoreau would be thrown off balance by the fantastic sights and sounds of the twentieth century. "The Concord nights," he once wrote, "are stranger than the Arabian nights." A four-engined airliner would merely serve to confirm his early views on travel. Everywhere he would observe, in new shapes and sizes, the old predicaments and follies of men—the desperation, the impedimenta, the meanness—along with the visible capacity for elevation of the mind and soul. "This curious world which we inhabit is more wonderful than it is convenient; more beautiful than it is useful; it is more to be admired and enjoyed than used." He would see that today ten thousand engineers are busy making sure that the world shall be convenient even if it is destroyed in the process, and others are determined to increase its usefulness even though its beauty is lost somewhere along the way.

At any rate, I'd like to stroll about the countryside in Thoreau's company for a day, observing the modern scene, inspecting today's snowstorm, pointing out the sights, and offering belated apologies for my sins. Thoreau is unique among writers in that those who admire him find him uncomfortable to live with—a regular hairshirt of a man. A little band of dedicated Thoreauvians would be a sorry sight indeed: fellows who hate compromise and have compromised, fellows who love wildness and have lived tamely, and at their side, censuring them and chiding them, the ghostly figure of this upright man, who long ago gave corroboration to impulses they perceived were right and issued warnings against the things they instinctively knew to be their enemies. I should hate to be called a Thoreauvian, yet I wince every time I walk into the barn I'm pushing before me, seventy-five feet by forty, and the author of *Walden* has served as my conscience through the long stretches of my trivial days.

Hairshirt or no, he is a better companion than most, and I would not swap him for a soberer or more reasonable friend even if I could.

I can reread his famous invitation with undiminished excitement. The sad thing is that not more acceptances have been received, that so many decline for one reason or another, pleading some previous engagement or ill health. But the invitation stands. It will beckon as long as this remarkable book stays in print—which will be as long as there are August afternoons in the intervals of a gentle rainstorm, as long as there are ears to catch the faint sounds of the orchestra. I find it agreeable to sit here this morning, in a house of correct proportions, and hear across a century of time his flute, his frogs, and his seductive summons to the wildest revels of them all.

# SOME REMARKS ON HUMOR*

Analysts have had their go at humor, and I have read some of this interpretative literature, but without being greatly instructed. Humor can be dissected, as a frog can, but the thing dies in the process and the innards are discouraging to any but the pure scientific mind.

In a newsreel theater the other day I saw a picture of a man who had developed the soap bubble to a higher point than it had ever before reached. He had become the ace soap bubble blower of America, had perfected the business of blowing bubbles, refined it, doubled it, squared it, and had even worked himself up into a convenient lather. The effect was not pretty. Some of the bubbles were too big to be beautiful, and the blower was always jumping into them or out of them, or playing some sort of unattractive trick with them. It was, if anything, a rather repulsive sight. Humor is a little like that: it won't stand much blowing up, and it won't stand much poking. It has a certain fragility, an evasiveness, which one had best respect. Essentially, it is a complete mystery. A human frame convulsed with laughter, and the laughter becoming hysterical and uncontrollable, is as far out of balance as one shaken with the hiccoughs or in the throes of a sneezing fit.

One of the things commonly said about humorists is that they are really very sad people—clowns with a breaking heart. There is some truth in it, but it is badly stated. It would be more accurate, I think, to say that there is a deep vein of melancholy running through everyone's life and that the humorist, perhaps more sensible of it than some others, compensates for it actively and positively. Humorists fatten on

---

* Adapted from the preface to *A Subtreasury of American Humor*, Coward-McCann, 1941.

trouble. They have always made trouble pay. They struggle along with a good will and endure pain cheerfully, knowing how well it will serve them in the sweet by and by. You find them wrestling with foreign languages, fighting folding ironing boards and swollen drainpipes, suffering the terrible discomfort of tight boots (or as Josh Billings wittily called them, "tite" boots). They pour out their sorrows profitably, in a form that is not quite fiction nor quite fact either. Beneath the sparkling surface of these dilemmas flows the strong tide of human woe.

Practically everyone is a manic depressive of sorts, with his up moments and his down moments, and you certainly don't have to be a humorist to taste the sadness of situation and mood. But there is often a rather fine line between laughing and crying, and if a humorous piece of writing brings a person to the point where his emotional responses are untrustworthy and seem likely to break over into the opposite realm, it is because humor, like poetry, has an extra content. It plays close to the big hot fire which is Truth, and sometimes the reader feels the heat.

The world likes humor, but it treats it patronizingly. It decorates its serious artists with laurel, and its wags with Brussels sprouts. It feels that if a thing is funny it can be presumed to be something less than great, because if it were truly great it would be wholly serious. Writers know this, and those who take their literary selves with great serious-ness are at considerable pains never to associate their name with anything funny or flippant or nonsensical or "light." They suspect it would hurt their reputation, and they are right. Many a poet writing today signs his real name to his serious verse and a pseudonym to his comical verse, being unwilling to have the public discover him in any but a pensive and heavy moment. It is a wise precaution. (It is often a bad poet, too.)

When I was reading over some of the parody diaries of Franklin P. Adams, I came across this entry for April 28, 1926:

> Read H. Canby's book, *Better Writing*, very excellent. But when he says, "A sense of humour is worth gold to any writer," I disagree with him vehemently. For the writers who amass the greatest gold have, it seems to me, no sense of humour; and I think also that if they had, it would be a terrible thing for them, for it would paralyze them so that they would not write at all. For in writing, emotion is more to be treas-ured than a sense of humour, and the two are often in conflict.

That is a sound observation. The conflict is fundamental. There constantly exists, for a certain sort of person of high emotional content, at work creatively, the danger of coming to a point where something cracks within himself or within the paragraph under construction—

cracks and turns into a snicker. Here, then, is the very nub of the con-flict: the careful form of art, and the careless shape of life itself. What a man does with this uninvited snicker (which may closely resemble a sob, at that) decides his destiny. If he resists it, conceals it, destroys it, he may keep his architectural scheme intact and save his building, and the world will never know. If he gives in to it, he becomes a humor-ist, and the sharp brim of the fool's cap leaves a mark forever on his brow.

I think the stature of humor must vary some with the times. The court fool in Shakespeare's day had no social standing and was no better than a lackey, but he did have some artistic standing and was listened to with considerable attention, there being a well-founded be-lief that he had the truth hidden somewhere about his person. Artisti-cally he stood probably higher than the humorist of today, who has gained social position but not the ear of the mighty. (Think of the trouble the world would 'ave itself if it would pay some attention to nonsense!) A narrative poet at court, singing of great deeds, enjoyed a higher standing than the fool and was allowed to wear fine clothes; yet I suspect that the ballad singer was more often than not a second-rate stooge, flattering his monarch lyrically, while the fool must often have been a first-rate character, giving his monarch good advice in bad puns.

In the British Empire of our time, satirical humor of the Gilbert and Sullivan sort enjoys a solid position in the realm, and *Punch,* which is as British as vegetable marrow, is socially acceptable every-where an Englishman is to be found. The *Punch* editors not only write the jokes but they help make the laws of England. Here in America we have an immensely humorous people in a land of milk and honey and wit, who cherish the ideal of the "sense" of humor and at the same time are highly suspicious of anything that is nonserious. Whatever else an American believes or disbelieves about himself, he is absolutely sure he has a sense of humor.

Frank Moore Colby, one of the most intelligent humorists operating in this country in the early years of the century, in an essay called "The Pursuit of Humor" described how the American loves and guards his most precious treasure:

> . . . Now it is the commonest thing in the world to hear people call the absence of a sense of humor the one fatal defect. No matter how owlish a man is, he will tell you that. It is a miserable falsehood, and it does incalculable harm. A life without humor is like a life with-out legs. You are haunted by a sense of incompleteness, and you cannot go where your friends go. You are also somewhat of a burden. But the

only really fatal thing is the shamming of humor when you have it not. There are people whom nature meant to be solemn from their cradle to their grave. They are under bonds to remain so. In so far as they are true to themselves they are safe company for any one; but outside their proper field they are terrible. Solemnity is relatively a blessing, and the man who was born with it should never be encouraged to wrench himself away.

We have praised humor so much that we have started an insincere cult, and there are many who think they must glorify it when they hate it from the bottom of their hearts. False humor-worship is the deadliest of social sins, and one of the commonest. People without a grain of humor in their composition will eulogize it by the hour. Men will confess to treason, murder, arson, false teeth, or a wig. How many of them will own up to a lack of humor? The courage that could draw this confession from a man would atone for everything.

Relatively few American humorists have become really famous, so that their name is known to everyone in the land in the way that many novelists and other solemn literary characters have become famous. Mark Twain made it. He had, of course, an auspicious start, since he was essentially a storyteller and his humor was an added attraction. (It was also very, very good.) In the nineteen twenties and thirties Ring Lardner was the idol of professional humorists and of plenty of other people, too; but I think I am correct in saying that at the height of his career he was not one of the most widely known literary figures in this country, and the name Lardner was not known to the millions but only to the thousands. He never reached Mr. and Mrs. America and all the ships at sea, to the extent that Mark Twain reached them, and I doubt if he ever will. On the whole, humorists who give pleasure to a wide audience are the ones who create characters and tell tales, the ones who are storytellers at heart. Lardner told stories and gave birth to some characters, but I think he was a realist and a parodist and a satirist first of all, not essentially a writer of fiction. The general public needs something to get a grip on—a Penrod, a Huck Finn, a Br'er Rabbit, or a Father Day. The subtleties of satire and burlesque and nonsense and parody and criticism are not to the general taste; they are for the top (or, if you want, for the bottom) layer of intellect. Clarence Day, for example, was relatively inconspicuous when he was oozing his incomparable "Thoughts without Words," which are his best creations; he became generally known and generally loved only after he had brought Father to life. (Advice to young writers who want to get ahead without any annoying delays: don't write about Man, write about *a* man.)

I was interested, in reading DeVoto's "Mark Twain in Eruption," to come across some caustic remarks of Mr. Clemens's about an anthology of humor which his copyright lawyer had sent him and which Mark described as "a great fat, coarse, offensive volume." He was not amused. "This book is a cemetery," he wrote.

> In this mortuary volume [he went on] I find Nasby, Artemus Ward, Yawcob Strauss, Derby, Burdette, Eli Perkins, the Danbury News Man, Orpheus C. Kerr, Smith O'Brien, Josh Billings, and a score of others, maybe two score, whose writings and sayings were once in everybody's mouth but are now heard of no more and are no longer mentioned. Seventy-eight seems an incredible crop of well-known humorists for one forty-year period to have produced, and yet this book has not harvested the entire crop—far from it. It has no mention of Ike Partington, once so welcome and so well known; it has no mention of Doesticks, nor of the Pfaff crowd, nor of Artemus Ward's numerous and perishable imitators, nor of three very popular Southern humorists whose names I am not able to recall, nor of a dozen other sparkling transients whose light shone for a time but has now, years ago, gone out.
>
> Why have they perished? Because they were merely humorists. Humorists of the "mere" sort cannot survive. Humor is only a fragrance, a decoration. Often it is merely an odd trick of speech and of spelling, as in the case of Ward and Billings and Nasby and the "Disbanded Volunteer," and presently the fashion passes and the fame along with it.

Not long ago I plunged back fifty to a hundred years into this school of dialect humor that Mark Twain found perishable. Then was the heyday of the crackerbarrel philosopher, sometimes wise, always wise-seeming, and when read today rather dreary. It seemed to me, in reading the dialect boys, that a certain basic confusion often exists in the use of tricky or quaint or illiterate spelling to achieve a humorous effect. I mean, it is not always clear whether the author intends his character to be writing or speaking—and I, for one, feel that unless I know at least this much about what I am reading, I am off to a bad start. For instance, here are some spellings from the works of Petroleum V. Nasby: he spells "would" *wood*, "of" *uv*, "you" *yoo*, "hence" *hentz*, "office" *offis*.

Now, it happens that I pronounce "office" *offis*. And I pronounce "hence" *hentz*, and I even pronounce "of" *uv*. Therefore, I infer that Nasby's character is supposed not to be speaking but to be writing. Yet in either event, justification for this perversion of the language is lacking; for if the character is speaking, the queer spelling is unnecessary, since the pronunciation is almost indistinguishable from the natural or ordinary pronunciation, and if the character is writing, the spelling is most unlikely. Who ever wrote "uv" for "of"? Nobody. Anyone who knows how to write at all knows how to spell a simple word like "of." If you can't spell "of" you wouldn't be able to spell anything and wouldn't be attempting to set words to paper—much less words like "solissitood." A person who can't spell "of" is an illiterate, and the only time such a person attempts to write anything down is in a great crisis. He doesn't write political essays or diaries or letters or satirical paragraphs.

In the case of Dooley, the Irish dialect is difficult but worth the effort, and it smooths out after the first hundred miles. Finley Peter Dunne was a sharp and gifted humorist, who wrote no second-rate stuff, and he had the sympathetic feeling for his character which is indispensable. This same sympathy is discernible in contemporary Jewish humor—in the work of Milt Gross, Arthur Kober, Leonard Q. Ross. It is sympathy, not contempt or derision, that makes their characters live. Lardner's ballplayer was born because the author had a warm feeling for ballplayers, however boyish or goofy. The spelling in all these cases is not a device for gaining a humorous effect but a necessary tool for working the material, which is inherently humorous.

I suspect that the popularity of all dialect stuff derives in part from flattery of the reader—giving him a pleasant sensation of superiority which he gets from working out the intricacies of misspelling, and the satisfaction of detecting boorishness or illiteracy in someone else. This is not the whole story but it has some bearing in the matter. Incidentally, I am told by an authority on juvenile literature that dialect is tops with children. They like to puzzle out the words. When they catch on to the thing, they must feel that first fine glow of maturity—the ability to exercise higher intellectual powers than those of the character they are looking at.

But to get back to Mark Twain and the "great fat, coarse volume" that offended him so:

> There are those [he continued], who say that a novel should be a work of art solely, and you must not preach in it, you must not teach in it. That may be true as regards novels but it is not true as regards humor. Humor must not professedly teach, and it must not professedly preach, but it must do both if it would live forever. By forever I mean thirty years. With all its preaching it is not likely to outlive so long a term as that. The very things it preaches about, and which are novelties when it preaches about them, can cease to be novelties and become commonplaces in thirty years. Then that sermon can thenceforth interest no one.
>
> I have always preached. That is the reason that I have lasted thirty years. If the humor came of its own accord and uninvited, I have allowed it a place in my sermon, but I was not writing the sermon for the sake of humor. I should have written the sermon just the same,

whether any humor applied for admission or not. I am saying these vain things in this frank way because I am a dead person speaking from the grave. Even I would be too modest to say them in life. I think we never become really and genuinely our entire and honest selves until we are dead—and not then until we have been dead years and years. People ought to start dead, and then they would be honest so much earlier.

I don't think I agree that humor must preach in order to live; it need only speak the truth—and I notice it usually does. But there is no question at all that people ought to start dead.

# DON MARQUIS*

❧✦☙

Among books of humor by American authors, there are only a handful that rest solidly on the shelf. This book about Archy and Mehitabel, hammered out at such awful cost by the bug hurling himself at the keys, is one of those books. It is funny, it is wise; it goes right on selling, year after year. The sales do not astound me; only the author astounds me, for I know (or think I do) at what cost Don Marquis produced these gaudy and irreverent tales. He was the sort of poet who does not create easily; he was left unsatisfied and gloomy by what he produced; day and night he felt the juices squeezed out of him by the merciless demands of daily newspaper work; he was never quite certified by intellectuals and serious critics of *belles lettres*. He ended in an exhausted condition—his money gone, his strength gone. Describing the coming of Archy in the Sun Dial column of the New York *Sun* one afternoon in 1916, he wrote: "After about an hour of this frightfully difficult literary labor he fell to the floor exhausted, and we saw him creep feebly into a nest of the poems which are always there in profusion." In that sentence Don Marquis was writing his own obituary notice. After about a lifetime of frightfully difficult literary labor keeping newspapers supplied with copy, he fell exhausted.

I feel obliged, before going any further, to dispose of one troublesome matter. The reader will have perhaps noticed that I am capitalizing the name Archy and the name Mehitabel. I mention this because the capitalization of Archy is considered the unforgivable sin by a whole raft of old Sun Dial fans who have somehow nursed the illogical

---

* This essay, in a slightly different form, appeared as the introduction to Doubleday's 1950 edition of *the lives and times of archy and mehitabel*.

idea that because Don Marquis's cockroach was incapable of operating the shift key of a typewriter, nobody else could operate it. This is preposterous. Archy himself wished to be capitalized—he was no e. e. cummings. In fact he once flirted with the idea of writing the story of his life all in capital letters, if he could get somebody to lock the shift key for him. Furthermore, I capitalize Archy on the highest authority: wherever in his columns Don Marquis referred to his hero, Archy was capitalized by the boss himself. What higher authority can you ask?

The device of having a cockroach leave messages in his typewriter in the *Sun* office was a lucky accident and a happy solution for an acute problem. Marquis did not have the patience to adjust himself easily and comfortably to the rigors of daily columning, and he did not go about it in the steady, conscientious way that (for example) his contemporary Franklin P. Adams did. Consequently Marquis was always hard up for stuff to fill his space. Adams was a great editor, an insatiable proofreader, a good makeup man. Marquis was none of these. Adams, operating his Conning Tower in the *World*, moved in the commodious margins of column-and-a-half width and built up a reliable stable of contributors. Marquis, cramped by single-column width, produced his column largely without outside assistance. He never assembled a hardhitting bunch of contributors and never tried to. He was impatient of hard work and humdrum restrictions, yet expression was the need of his soul. (It is significant that the first words Archy left in his machine were "expression is the need of my soul.")

The creation of Archy, whose communications were in free verse, was part inspiration, part desperation. It enabled Marquis to use short (sometimes very, very short) lines, which fill space rapidly, and at the same time it allowed his spirit to soar while viewing things from the under side, insect fashion. Even Archy's physical limitations (his inability to operate the shift key) relieved Marquis of the toilsome business of capital letters, apostrophes, and quotation marks, those small irritations that slow up all men who are hoping their spirit will soar in time to catch the edition. Typographically, the *vers libre* did away with the turned or runover line that every single-column practitioner suffers from.

Archy has endeared himself in a special way to thousands of poets and creators and newspaper slaves, and there are reasons for this beyond the sheer merit of his literary output. The details of his creative life make him blood brother to writing men. He cast himself with all his force upon a key, head downward. So do we all. And when he was through his labors, he fell to the floor, spent. He was vain (so are we all), hungry, saw things from the under side, and was continually bringing up the matter of whether he should be paid for his work. He was bold, disrespectful, possessed of the revolutionary spirit (he organized the Worms Turnverein), was never subservient to the boss yet always trying to wheedle food out of him, always getting right to the heart of the matter. And he was contemptuous of those persons who were absorbed in the mere technical details of his writing. "The question is whether the stuff is literature or not." That question dogged his boss, it dogs us all. This book—and the fact that it sells steadily and keeps going into new editions—supplies the answer.

In one sense Archy and his racy pal Mehitabel are timeless. In another sense, they belong rather intimately to an era—an era in American letters when this century was in its teens and its early twenties, an era before the newspaper column had degenerated. In 1916 to hold a job on a daily paper, a columnist was expected to be something of a scholar and a poet—or if not a poet at least to harbor the transmigrated soul of a dead poet. Nowadays, to get a columning job a man need only have the soul of a Peep Tom or a third-rate prophet. There are plenty of loud clowns and bad poets at work on papers today, but there are not many columnists adding to *belles lettres*, and certainly there is no Don Marquis at work on any big daily, or if there is, I haven't encountered his stuff. This seems to me a serious falling off of the press. Mr. Marquis's cockroach was more than the natural issue of a creative and humorous mind. Archy was the child of compulsion, the stern compulsion of journalism. The compulsion is as great today as it ever was, but it is met in a different spirit. Archy used to come back from the golden companionship of the tavern with a poet's report of life as seen from the under side. Today's columnist returns from the platinum companionship of the night club with a dozen pieces of watered gossip and a few bottomless anecdotes. Archy returned carrying a heavy load of wine and dreams. These later cockroaches come sober from their taverns, carrying a basket of fluff. I think newspaper publishers in this decade ought to ask themselves why. What accounts for so great a falling off?

To interpret humor is as futile as explaining a spider's web in terms of geometry. Marquis was, and is, to me a very funny man, his product rich and satisfying, full of sad beauty, bawdy adventure, political wisdom, and wild surmise; full of pain and jollity, full of exact and inspired writing. The little dedication to this book

.  .  .   to babs
          with babs knows what
          and babs knows why

is a characteristic bit of Marquis madness. It has the hasty despair, the quick anguish, of an author who has just tossed another book to a publisher. It has the unmistakable whiff of the tavern, and is free of the pretense and the studied affection that so often pollute a dedicatory message.

The days of the Sun Dial were, as one gazes back on them, pleasantly preposterous times and Marquis was made for them, or they for him. *Vers libre* was in vogue, and tons of souped-up prose and other dribble poured from young free-verse artists who were suddenly experiencing a gorgeous release in the disorderly high-sounding tangle of nonmetrical lines. Spiritualism had captured people's fancy also. Sir Arthur Conan Doyle was in close touch with the hereafter, and received frequent communications from the other side. Ectoplasm swirled around all our heads in those days. (It was great stuff, Archy pointed out, to mend broken furniture with.) Souls, at this period, were being transmigrated in Pythagorean fashion. It was the time of "swat the fly," dancing the shimmy, and speakeasies. Marquis imbibed freely of this carnival air, and it all turned up, somehow, in Archy's report. Thanks to Archy, Marquis was able to write rapidly and almost (but not quite) carelessly. In the very act of spoofing free verse, he was enjoying some of its obvious advantages. And he could always let the chips fall where they might, since the burden of responsibility for his sentiments, prejudices, and opinions was neatly shifted to the roach and the cat. It was quite in character for them to write either beautifully or sourly, and Marquis turned it on and off the way an orchestra plays first hot, then sweet.

Archy and Mehitabel, between the two of them, performed the inestimable service of enabling their boss to be profound without sounding self-important, or even self-conscious. Between them, they were capable of taking any theme the boss threw them, and handling it. The piece called "the old trouper" is a good example of how smoothly the combination worked. Marquis, a devoted member of The Players, had undoubtedly had a bellyful of the lamentations of aging actors who mourned the passing of the great days of the theater. It is not hard to imagine him hastening from his club on Gramercy Park to his desk in the *Sun* office and finding, on examining Archy's report, that Mehitabel was inhabiting an old theater trunk with a tom who had given his life to the theater and who felt that actors today don't have it any more— "they don't have it here." (Paw on breast.) The conversation in the trunk is Marquis in full cry, ribbing his nostalgic old actors all in the most wildly fantastic terms, with the tomcat's grandfather (who trooped with Forrest) dropping from the fly gallery to play the beard. This is double-barreled writing, for the scene is funny in itself, with the disreputable cat and her platonic relationship with an old ham, and the implications are funny, with the author successfully winging a familiar type of bore. Double-barreled writing and, on George Herriman's part, double-barreled illustration. It seems to me Herriman deserves much credit for giving the right form and mien to these willful animals. They possess (as he drew them) the great soul. It would be hard to take Mehitabel if she were either more catlike or less. She is cat, yet not cat; and Archy's lineaments are unmistakably those of poet and pest.

Marquis was by temperament a city dweller, and both his little friends were of the city: the cockroach, most common of city bugs; the cat, most indigenous of city mammals. Both, too, were tavern habitués, as was their boss. Here were perfect transmigrations of an American soul, this dissolute feline who was a dancer and always the lady, *toujours gai*, and this troubled insect who was a poet—both seeking expression, both vainly trying to reconcile art and life, both finding always that one gets in the way of the other.

Marquis moved easily from one literary form to another. He was parodist, historian, poet, clown, fable writer, satirist, reporter, and teller of tales. He had everything it takes and more. In this book you will find prose in the guise of bad *vers libre*, you will find poetry that is truly free verse, and you will find rhymed verse. Whatever fiddle he plucked, he always produced a song. I think he was at his best in a piece like "warty bliggens," which has the jewel-like perfection of poetry and contains cosmic reverberations along with high comedy. Beautiful to read, beautiful to think about.

At bottom Don Marquis was a poet, and his life followed the precarious pattern of a poet's existence. He danced on bitter nights with Boreas, he ground out copy on drowsy afternoons when he felt no urge to write and in newspaper offices where he didn't want to be. After he had exhausted himself columning, he tried playwriting and made a pot of money (on *The Old Soak*) and then lost it all on another play (about the Crucifixion). He tried Hollywood and was utterly miserable and angry, and came away with a violent, unprintable poem in his pocket describing the place. In his domestic life he suffered one tragedy after another—the death of a young son, the death of his first wife, the death of his daughter, finally the death of his second wife. Then sickness and poverty. All these things happened in the space of a few years. He was never a robust man—usually had a puffy, overweight look and a gray complexion. He loved to drink, and was told by doctors that he mustn't. Some of the old tomcats at The Players remember the day when he came downstairs after a month on the wagon, ambled over to the bar, and announced: "I've conquered that god-damn will power of mine. Gimme a double scotch."

I think the new generation of newspaper readers is missing a lot that we used to have, and I am deeply sensible of what it meant to be a young man when Archy was at the top of his form and when Marquis was discussing the Almost Perfect State in the daily paper. Buying a paper then was quietly exciting, in a way that it has ceased to be.

# WILL STRUNK

✦✦✦

AUTHOR'S NOTE. Soon after this piece about Professor Strunk appeared in *The New Yorker*, a publisher asked me to revise and amplify *The Elements of Style* in order that it might be reissued. I agreed to do this and did it, but the job, which should have taken about a month's time, took me a year. I discovered that for all my fine talk I was no match for the parts of speech—was, in fact, over my depth and in trouble. Not only that, I felt uneasy at posing as an expert on rhetoric, when the truth is I write by ear, always with difficulty and seldom with any exact notion of what is taking place under the hood.

The Strunk book, which is a "right and wrong" book, arrived on the scene at a time when a wave of reaction was setting in against the permissive school of rhetoric, the Anything Goes school where right and wrong do not exist and there is no foundation all down the line. The little book climbed on this handy wave and rode it in.

It was during the permissive years that the third edition of Webster's *New International Dictionary* was being put together, along new lines of lexicography, and it was Dr. Gove, the head man, who perhaps expressed the whole thing most succinctly when he remarked that a dictionary "should have no traffic with . . . artificial notions of correctness or superiority. It must be descriptive and not prescriptive." This approach struck many people as chaotic and degenerative, and that's the way it struck me. Strunk was a fundamentalist; he believed in right and wrong, and so, in the main, do I. Unless someone is willing to entertain notions of superiority, the English language disintegrates, just as a home disintegrates unless someone in the family sets standards of good taste, good conduct, and simple justice.

*Turtle Bay, July 15, 1957*

Mosquitoes have arrived with the warm nights, and our bedchamber is their theater under the stars. I have been up and down all night, swinging at them with a face towel dampened at one end to give it authority. This morning I suffer from the lightheadedness that comes from no sleep—a sort of drunkenness, very good for writing because all sense of responsibility for what the words say is gone. Yesterday evening my wife showed up with a few yards of netting, and together we knelt and covered the fireplace with an illusion veil. It looks like a bride. (One of our many theories is that mosquitoes come down chimneys.) I bought a couple of adjustable screens at the hardware store on Third Avenue and they are in place in the windows; but the window sashes in this building are so old and irregular that any mosquito except one suffering from elephantiasis has no difficulty walking into the room through the space between sash and screen. (And then there is the even larger opening between upper sash and lower sash when the lower sash is raised to receive the screen—a space that hardly ever occurs to an apartment dweller but must occur to all mosquitoes.) I also bought a very old air-conditioning machine for twenty-five dollars, a great bargain, and I like this machine. It has almost no effect on the atmosphere of the room, merely chipping the edge off the heat, and it makes a loud grinding noise reminiscent of the subway, so that I can snap off the lights, close my eyes, holding the damp towel at the ready, and imagine, with the first stab, that I am riding in the underground and being pricked by pins wielded by angry girls.

Another theory of mine about the Turtle Bay mosquito is that he is swept into one's bedroom through the air conditioner, riding the cool indraft as an eagle rides a warm updraft. It is a feeble theory, but a man has to entertain theories if he is to while away the hours of sleeplessness. I wanted to buy some old-fashioned bug spray, and went to the store for that purpose, but when I asked the clerk for a Flit gun and some Flit, he gave me a queer look, as though wondering where I had been keeping myself all these years. "We got something a lot stronger than that," he said, producing a can of stuff that contained chlordane and several other unmentionable chemicals. I told him I couldn't use it because I was hypersensitive to chlordane. "Gets me right in the liver," I said, throwing a wild glance at him.

The mornings are the pleasantest times in the apartment, exhaustion having set in, the sated mosquitoes at rest on ceiling and walls, sleeping it off, the room a swirl of tortured bedclothes and abandoned garments, the vines in their full leafiness filtering the hard light of day, the air conditioner silent at last, like the mosquitoes. From Third Avenue comes the sound of the mad builders—American cicadas, out in the noonday sun. In the garden the sparrow chants—a desultory second courtship, a subdued passion, in keeping with the great heat, love in summertime, relaxed and languorous. I shall miss this apartment when it is gone; we are quitting it come fall, to turn ourselves out to pasture. Every so often I make an attempt to simplify my life, burning my books behind me, selling the occasional chair, discarding the accumulated miscellany. I have noticed, though, that these purifications of mine—to which my wife submits with cautious grace—have usually led to even greater complexity in the long pull, and I have no doubt this one will, too, for I don't trust myself in a situation of this sort and suspect that my first act as an old horse will be to set to work improving the pasture. I may even join a pasture-improvement society. The last time I tried to purify myself by fire, I managed to acquire a zoo in the process and am still supporting it and carrying heavy pails of water to the animals, a task that is sometimes beyond my strength.

A book I have decided not to get rid of is a small one that arrived in the mail not long ago, a gift from a friend in Ithaca. It is *The Elements of Style*, by the late William Strunk, Jr., and it was known on the Cornell campus in my day as "the little book," with the stress on the word "little." I must have once owned a copy, for I took English 8 under Professor Strunk in 1919 and the book was required reading, but my copy presumably failed to survive an early purge. I'd not laid eyes on it in thirty-eight years. Am now delighted to study it again and rediscover its rich deposits of gold.

*The Elements of Style* was Will Strunk's *parvum opus*, his attempt to cut the vast tangle of English rhetoric down to size and write its rules and principles on the head of a pin. Will himself hung the title "little" on the book: he referred to it sardonically and with secret pride as "the *little* book," always giving the word "little" a special twist, as though he were putting a spin on a ball. The title page reveals that the book was privately printed (Ithaca, N.Y.) and that it was copyrighted in 1918 by the author. It is a forty-three-page summation of the case for cleanliness, accuracy, and brevity in the use of English. Its vigor is unimpaired, and for sheer pith I think it probably sets a record that is not likely to be broken. The Cornell University Library has one copy. It had two, but my friend pried one loose and mailed it to me.

The book consists of a short introduction, eight rules of usage, ten principles of composition, a few matters of form, a list of words and expressions commonly misused, a list of words commonly misspelled. That's all there is. The rules and principles are in the form of direct commands, Sergeant Strunk snapping orders to his platoon. "Do not join independent clauses with a comma." (Rule 5.) "Do not break sentences in two." (Rule 6.) "Use the active voice." (Rule 11.)

"Omit needless words." (Rule 13.) "Avoid a succession of loose sentences." (Rule 14.) "In summaries, keep to one tense." (Rule 17.) Each rule or principle is followed by a short hortatory essay, and the exhoration is followed by, or interlarded with, examples in parallel columns—the true vs. the false, the right vs. the wrong, the timid vs. the bold, the ragged vs. the trim. From every line there peers out at me the puckish face of my professor, his short hair parted neatly in the middle and combed down over his forehead, his eyes blinking incessantly behind steel-rimmed spectacles as though he had just emerged into strong light, his lips nibbling each other like nervous horses, his smile shuttling to and fro in a carefully edged mustache.

"Omit needless words!" cries the author on page 21, and into that imperative Will Strunk really put his heart and soul. In the days when I was sitting in his class, he omitted so many needless words, and omitted them so forcibly and with such eagerness and obvious relish, that he often seemed in the position of having short-changed himself, a man left with nothing more to say yet with time to fill, a radio prophet who had outdistanced the clock. Will Strunk got out of this predicament by a simple trick: he uttered every sentence three times. When he delivered his oration on brevity to the class, he leaned forward over his desk, grasped his coat lapels in his hands, and in a husky, conspiratorial voice said, "Rule Thirteen. Omit needless words! Omit needless words! Omit needless words!"

He was a memorable man, friendly and funny. Under the remembered sting of his kindly lash, I have been trying to omit needless words since 1919, and although there are still many words that cry for omission and the huge task will never be accomplished, it is exciting to me to reread the masterly Strunkian elaboration of this noble theme. It goes:

> Vigorous writing is concise. A sentence should contain no unnecessary words, a paragraph no unnecessary sentences, for the same reason that a drawing should have no unnecessary lines and a machine no unnecessary parts. This requires not that the writer make all his sentences short, or that he avoid all detail and treat his subjects only in outline, but that every word tell.

There you have a short, valuable essay on the nature and beauty of brevity—sixty-three words that could change the world. Having recovered from his adventure in prolixity (sixty-three words were a lot of words in the tight world of William Strunk, Jr.), the Professor proceeds to give a few quick lessons in pruning. The student learns to cut the deadwood from "This is a subject which . . ." reducing it to "This subject . . .," a gain of three words. He learns to trim ". . . used for fuel purposes" down to "used for fuel." He learns that he is being a chatterbox when he says "The question as to whether" and that he should just say "Whether"—a gain of four words out of a possible five.

The Professor devotes a special paragraph to the vile expression "the fact that," a phrase that causes him to quiver with revulsion. The expression, he says, should be "revised out of every sentence in which it occurs." But a shadow of gloom seems to hang over the page, and you feel that he knows how hopeless his cause is. I suppose I have written "the fact that" a thousand times in the heat of composition, revised it out maybe five hundred times in the cool aftermath. To be batting only .500 this late in the season, to fail half the time to connect with this fat pitch, saddens me, for it seems a betrayal of the man who showed me how to swing at it and made the swinging seem worth while.

I treasure *The Elements of Style* for its sharp advice, but I treasure it even more for the audacity and self-confidence of its author. Will knew where he stood. He was so sure of where he stood, and made his position so clear and so plausible, that his peculiar stance has continued to invigorate me—and, I am sure, thousands of other ex-students —during the years that have intervened since our first encounter. He had a number of likes and dislikes that were almost as whimsical as the choice of a necktie, yet he made them seem utterly convincing. He disliked the word "forceful" and advised us to use "forcible" instead. He felt that the word "clever" was greatly overused; "it is best restricted to ingenuity displayed in small matters." He despised the expression "student body," which he termed gruesome, and made a special trip downtown to the *Alumni News* office one day to protest the expression and suggest that "studentry" be substituted, a coinage of his own which he felt was similar to "citizenry." I am told that the *News* editor was so charmed by the visit, if not by the word, that he ordered the student body buried, never to rise again. "Studentry" has taken its place. It's not much of an improvement, but it does sound less cadaverous, and it made Will Strunk quite happy.

A few weeks ago I noticed a headline in the *Times* about Bonnie Prince Charlie: "CHARLES' TONSILS OUT." Immediately Rule 1 leapt to mind.

> 1. Form the possessive singular of nouns with 's. Follow this rule whatever the final consonant. Thus write,
> > Charles's friend
> > Burns's poems
> > the witch's malice.

Clearly Will Strunk had foreseen, as far back as 1918, the dangerous tonsillectomy of a prince, in which the surgeon removes the tonsils and the *Times* copy desk removes the final "s." He started his book with it.

I commend Rule 1 to the *Times* and I trust that Charles's throat, not Charles' throat, is mended.

Style rules of this sort are, of course, somewhat a matter of individual preference, and even the established rules of grammar are open to challenge. Professor Strunk, although one of the most inflexible and choosy of men, was quick to acknowledge the fallacy of inflexibility and the danger of doctrine.

"It is an old observation," he wrote, "that the best writers sometimes disregard the rules of rhetoric. When they do so, however, the reader will usually find in the sentence some compensating merit, attained at the cost of the violation. Unless he is certain of doing as well, he will probably do best to follow the rules."

It is encouraging to see how perfectly a book, even a dusty rulebook, perpetuates and extends the spirit of a man. Will Strunk loved the clear, the brief, the bold, and his book is clear, brief, bold. Boldness is perhaps its chief distinguishing mark. On page 24, explaining one of his parallels, he says, "The left-hand version gives the impression that the writer is undecided or timid; he seems unable or afraid to choose one form of expression and hold to it." And his Rule 12 is "Make definite assertions." That was Will all over. He scorned the vague, the tame, the colorless, the irresolute. He felt it was worse to be irresolute than to be wrong. I remember a day in class when he leaned far forward in his characteristic pose—the pose of a man about to impart a secret—and croaked, "If you don't know how to pronounce a word, say it loud! If you don't know how to pronounce a word, say it loud!" This comical piece of advice struck me as sound at the time, and I still respect it Why compound ignorance with inaudibility? Why run and hide?

All through *The Elements of Style* one finds evidences of the author's deep sympathy for the reader. Will felt that the reader was in serious trouble most of the time, a man floundering in a swamp, and that it was the duty of anyone attempting to write English to drain this swamp quickly and get his man up on dry ground, or at least throw him a rope.

"The little book" has long since passed into disuse. Will died in 1946, and he had retired from teaching several years before that. Longer, lower textbooks are in use in English classes nowadays, I daresay—books with upswept tail fins and automatic verbs. I hope some of them manage to compress as much wisdom into as small a space, manage to come to the point as quickly and illuminate it as amusingly. I think, though, that if I suddenly found myself in the, to me, unthinkable position of facing a class in English usage and style, I would simply lean far out over the desk, clutch my lapels, blink my eyes, and say, "Get the *little* book! Get the *little* book! Get the *little* book!"

# MR. FORBUSH'S FRIENDS

As a boy, Edward Howe Forbush, the ornithologist, was up and away at daybreak every fine spring morning, exploring the woods and fields of West Roxbury. At thirteen, he stuffed a song sparrow—his first attempt at taxidermy. At fifteen, he gave up school in favor of birds. At sixteen, he was appointed Curator of Ornithology of the Worcester Natural History Society's museum—undoubtedly one of the youngest curators anywhere about. He began "collecting," which means shooting birds to get a closer look at them, and he continued to experiment with taxidermy after reading a book on it. "Such mummies," he wrote of his mounted birds, "have their uses, but later I came to see that life, not death, would solve all riddles; that an examination of the dead was merely a preliminary to a study of the living, and that it was more essential to preserve the living than the dead."

Even when he ate a bird (he was a hungry man and ate his share of birds), Mr. Forbush always saved the skin to further his scientific researches. His life was bound up with everything on wings, and his career culminated in the great *Birds of Massachusetts and Other New England States*, a three-volume summation of the avian scene. Mr. Forbush died in 1929, aged seventy-one, when the work was within a few pages of completion.

When I am out of joint, from bad weather or a poor run of thoughts, I like to sit and think about Edward Howe Forbush. I like to think of him on that June morning in 1908 when, marooned on a sandy islet near the elbow of Cape Cod, his stranded skiff awash, his oars carried to sea, a stiff sou'wester blowing, drifting sand cutting his face, sea rising, he allowed himself to become utterly absorbed in "an immense concourse of birds" resting on the sands, most of them common terns. I see him,

again, concealed in the lowest branches of a spruce on a small island off the Maine coast—a soft, balmy night. He is observing the arrival of Leach's petrels, whose burrows are underneath the tree—eerie, strange birds, whose chucklings and formless sounds might have been the conversation of elves. Or on that night when he visited a heronry among the sand dunes of Sandy Neck, Barnstable: "The windless air was stagnant and fetid; swarms of stinging midges, deerflies, and mosquitoes attacked at will; and vicious wood-ticks, hanging from the vegetation, reached for me with their clinging claws, and crawled upon my limbs, seeking an opening to bury their heads in my flesh." In such uncomfortable situations, birds being near, Mr. Forbush found the purest delight.

I managed to acquire a set of *Birds of Massachusetts* about twenty years ago, and have been reading around in the books ever since, for refreshment and instruction. The first entry in Volume I is Holbœll's grebe (grebes seem to rank nearest to the reptiles from which birds sprang). The last entry in Volume III is the golden-crowned sparrow, an accidental visitor to New England. In between these two entries are descriptive accounts and anecdotal reports of all the species known to visit New England, whether on business or on pleasure or through the accident of great storms. Although not a student of birds, I am thrown with them a good bit. It is much the same sort of experience as being thrown with people in the subway: I gaze at a female, and am filled with curiosity and a wish to know more than I do about her nesting site, breeding habits, measurements, voice, and range. In the subway, gazing at an interesting face, I have nothing to help me but my imagination. But among birds, when I encounter a new face or renew my acquaintance with an old one, I turn to Forbush for help in comprehending what I have been looking at. The information he imparts is, of course, reliable and often fascinating, but for the casual reader his great gift is his immense enthusiasm for anything that has feathers. I suppose all ornithologists rather approve of birds or they wouldn't pursue the thing, but Edward Howe Forbush during his long and busy life was obviously enchanted with them. He was the champion of birds as well as their interpreter.

A certain tidiness infects *Birds of Massachusetts*. The arrangement is calming to the nerves. You always know what you are going to get and the order in which you will get it. Let us say you wish to satisfy an idle curiosity about the barn owl and you take out Volume II and turn to page 189. First, the Latin name. Then the common name. Then the "other" name (or names)—in this case, monkey-faced owl. Then comes a section in small type: description, measurements, molts, field marks,

voice, breeding, range, distribution in New England, and season in Massachusetts. This fine-print section goes into great detail. The barn owl, for instance, is such an infrequent visitor to New England that Mr. Forbush lists the names of the persons who have observed him or taken him, and the dates ("Lexington, June 10, 1915, female taken by Chas. Fowle," and so on). When it comes to describing the sounds a bird makes, Mr. Forbush is seldom content with giving his own rendition; instead, he assembles a company of listeners and lets each one do an imitation. The voice of the barn owl, depending on who is trying to get it on paper, is "a weird scream; a nasal snore; a loud, prolonged rasping *sksck*; a series of notes *click, click, click, click, click,* resembling in character the notes of a Katydid, but delivered with diminishing emphasis and shortening intervals during the end of the series." The song of the black-throated green warbler: Bradford Torrey translates it as "trees, trees, murmuring trees," a pleasing, dreamy, drawling, reed-like lay; others change it to "cheese, cheese, a little more cheese"; and Dr. C. W. Townsend sets it down as "Hear me, Saint Theresa." (Mrs. M. M. Nice recorded two hundred and seventy-four repetitions of the song in one hour.) If you have any questions about nesting sites, eggs, period of incubation, breeding habits, breeding dates, appearance of young in juvenile plumage, range, or distribution, the answers will almost certainly be here in this section.

But when he's all through with the monumental task of delineating his bird in fine print, Mr. Forbush cuts loose with larger type and wider thoughts. Under the heading "Haunts and Habits" he writes an essay about the bird, dropping his tight scientific detachment and indulging himself as stylist, enthusiast, and footloose reporter. It is in these free-swinging essays that the fun is—for me, anyway. The style of the pieces is peculiarly the author's own—a rich prose occasionally touched with purple but never with dullness or disenchantment. A devotee of the periodic sentence, he often begins his report by setting the stage, leaving the bird out of it for a few moments, as in the very first entry (Holbœll's grebe): "A bright clear day in January, a gentle breeze, a river mouth where the rippling flood flows into the sparkling sea, a lazy swell washing gently on the bar where a herd of mottled seals is basking in the sun, Old-squaws and Golden-eyes in small parties—such a scene at Ipswich is a fit setting for the great Grebe that winters on our coasts." Or the entry for the ivory gull: "In spring dawns, fair and rosy, when the sun rising over the blue Arctic, magnificent with floating ice, reveals scene of gorgeous splendor; where ice lies in innumerable shapes, some sparkling like gems and prisms, others rearing vast, white, phantasmal forms; on the edge of the ice pack where the wind opens

vast sea-lanes; where the mirage shows towering mountains that never were on land or sea; in summer or winter, in storm or sunshine, there dwells the white Gull, bird of the ice and snow."

Sometimes, ignoring the scene, he leaps to the side of his bird and launches an attack on its detractors, as with the barn owl: "Since the dawn of history, owls have been the pitiable victims of ignorance and superstition. Hated, despised, and feared by many peoples, only their nocturnal habits have enabled them to survive in company with civilized man. In the minds of mankind they have been leagued with witches and malignant evil spirits, or even have been believed to personify the Evil One. They have been regarded as precursors of sorrow and death, and some savage tribes have been so fixed in the belief that a man will die if an owl alights on the roof of his dwelling that, it is said, some Indians having actually seen the owl on the roof-tree have pined away and died. Among all these eerie birds, the Barn Owl has been the victim of the greatest share of obloquy and persecution, owing to its sinister appearance, its weird night cries, its habit of haunting dismal swamps and dank quagmires, where an incautious step may precipitate the investigator into malodorous filth or sucking quicksands, and its tendency to frequent the neighborhood of man's dwellings, especially unoccupied buildings and ghostly ruins. Doubtless the Barn Owl is responsible for some of the stories of haunted houses which have been current through the centuries. When divested by science of its atmosphere of malign mystery, however, this owl is seen to be not only harmless but a benefactor to mankind and a very interesting fowl that will well repay close study."

Sometimes Mr. Forbush devotes most of his essay to some peculiarity of the bird: how the bittern produces its famous sounds of pumping and of stake-driving; whether the night heron really can throw out a light from its breast, as some believe; whether the cedar waxwing's dizzy spells are caused by its drinking too much fermented juice or by plain gluttony. Sometimes he starts his essay off with a bit of plain talk, straight from the shoulder, to clear up any misconception about the subject: "Cowbirds are free lovers. They are neither polygamous nor polyandrous—just promiscuous. They have no demesne and no domicile; they are entirely unattached. Their courting is brief and to the point. In this pleasant pastime the male usually takes the lead."

When he has finished with one of these rambling essays, Mr. Forbush winds up his study of the species with a short, businesslike paragraph headed "Economic Status." Here he weighs the bird's usefulness against its crimes, and it is in these concluding paragraphs, in which the bird is usually subjected to the ordeal of having the contents of its stomach examined, that you see Mr. Forbush the partisan wrestling with Mr. Forbush the scientist. The two are evenly matched, and they struggle manfully. Not all birds are popular in this world, and a number of them have police records. The crow is a cornpatch vandal. The jay is a common thief. The cormorant poses a threat to the salmon fishery. The shrike catches other birds and impales them in a thornbush for future reference. The bobolink knocks the spots out of a rice harvest. The owl presages death. The herring gull annoys commercial fishermen and befouls the decks of yachts at anchor. And so on—a long list of crimes and misdeeds. Edward Howe Forbush, however, during his long life of studying birds, managed to see more good in them than bad, and the dark chapters in the avian book are deeply challenging to him. Of the cruel shrike he says that "though we may deplore his attack on the smaller birds, we can but admire his self-reliance, audacity and courage," and that "all economic ornithologists who have investigated the food of this species regard it as a useful bird." Yet the author is scrupulously fair—he ends his defense by quoting Mr. W. L. Dawson, author of *Birds of Ohio*, who finds the shrike's offenses hard to forgive, and who says he keeps his gun loaded.

Of the mischievous crow Mr. Forbush says, "Its habit of eating eggs and young of other birds should not count too heavily against it, as the birds thus molested usually have an opportunity to raise young later in the season, when the young Crows have been reared, and natural enemies of birds are necessary to keep their numbers within bounds." Mr. Forbush also recalls with relish the case of a sheepman who annihilated the crows in his region because they killed newborn lambs, only to discover that the grass in his pastures was dying from white grubs, which had increased rapidly following the destruction of the crows. You can feel his heart rise up at this bit of ecological justice.

In his role as defense attorney for the birds, Mr. Forbush is not merely spirited, he is wonderfully resourceful. He thinks of everything. After listing the obvious benefactions of gulls (they destroy grasshoppers and locusts, dispose of dead fish and garbage, eat field mice and other pests, and in foggy weather enable mariners to locate dangerous rocks and ledges by their shrill cries), he springs a surprise. "In war time," he says, triumphantly, "gulls show the location of drifting mines by perching upon them." What jury would convict a seagull after that piece of testimony?

The common tern: "It never eats marketable fish."

The blue jay: "Jays bury nuts and seeds in the ground, thus planting forests. They also regurgitate smaller seeds and so distribute them."

The cedar waxwing: "If the cherry grower, when planting an orchard, would first set out a row of soft early cherries or early mulberries around his orchard, and allow the birds to take the fruit from those trees, he might thereby save the main crop of later, harder, and more marketable fruit."

The sharp-shinned hawk: "It is not a bird for the farmer to tolerate about his chicken coops nor is it desirable about a bird preserve. Nevertheless, in the eternal scheme of the universe, its existence serves to check the undue increase of small birds and to prevent the propagation of unfitness and disease among them."

When Mr. Forbush came to the economic status of the brown pelican, which not only loves fish but boldly advertises the fact by carrying a pouch to hold them in, he knew he was in a tough spot. Without hesitation, he called to his assistance Mr. T. Gilbert Pearson, onetime president of the National Association of Audubon Societies, who, in the spring of 1918, had investigated the pelican's criminal record and reported on it to the Federal Food Administrator. Mr. Pearson proved every bit as slippery in arguing a case as Mr. Forbush himself. He first testified that the stomachs of pelicans contained no trout, mackerel, or pompano; instead, they were loaded with mullet, pigfish, Gulf menhaden, pinfish, and thread herring. Then he introduced an exciting new theme. "These large, grotesque-looking birds," he wrote, "afford winter tourists much interest as they flop about the docks . . . and many postcards bearing pictures of pelicans are sent north every year. It is quite possible that the profits made on pelican postcards at Florida newsstands exceed in value the total quantity of food fish captured by the pelicans in the waters along its charming coast."

A wanderer in the pages of Forbush is rewarded with many delights and surprises, not the least of which are the peerless illustrations by Louis Agassiz Fuertes and Allan Brooks. To me, one of the chief amusements of the work is the presence of Mr. Forbush's large company of informers, or tipsters: people who at one time or another wrote him or phoned him to tell of an encounter with a bird—a strange doing, an odd fact, a bizarre occurrence. By paying heed to these people and giving them house-room, Mr. Forbush adds greatly to his own abundant store of knowledge besides livening things up for the reader. He welcomes tipsters just as a newspaper columnist welcomes them. Some of his are professional bird people, known to him. Some are contributors of articles to nature publications, from which Mr. F. has lifted a juicy passage. But scattered through the three volumes are the names of hundreds of amateurs and strangers, who by reporting some oddity of bird behavior or recording an unlikely arrival have achieved immortality; their names are embedded in the text of *Birds of Massachusetts* as firmly as a bottle cap in a city pavement, and they are for the ages. Their lives, from the evidence, appear to be wonderfully haphazard and fortuitous. One of them will be "sharpening a sickle" when he looks up to see a girl attacked by an eagle; one of them will "happen to be" in a little outbuilding at precisely the right moment to witness the courtship of whippoorwills; one of them will chance to step from a clump of small pines facing an alder run, and there, right before his eyes, will be the nest of a least flycatcher. The reader has hardly got started on Volume I before the first of these tipsters pops up: "Mr. Wilbur F. Smith, of South Norwalk, Connecticut, wrote to me March 27, 1916, that he had observed Holbœll's Grebes fishing near an anchored boat on which a fisherman lived. . . . Mr. Smith noted that when a bird had swallowed a particularly large fish, it put its head on its back and went to sleep."

Well, there you are. It'll be fifty years next month that Smith of South Norwalk discovered that a grebe grabs a little shut-eye after a heavy fish dinner, but the news comes as fresh today as when the letter was dropped in the mail. (I called the informant "Smith" just now, but Mr. Forbush was a courtly man and always used the polite "Mr." or "Miss" or "Mrs." or "Dr." in introducing his people.)

I have taken it on myself to bring a few of Forbush's friends together—a sort of convention of tipsters, pros and amateurs alike—and will here summarize their findings about birds. My list is necessarily selective; out of perhaps a thousand I've chosen a handful. And I have shortened their tales, giving merely the gist of the observations. Here they are, a goodly company, bright of eye, quick to take pen in hand:

Mr. Sidney Chase, of Nantucket. Saw loon rinse mouth after repast. May 3, 1922.

Mr. Harold Cooke, of Kingston. Found puffin in garage, offered it spaghetti. Spaghetti was accepted. February 1, 1922.

Mrs. Lidian E. Bridge, of Rockport. While standing on rock overlooking sea, saw two dovekies meet underwater. As they met, they uttered "an absurd little screech." No date.

Mr. Horace Bearse, of Chatham. Saw starving crow attack starving herring gull after clash at garbage heap. Winter of 1919–20, a hard winter.

Mr. J. A. Farley. In the Gulf of St. Lawrence saw ring-billed gull scratch its face with its claw as it flew. Insouciance. No date.

Mr. Allan Keniston. While visiting Muskeget Island saw young laughing gulls eject the remains of cicadas. Insects had been flown twenty miles from Cape Cod by the gulls' parents. 1923.

Captain B. F. Goss. Saw Caspian terns dive on their own eggs, break them. Terns apparently did not want eggs to fall into hands of intruders. No date.

Mr. David Gould. At Nauset, watched newly hatched common terns during windstorm. Blowing sand adhered to wet plumage, many babies buried alive. No date.

Dr. L. B. Bishop. At Stump Lake, North Dakota, saw terns strike and kill young ring-billed gulls in retaliation for adult gulls' eating terns' eggs. No date.

Dr. Joseph Grinnell. Passed night on island of St. Lazaria, Alaska. Found it impossible to keep campfire alight because Leach's petrels, who stay out all night, flew into fire in such numbers as to extinguish it. June 1896.

Mr. Frank A. Brown. On Machias Seal Island, found dog that was killing average of ten petrels a day by digging them out of their burrows. No date.

Reverend J. H. Linsley. Opened the stomach of a gannet, found bird. Opened stomach of *that* bird, found another bird. Bird within bird within bird. No date.

Mr. George H. Mackay. On Cormorant Rock, off Newport, found large number of curious balls. Appeared to have been ejected by cormorants. One ball, 5.25 inches in circumference, contained three crabs. April 1892.

Mr. Stanley C. Jewett. Asserts that wounded red-breasted merganser at Netarts Bay, Oregon, dived to submerged root in three feet of water and died while clinging there. Apparent suicide. May 1915.

Mr. J. A. Munro, of Okanagan Landing, British Columbia. Watched male bufflehead, far gone in passion, dive under another male, toss him into air. Sexual jealousy. No date.

Mr. G. Dallas Hanna. At Pribilof Islands, sought wounded harlequin duck that dived and failed to reappear. Found it dead in eight feet of water, clinging with bill to kelp near bottom. Apparent suicide. No date.

Mr. George H. Mackay again. Presented Mr. Forbush with head of female eider duck that had been found dying on Nantucket with large mussel in mouth. Mussel had closed on bird's tongue. Bird starved. Mussel remained alive, did not relax grip. January 3, 1923.

Mr. W. Sprague Brooks. In Alaska lagoon saw three male king eiders courting one female. Much neck stretching and bowing of heads. Occasionally, one male would interrupt courtship long enough to take a bath. Female unimpressed by this bathing ploy. June 14, 1915.

Mr. George W. Morse, of Tulsa, Oklahoma. Saw great blue heron strike at small fish between own legs, tripping self up. Heron was carried downstream in capsized position with legs in air. It held on to the fish. No date.

Mrs. L. H. Touissaint. States that in one morning a pet sand-hill crane captured and consumed 148 grasshoppers, 2 moths, a roach, a lizard, 2 grubs, and 11 spiders. No date.

Mr. Isador S. Trostler. Says woodcocks often play in very droll manner, run round and round each other in small circles, with wings lifted and bills pointed nearly to the zenith.

Mr. E. O. Grant. While kneeling on ground imitating squeal of spruce-grouse chick, had mother grouse fly directly at his head. No damage. No date.

Mr. W. L. Bishop. Found ruffed grouse submerged in brook, except for head, to escape goshawk. No date.

Mr. Charles Hayward. Examined crop of a ruffed grouse. Found 140 apple buds, 134 pieces of laurel leaves, 28 wintergreen leaves, 69 birch buds, 205 blueberry buds, 201 cherry buds, and 109 blueberry stems. Splendid appetite. No date.

Mrs. Eliza Cabot. Saw heath hen in her youth, another after her marriage. Late eighteenth century, early nineteenth century.

Mr. T. Gilbert Pearson. Lady of his acquaintance, while sitting alone in her room, was startled when beef bone fell out onto hearth. Went outside, discovered turkey buzzard peering down chimney. Carelessness on part of bird. No date.

Mr. William Brewster, of Concord. Was standing by corner of one of his barns. Phoebe pursued by sharp-shinned hawk used Brewster's body as shield in eluding hawk. No date.

Dr. P. L. Hatch. While riding across Minnesota prairie during winter gale, temperature 46° below zero, saw sharp-shinned hawk seize snow bunting at high speed. No date.

Mr. H. H. Waterman, of Auburn, Maine. Saw Cooper's hawk plunge flicker in roadside ditch containing one foot of water, hold it under for three minutes. May 15, 1921.

Dr. C. Hart Merriam. Attacked by enraged goshawk for defending hen. Hen hid under catnip plant during melee, remained there for five hours following encounter. October 3, 1882.

Mr. M. Semper, of Mapes P.O., British Columbia. Was at neighbor's house sharpening a mower sickle, saw golden eagle seize neighbor's little girl, Ellen Gibbs, by arm. Mr. Semper kicked eagle with no effect. Girl's mother appeared, decapitated eagle with good effect. No date.

Mrs. Elizabeth Caswell. Saw bald eagle fly directly at her house. Before reaching house, eagle swooped down, picked up what seemed to be large rat. Mrs. Caswell surprised at this. No date.

Mr. Eugene P. Bicknell. Saw duck hawk capture monarch butterfly on the wing. Hawk appeared to release prey in disgust. November 12, 1922.

Mr. Aretas A. Saunders. Heard sparrow hawk, while hovering, squeal like mouse. Hawk possibly trying to entice mouse from concealment. No date.

Friend of Mr. Forbush's, no name. Bought farm in Touisset, found osprey's nest atop chimney. Ospreys in charge of premises. Owner removed nest. Birds immediately began rebuilding, using sticks, clods, and stones. Owner, now desperate, shot female. Male went off, returned a few hours later with another mate. Pair went on with rebuilding operations. Filled chimney from bottom to top with sticks, stones, and rubbish. Owner accepted challenge, shot both birds. Large section of chimney had to be removed on one side, for removal of material choking flue. Perseverance. No date.

Dr. Anne E. Perkins, in letter from Helmuth, New York. Picked up pellets of barred owl, found they contained pig bristles and a piece of broken bone. March 23, 1925.

Mr. Joseph B. Underhill. Caught and confined male great horned owl. In return, was struck and injured by female owl. Much blood spilled. 1885.

Miss Florence Pease. Reported large owl with steel trap on one leg alighted on factory in Connecticut. Incident caused so much excitement among workers, plant was shut down for the day. 1919.

Mr. Zenas Langford, of Plymouth. Told Mr. J. A. Farley he witnessed struggle between great horned owl and blacksnake. Owl caught snake, snake twisted self around owl so latter unable to fly, fell to ground with prey. Owl held snake six inches below head, snake threw turn around owl's neck. Owl nearly exhausted but retained grip. Mr. Langford killed snake (four feet), wrapped owl in blanket, took it home, kept it a week, let it go. No date.

Mr. R. J. Gregory, of Princeton. Saw snowy owl perch in tree, devour a bird—a meadowlark. After the meal, owl dropped to ground, washed face in snow, pushing its head through the snow "in a manner similar to the way cats have been known to act." (Author's note: Dachshunds have also been known to act this way, using broadloom carpet instead of snow.)

Mr. F. H. Mosher ("a competent observer"). Watched yellow-billed cuckoo eat 41 gypsy caterpillars in fifteen minutes. Later saw another cuckoo eat 47 forest tent caterpillars in six minutes.

Mr. J. L. Davison, of Lockport, New York. Found a black-billed cuckoo and a mourning dove sitting together in a robin's nest. Nest contained two eggs of cuckoo, two of dove, one of robin. Bad management. June 17, 1882.

Mrs. Mary Treat. Watched kingfisher that commonly fished near her windows, observed that when water was too rough for fishing, bird visited sour-gum tree (*Nyssa aquatica*) and greedily devoured berries, afterward regurgitated pellets of seeds in same manner it ejected scales and bones of fish. No date.

Mrs. Gene Stratton Porter. Examined food remains in nest of kingfisher, found one-tenth of them to be nearly equally divided between berry seeds and the hard parts of grasshoppers. Exacting work but easier than writing. No date.

Mrs. W. F. Eldredge, of Rockport. Reported downy woodpecker had chiselled nest hole through cement filling of hollow limb. Spring of 1919.

Mrs. Arthur Caswell, of Athol. Saw three downy woodpeckers busy tapping maple trees near her windows. Suet was fastened to tree trunks. Woodpeckers would fill up on suet, then chase it with deep draughts of sap. No date.

Mr. Charles E. Bailey, assistant to Mr. Forbush. Observed downy woodpecker climb over and inspect 181 woodland trees between 9:40 A.M. and 12:15 P.M. and make 26 excavations for food. (At this point, Mr. Bailey presumably began thinking about food himself.) March 28, 1899.

Mr. Harry E. Woods, of Huntington. Watched pair of yellow-bellied sapsuckers feeding their young on insects. Each insect was taken by the bird to a tree in which was a hole the size of a quarter; insect was soaked in sap, then fed to young. Principle of the cocktail-hour dip. No date.

Major Charles Bendire. Witnessed tryst of whippoorwills. "I happened to be in a little outbuilding, some 20 feet in the rear of the house at which we were stopping, early on the evening of the 24th, about half an hour after sundown, when I heard a peculiar, low, clucking noise outside, which was directly followed by the familiar call of 'whip-poor-will.' . . . Directly alongside of the small outbuilding previously referred to, a barrel of sand and lime had been spilled, and from the numerous tracks of these birds, made by them nightly afterwards, it was evident that this spot was visited regularly, and was the trysting place of at least one pair. Looking through a small aperture, I saw one of the birds waddling about in a very excited manner over the sand-covered space, which was perhaps 2 by 3 feet square, and it was so much interested in its own performance that it did not notice me, although I made some noise trying to fight off a swarm of mosquitoes which assailed me from all sides. Its head appeared to be all mouth, and its notes were uttered so rapidly that, close as I was to the bird, they sounded like one long, continuous roll. A few seconds after his first effort (it was the male) he was joined by his mate, and she at once commenced to respond with a peculiar, low, buzzing or grunting note, like 'gaw-gaw-gaw,' undoubtedly a note of approval or endearment. This evidently cost her considerable effort; her head almost touched the ground while uttering it, her plumage was relaxed, and her whole body seemed to be in a violent tremble. The male in the meantime had sidled up to her and touched her bill with his, which made her move slightly to one side, but so slowly that he easily kept close alongside of her. These sidling movements were kept up for a minute or more each time; first one would move away, followed by the other, and then it would be reversed; both were about equally bold and coy at the same time. Their entire lovemaking looked exceedingly human, and the female acted as timid and bashful as many young maidens would when receiving the first declarations of their would-be lovers, while the lowering of her head might easily be interpreted as being done to hide her blushes. Just about the time I thought this courtship would reach its climax, a dog ran out of the house and caused both to take flight." 1895.

Mr. Manly Hardy. Camped on island off Maine coast. The discarded red shells of cooked lobsters were all about. Ruby-throated hummingbird suddenly appeared out of fog, went from shell to shell under impression they were flowers. 1895.

Miss Inez A. Howe. Observed courtship of pileated woodpeckers. Birds met in treetop, spread wings to full width, danced, balanced before each other, bowed to each other, kissed, then repeated performance. Miss Howe greatly impressed by this pretty sight. April 23, 1921, in the morning.

Mr. Franklin P. Cook, of Lawrenceville, New Jersey. Found phoebe's nest inside field-telephone box on rifle range. Firing of long-range rifles did not disturb birds in the least. No date.

Mr. Frithof Kumlien. Tells of an old, worn, partly blind blue jay that was fed, tended, and guarded by his companions, who never deserted him. They regularly guided him to a spring, where he bathed.

Mr. J. N. Baskett. Saw blue jay lift wing, rub walnut leaves into feathers underneath. No date.

Miss Grace Ellicott, of Newcastle, Indiana. Saw blue jay pick ants from anthill, tuck them under wing for safekeeping. 1908.

Mrs. Arthur Caswell, of Athol, again. Three crows came to large oak tree near her home. First one, then another held its head down to have its feathers dressed by the others. Afterward, they presented one another with little sticks, and touched beaks together. No date.

Mr. Adelbert Temple, of Hopkinton. Pet crow went ice fishing with Temple's son. Crow sprang the tilts, one after another; laughed after each episode. No date.

Mr. Frank E. Peck, of Wareham. As child, was playing with silver shoe buckle tied to ribbon. Male Baltimore oriole spied ribbon, swooped down, seized it. Later, ribbon and buckle were seen to be woven into nest, giving nest bright appearance. No date.

Mr. E. O. Grant again. Saw farmer near Patten, Maine, sitting on a snowdrift about fifteen feet high, surrounded by a hundred redpolls. Birds perched on farmer's head and shoulders. One sat on knee. Farmer told Grant he had enjoyed the previous half hour more than any other period in his life. March 23, 1926.

Mr. William Holden, of Leominster, and neighbor Mr. E. R. Davis. These two men had fed birds, including pine siskins. Because Mr. Davis was late riser, siskins entered his bedroom, pulled his hair, tweaked his ears, to induce him to uncover seed dish. One morning, Mr. Davis, in an experimental mood, covered his head, leaving only small hole through which to observe birds. One bird discovered peephole, reached in, tapped Mr. Davis on forehead. March 1926.

Mr. B. H. Newell, of City Point, Maine. Female house sparrow removed eggs from thirty-five cliff swallows' nests at his place. Sparrow drove bill into egg after egg, dropped eggs to ground. No date.

Mr. H. C. Denslow. Timed the chirps of a Henslow's sparrow, which sings in its sleep. Found they came eight to the minute.

Miss Viola E. Crittenden, of North Adams. Chipping sparrow had nest not far from robin's nest under construction. Chippy very kindly brought straws, dropped them into unfinished structure for convenience of robin. This occurrence considered unique by Mr. Forbush. No date.

Mr. Henry Hales, of Ridgewood, New Jersey. Male scarlet tanager so anxious to become father that he started tending young chipping sparrows nearby, who hatched before his own brood.

Miss Clara E. Reed. Tells of cliffswallow nest that fell, carrying young birds along with it. Birds were put in strawberry basket, which was then hung where nest had been. Parent birds accepted situation, lined basket with mud, raised young. Liked basket-nest well enough to return to it next year. No date.

Mrs. Chester Bancroft, of Tyngsborough. Reported to Thornton Burgess she saw large bullfrog with barn swallow in mouth. Mr. Burgess relayed information to Mr. Forbush. Summer of 1927.

Miss Dorothy A. Baldwin, of Hardwick. Observed inconstancy in female tree swallow. Entertained young male when husband off somewhere. Happened again and again. One day, female left with interloper. Mate mourned for day, then disappeared, leaving eggs cold in deserted nest. Broken home. No date.

Mr. John Willison. In woods behind Mayflower Inn, at Manomet Point, came upon gay crowd of cedar waxwings swigging ripe chokecherry juice. All birds had had one too many, were falling-down drunk. (Social drinking a common failing of waxwings.) No date.

Mr. William C. Wheeler. Whistled song of robin as he approached northern shrike. (There are all kinds of bird people and they are up to all kinds of stunts.) Shrike mimicked song, repeated it three times. No date.

Mr. Neil F. Posson. Credits yellow warbler with 3,240 songs a day, or 22,680 a week. 1892.

Dr. H. F. Perkins. Found yellow warbler's nest six stories high with a cowbird's egg on every floor. The warblers, each time they discovered a stranger's egg in the nest, built on top of it, thus burying the egg. No date.

Miss Fannie A. Stebbins. Young pine warbler was detained for three days in schoolroom in Springfield. Parents flew in at the window during school sessions, fed bird. No date.

Mr. Arthur T. Wayne. Wore out suit of clothes pursuing Louisiana water thrush through dense swamp in South Carolina during one entire week. Failed to get bird. No date.

Mr. Arthur W. Brockway. Female Maryland yellowthroat found shoe left out on underpinning of house. Bird built nest in shoe, laid five eggs, began to incubate, was attacked by dog. 1899.

Mrs. George H. McGregor, of Fall River. While sitting on front porch one evening, heard catbird sound "Taps." Believes bird picked it up from hearing it played at burial services in nearby cemetery. No date.

Mrs. Jean E. Carth. Heard brown thrasher imitate frog. No date.

Owner of a barn in Fairhaven (no name given). Had pair of Carolina wrens build nest in basket containing sticks of dynamite. No untoward results. No date.

Mrs. Daisy Dill Norton. Found female house wren nesting in bluebird nest box, with no mate. Little wren busy and happy with domestic chores, allowed no other bird near, male or female; whiled away time by laying eggs. Laid, it turned out later, twelve. No date.

Miss Elizabeth Dickens. While on Block Island saw brown creeper climbing cow's tail. No date.

Miss Mabel T. Tilton, of Vineyard Haven. Became friendly with redbreasted nuthatch. Bird made use of her hand to warm its feet, took many liberties with her fingernails. No date.

Mrs. Olive Thorne Miller. Reported case of female tufted titmouse stealing hair from gentleman in Ohio for use in nest building. Bird lit on gentleman's head, seized a beakful, braced itself, jerked lock out, flew away, came back for more. Gentleman a bird lover, consented to give hair again. No date.

Reverend William R. Lord. Talked to robin in low, confidential tone. Bird liked this, followed Lord. No date.

Mrs. Elizabeth L. Burbank, of Sandwich. Observed male robin act in peculiar manner. While female incubated eggs on nest, male crouched on lawn, imitated her—fluffing out feathers, rising up, pretending to turn eggs. No date.

Mr. Fred G. Knaub, of New Haven. Male bluebird neglected own family in order to tend young house wrens in nest box nearby. Fought wren parents to a fare-thee-well. No date.

Dr. Mary F. Hobart, of Needham. Male bluebird became infatuated with caged canary. Began flirtation on May 16th, continued it while own mate was busy incubating eggs. Frequently alighted on canary's cage, offered worms, caterpillars. July 1st, saw error of ways or tired of color yellow, returned to mate, resumed parental duties. No date.

Of all Mr. Forbush's tipsters, the only one I am jealous of is Fred G. Floyd, of Hingham. Mr. Floyd beat me to a very fine niche in *Birds of Massachusetts*—he beat me by some thirty years. There is just one record of a Harris's sparrow in *Birds*, and Mr. Floyd, along with his wife, gets the credit for it. The bird was seen in Hingham in April 1929, shortly after Mr. Forbush's death but still in time to get into the unfinished Volume III. Five or six years ago, I, too, was visited by a Harris's sparrow; one showed up at my home in Maine and hung around the feeding station for three days—a beautifully turned-out bird, reddish-brown, with a black face and throat and a white waistcoat. At first I didn't know what I was looking at, but I soon found out. The bird is almost unknown in New England, and this one was at least a thousand miles from where he belonged. We had had a gale not long before, and he must have ridden it all the way from Nebraska or Kansas.

I have never seen a loon rinse its mouth, but once I liberated a hummingbird from a spider's web. Mr. Forbush, I think, would have wanted to hear about that. I have never watched a merganser commit suicide, but once, in Florida, I saw two flickers dancing at one end of a tin rain gutter to music supplied by a red-bellied woodpecker, who was drumming on the gutter at the other end. Mr. Forbush came instantly to mind. I have never seen a bullfrog with a swallow in its mouth, but the first cast I ever made with a spinning reel (it was a practice shot on a lawn) was taken by a mockingbird, who swept down out of a bush and grabbed the bob. These are my noteworthy bird experiences. Alas, they are too late. (And I should add that I know a man who, while hunting in the woods, leaned over to pick up a glove and was bit on the nose by a bittern. He is Mr. Ward F. Snow, of Blue Hill, Maine. November 1965.)

If Edward Howe Forbush's prose is occasionally overblown, this results from a genuine ecstasy in the man, rather than from lack of discipline. Reading the essays, one shares his ecstasy. I have nothing in my bookshelves that I turn to more often or with greater satisfaction than his *Birds*. He is a man for all seasons, and, like a flight of geese, he carries his reader along into seasons yet to come. On a winter's evening, it is a pure pleasure to read, "When the spring rains and mounting sun begin to tint the meadow grass, when the alewives run up the streams, when the blackbirds and the spring frogs sing their full chorus, then the Snipe arrives at night on the south wind."